The Making of
John Lennon

The Making of John Lennon

The Untold Story of the Rise and Fall of The Beatles

FRANCIS KENNY

with a Foreword by BILL HARRY

Luath Press Limited

EDINBURGH

www.luath.co.uk

First published 2014

ISBN: 978-1-908373-90-8

The paper used in this book is recyclable. It is made from
low chlorine pulps produced in a low energy, low emissions manner
from renewable forests.

Printed and bound by
CPI Antony Rowe, Chippenham

Typeset in 11 point Sabon
by 3btype.com

Maps by Jim Lewis

To Eileen

Lennon is clearly on the road to failure.

QUARRY BANK HIGH SCHOOL REPORT

Contents

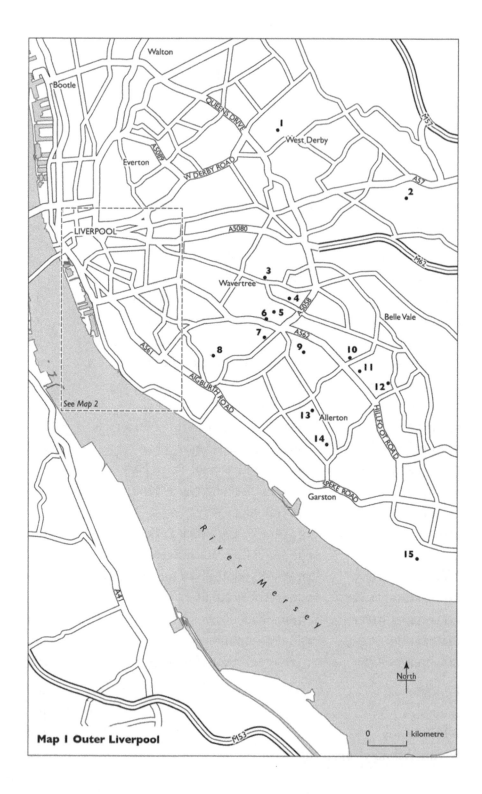

Map 1 Outer Liverpool

NOTE: These maps are not period maps. Rather, they show Liverpool as it is today to allow the reader to visit the important places in John's life mentioned throughout this book, and see the legacy that he has left on his city.

Map 1 – Outer Liverpool

1 **The Casbah Coffee Club** – The Quarrymen (John Lennon, Paul McCartney, George Harrison, and Ken Brown) played at the Casbah Coffee Club when it first opened in 1959.

2 **Paul McCartney's Auntie Jin's house** – This is where Paul McCartney's 21st birthday party was thrown, at which a drunken John Lennon attacked Cavern DJ Bob Wooler over a comment he made about John's holiday in Barcelona with Brian Epstein.

3 **12 Arnold Grove** – George Harrison's childhood home.

4 **Mosspits Lane Primary School** – John Lennon's primary school.

5 **9 Newcastle Road** – John lived here until he was five years old, when he was moved to stay with his Aunt Mimi at Mendips.

6 **Penny Lane**

7 **Dovedale Infant School** – The primary school which John Lennon and George Harrison attended.

8 **Sefton Park Boating Lake** – This is where John Lennon's mother and father met and began courting.

9 **Quarry Bank High School** – The grammar school for boys which John Lennon attended. His record here was one of shoddy work and delinquent behaviour.

10 **Strawberry Field** – The Salvation Army children's home near John's high school, which inspired the 1967 Beatles song 'Strawberry Fields Forever'. John used to enjoy being taking by Aunt Mimi to garden parties that were held there.

11 **Mendips** – 251 Menlove Avenue. John was sent to live at his Aunt Mimi's house in leafy suburbia when he was five years old.

12 **St Peter's Church** – The very first meeting between John and Paul took place at a fete held in the grounds of this church in 1957.

13 **20 Forthlin Road** – Paul McCartney's childhood home.

14 **1 Blomfield Road** – John Lennon's mother's house. This is where John's mother Julia lived with Bobby Dykins, while John lived with his Aunt Mimi at Mendips.

15 **Liverpool John Lennon Airport** – Formerly Speke Airport. Renamed in honour of John Lennon in 2002. There is a seven-foot statue of John at check-in.

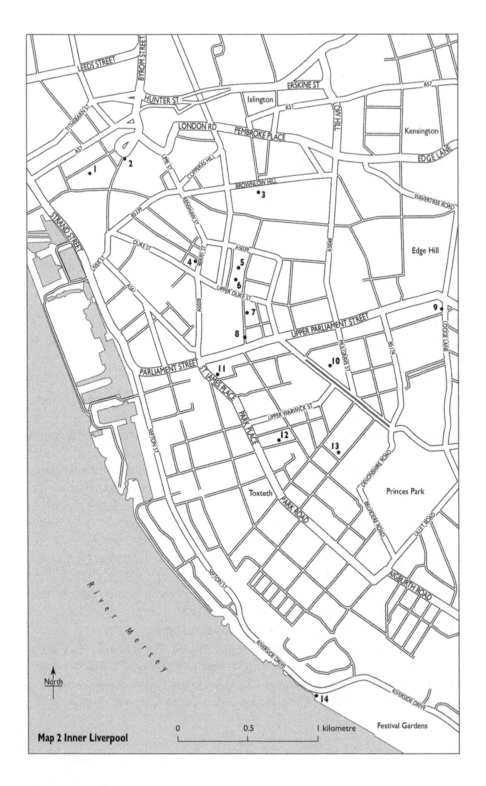

LEEDS STREET
BYROM STREET
TITHEBARN ST
A57
HUNTER ST
Islington
ERSKINE ST
A57
LONDON RD
PEMBROKE PLACE
A57
OW HILL
Kensington
EDGE LANE
•1
•2
LIME ST
COPPERAS HILL
BROWNLOW HILL
•3
WAVERTREE ROAD
STRAND STREET
BSS3P
RENSHAW ST
DUKE ST
A5039
BERRY ST
A5039
Edge Hill
LIVER ST
•4
•5
•6
A561
UPPER DUKE ST
A5039
•7
•8
UPPER PARLIAMENT STREET
•9
LODGE LANE
B5174
A5036
MULGRAVE ST
PARLIAMENT STREET
•11
•10
ST JAMES PLACE
PARK PLACE
UPPER WARWICK ST
ST JAMES ST
•12
•13
DEVONSHIRE ROAD
Toxteth
PARK ROAD
Princes Park
BELVIDERE ROAD
ULLET ROAD
SEFTON ST
AIGBURTH ROAD
RIVERSIDE DRIVE
R i v e r   M e r s e y
RIVERSIDE DRIVE
North
•14
0   0.5   1 kilometre
Festival Gardens

Map 2 Inner Liverpool

Map 2 – Inner Liverpool

1   **The Cavern – 10 Mathew Street**. The Beatles played this club frequently in their early years. They played their first gig as The Beatles here on 9 February 1961, but John and Paul had appeared previously as part of The Quarrymen in the late 1950s.

2   **NEMS** – The North End Music Stores offices where The Beatles signed a contract with Brian Epstein on 24 January 1962.

3   **John Lennon Art and Design Building at Liverpool John Moores University** – Duckinfield Street. Just down the road from John Lennon's former College of Art, this university building was renamed The John Lennon Art and Design Building in 2013. The front of the building features a line drawing self-portrait of John Lennon.

4   **The Blue Angel** – Club where Brian Epstein gave a press conference shortly after signing The Beatles. This was also where The Quarrymen unsuccessfully auditioned for Billy Fury's Northern Circuit rock extravaganza. The club was then known as the Wyvern Social Club.

5   **Ye Cracke Pub** – This pub was a regular haunt of John's when he was at Liverpool College of Art. John's tutor Arthur Ballard frequently held tutorials here.

6   **Liverpool Institute of Performing Arts** – This was formerly the Liverpool Institute High School for boys, the high school which Paul and George attended.

7   **Gambier Terrace** – John Lennon lived here as a student with original Beatles bassist Stuart Sutcliffe.

8   **Liverpool College of Art** – 68 Hope Street. Where John Lennon attended to study art. He met Cynthia Powell here, who he later married.

9   **The Pavilion** – The Quarrymen took part in various 'skiffle contests' at this venue in the 1950s. The Beatles on performed once at The Pavilion on 2 April 1962.

10 **Rosebery Street** – One of The Quarrymen's first appearances was at a street party in Rosebery Street in 1957, where they played on the back of a stationary coal lorry.

11 **Original site of the Flat Iron** – John Lennon's grandfather Jack used to perform song-and-dance routines regularly at this pub. In a strange coincidence, an illustration of this pub featured in the feature animation *Yellow Submarine* (1968).

12 Original site of John's father's family home at 27 Copperfield Street.

13 **10 Admiral Grove** – Ringo Starr's childhood home.

14 **Cast Iron Shore** – A strip of wasteland on the banks of the Mersey, referred to in John's 1968 song 'Glass Onion'.

Acknowledgements

The Making of John Lennon took over five years to complete. During this period, an old Liverpool Art College friend of John and Cynthia, Freddie O'Brien, gave his advice, time and energy, as did Tony Wailey, for which I am indebted and grateful.

I'd also like to give thanks to Bill Harry, another Art College friend and confidant of John, for his depth of knowledge in all things John Lennon and The Beatles, and for his generosity of spirit in providing a Foreword.

Thanks, as well, to Julia Baird, John Lennon's half-sister, for granting me an insightful interview as part of my research for this book.

I'm also thankful to my lifelong friend, Peter Devaney, who gave unstinting support and guidance on the book and helped circle the wagons when the going got rough.

I'd like to thank my son, Daniel, and daughters, Suzanna, Caroline, Lucy and Holly for their belief and encouragement, which helped me enormously.

And finally, to my wife, Eileen, without whose understanding, patience and love this book would never have found its way to completion: thanks with much love, and more.

Foreword by Bill Harry

JOHN LENNON COULD only have been born in Liverpool and Francis certainly provides an answer 'why' in this book, analysing John's life and what made John Lennon become John Lennon – not only the times John lived through and was born into, but the thread that wound throughout the city's history, including its Celtic heritage due to its existence as one of the greatest ports in the world.

Capturing history before it fades and disappears forever is difficult because even recent history has its many different aspects, seen from different points of view, which often distort the reality of events. However, dedicated research often continues to uncover facts which have been contrary to events which really happened, such as the fact that John was not born during a heavy air raid, which so many previous books have contended.

This isn't a roller-coaster ride, skipping through John's life, but a carefully prepared examination of his early years, slowly examining the general picture that surrounded John's life, rather than focusing on one specific aspect, wrapping the surroundings of the city, the family, the friends, the music and the events which forged the young man who became a 20th century icon, into a whole.

Some of the conclusions in John's personal story might prove controversial because time and the passing of many of the main characters, including John himself, leave us with no option but to analyse what has previously been said and documented, taking into consideration the different viewpoints about him.

Early in 1960 John Lennon, Stuart Sutcliffe, Rod Murray and I formed the Dissenters, whose aim was to make Liverpool famous! We figured that Liverpool had more than its fair share of musicians, writers, comedians, artists and sculptors. We four would attempt to do this in our various ways – John with his music, Stuart and Rod with their painting and me with my writing. (A plaque, made by my art school friend Fred O'Brien, dedicated to the place where we made our vow is to be found in Ye Cracke, Rice Street).

Francis Kenny is another example of what we were aiming to achieve – to put the light on creative people from the city. He was born in the

Toxteth area of the city and left school with no qualifications, worked for 15 years in the construction industry and then entered a vacuum of unemployment before attending Coleg Harlech, an adult residential college in North Wales where he achieved a Diploma in Political Philosophy and Economics. This was followed by a period at Liverpool University where he completed a BA Honours in Economics and Politics and Sociology. He also qualified as a teacher after completing a Post Graduate Course in Education at Bolton University.

Francis then completed MAs in Urban Regeneration at Hope University and Screen Writing at John Moores University.

He began writing 15 years ago and has penned a dozen screenplays, a novel *Waiting for the Beatles* and a crime novel *All I Ever Wanted*, among other works, including a stage play.

Francis was to tell me that his book: 'Aims to present a "below the surface" alternative view of John's creative and emotional makeup.'

This work is now endorsed by a former Dissenter. Read, enjoy and learn.

Regards,
Bill Harry, Founder of *Mersey Beat*.

BILL HARRY was born in Liverpool and attended Liverpool Art College where he met and became good friends with John Lennon and Stuart Sutcliffe. While at college Bill developed an interest in journalism which led to his founding of *Mersey Beat* magazine, which played a crucial role in supporting The Beatles during their early days.

Milestones in
The Making of John Lennon

1940   John born on 9 October to Julia and Freddie Lennon in war-torn Liverpool.

1941   John lived in Newcastle Road, Liverpool with his mother and maternal grandparents.

1942   John's seafaring father Freddie is still away at sea.

1943   Julia began a relationship with a Welsh soldier stationed in Liverpool, Taffy Williams.

1944   Julia gave birth to a girl (Victoria) with Williams the father; the child was given up for adoption.

1945   Julia and John move in with Bobby Dykins.

1946   Due to the intervention by Social Services over the common-law living arrangements of Julia and Bobby, John goes to live with Julia's sister Mimi and her husband George in the Liverpool suburb of Woolton.

1947   Mimi changes John's school, which meant he became further away from his mother's home.

1948   At school John becomes ill-disciplined and aggressive.

1949   John immerses himself in books, poetry and story writing, which became a refuge from his emotional turmoil.

1950   Mimi takes in lodgers from the local university, meaning she and George sleep downstairs while John's upstairs box room is flanked by rooms containing students.

1951   John passes the Eleven Plus exam, which gains him entrance into Quarry Bank, the local grammar school.

1952   John forms a gang: he is influenced by his story book hero *Just William*. John is the leader.

1953   John's poor discipline, shoddy class work and bullying behaviour continue at Quarry Bank.

1954   John discovers his mother lived only a mile away from Mendips.

1955   A skiffle craze hits the UK and John is one of the tens of thousands of youngsters who form skiffle groups.

1956   John discovers rock 'n' roll and Elvis.

1957   While playing at a local fête with his band The Quarrymen, John meets Paul McCartney. John starts at Liverpool College of Art. John's Quarrymen now include Paul's friend George Harrison.

1958   In the summer John, Paul and George 'cut a disc' at a local recording studio, the next day his mother is involved in a fatal car accident.

1959   The group change their name from The Quarrymen to The Silver Beetles and make a short tour of Scotland.

1960   The name of John's band changes again to The Beatles. Pete Best joins on drums as they embark on a 12-week engagement at the Indra Club in Hamburg.

1961   Brian Epstein visits the Cavern Club where The Beatles had become the club's resident band and offers to be their manager.

1962   Brian secures a recording contract with Parlophone Records for the band. John marries Cynthia. Ringo Starr joins The Beatles as Pete Best is sacked weeks before the release of group's first single 'Love Me Do'.

1963   The release of The Beatles' second and third singles, 'Please Please Me' and 'She Loves You' ignites the beginning of Beatle-mania. John's son Julian is born.

1964   The Beatles arrive in New York for the Ed Sullivan Show and a TV audience of 73 million. The same year sees the cinema release of the group's *A Hard Day's Night*.

1965   John's confessional song 'Help!' becomes the title for the band's next feature film of the same name. The Beatles become heavy users of marijuana and begin to experiment with LSD.

1966   The band stop touring and The Beatles' music takes on a major sea change with their album *Revolver*, its direction being foreshadowed by it precursor *Rubber Soul*, the previous year.

1967   The Beatles' album *Sergeant Pepper's Lonely Hearts Club Band* is released against the backdrop of the counter-culture the Hippy movement and alternative lifestyles of young people.

1968   The Beatles immerse themselves in Indian culture and meditation. In July of this year Brian Epstein dies due to an overdose of barbiturates. John takes a strong interest in the avant-garde and meets Yoko Ono. The band produce a double album commonly known as the *White Album*.

1969   The personal and musical differences in the band along with complex financial issues means that the last two Beatles albums come out in reverse order, the last album *Abbey Road* appearing before the previously recorded *Let it Be*. John marries Yoko and uses his honeymoon as a vehicle to promote his new found support for world peace.

1970   John continues to go his separate way from The Beatles socially and musically, committing himself more to Yoko and his solo efforts. On 31 December Paul applies to the High Court for the dissolution of The Beatles.

1980   John shot dead outside the Dakota building in New York.

Introduction

JOHN LENNON was one of the most radical and controversial musical icons of the 1960s. Even after his death over 30 years ago he still remains celebrated around the world as a figure of musical genius, and one of deep contradictions. Despite his global fame, John's 'real identity' has been notoriously difficult to pin down. His famously challenging and confrontational attitude can be readily linked, however, to his formative years in his hometown of Liverpool. John's life began, and tragically ended, in two different port cities – Liverpool and New York – each facing each other across the Atlantic Ocean, each on the edge of their own countries, ports whose histories were defined by the contradictory cultural norms of their home country – edgy cities, sister cities, bonded together by a transatlantic trade route and an Irish Diaspora.

As a child, John's mind seems to have been a fog of confusion, 'rejected' by both parents and forced to accept life under an aunt who was, by all accounts, a dictatorial head of household. This left him isolated and constrained. For the young John, the restrictive and critical atmosphere during his time being brought up at his aunt's home Mendips fashioned emotional scars that never fully healed. From almost the time of his separation from his mother, Julia, John began to develop defensive, hostile and aggressive behaviours. Even with the long-awaited success of The Beatles, he still couldn't shake off the dread of being unloved that he carried with him in his early years. Although he was known to wear his emotions on his sleeve, shown with brutal transparency in songs such as 'Help!' and 'Nowhere Man', to a large extent his childhood memories were so painful that most of the bruises remained on the inside. He may have remained forever hostage to his childhood, but it was during this time that the young John learned to use his talent as a barrier against the intermittent periods of despondency.

It was at Mendips that the apprenticeship of his creativity was to be found in the self-defence mechanism of isolation, of story writing, books and poetry. This insular but creative lifestyle was to nurture his art, and later, the studio would make this creativity available to a wider audience. In many ways, John fits neatly into the stereotype of the tortured artist. As John himself declared:

All art is pain expressing itself. I think all life is, everything we do, but particularly artists – that's why they're always vilified. They're always persecuted because they show pain, they can't help it. They express it in art and the way they live, and people don't like to see that reality that they're suffering.[1]

As a musician and artist he displayed a fierce independence and marched to the beat of his own drum, but at the same time he was dogged by insecurity, pessimism and depression. For all his musical and artistic success, John was forever haunted by fears, living most of his life shadowed by doubt. On meeting John, Stuart Sutcliffe's sister Pauline was to comment that 'John's whole history speaks to a desperate kind of nurturing'.[2]

As a teenager, John's character and musical creativity were strongly influenced by his attempts to gain access to and acceptance in a culture of rock 'n' roll. For John, this culture was to be found in a largely blue collar teenage population in Liverpool's inner city. He was determined to shed a background in the leafy boulevards and manicured parks of Woolton by adopting a smokescreen of rebelliousness, sarcastic wit and belligerence. He desperately needed to have a grounding to support his vulnerable self-esteem. It was in rock 'n' roll that he found an identity which was to be crucial and life-saving. John's life support of music and writing was also to be supplemented by the cultural impact of the city and port of Liverpool. John desperately needed and wanted the raucousness, spontaneous humour and vibrancy that could be found in Liverpool's blue collar life.

As a teenager, his early trips into inner-city Liverpool found John intrigued and in awe of the locals with their sharpness, wit and streetwise dialogue. As Paul Morley puts it:

Liverpool is always on guard. They know that the English look up and over with suspicion and doubt, stumped by the language, needled by the snappy, mongrel confidence, outmanoeuvred by the fast logic-shredding wit. The city is also always wary at what might appear over the horizon, from the endless heavy sea, at what unknown force, for good or evil, might wash up on their vulnerable, open shore.[3]

John adopted a Scouse accent, which came into conflict with his surrogate mother from the age of five, Aunt Mimi, and the conditioning of John towards King, Country, Empire and the linguistic fabric of these in the shape of 'BBC English'. John's conservative upbringing by his aunt left him ill-equipped for validation within the local rock 'n' roll community, and to win acceptance by his peers he proceeded to adopt an exaggerated toughness that he never fully abandoned.

Liverpool has always had a deep-seated historical Celtic connection – the city sits with its back to mainland Britain, looking out instead to the Atlantic Ocean, so much so that the Mersey was viewed as an inland river of the Irish Sea. This, combined with its sense of otherness and the outlook of defiance that existed in Liverpool's inner-city population's irreverence to status, bolshiness and verbal gymnastics, fitted John like a glove. His search for rebellion was nurtured by his embrace of Liverpool's Irish influence and the dynamic effect of the city's seafarer culture via the movement of ideas across oceans. 'We came from Liverpool,' John declared, 'and reflected our past'.[4]

As The Beatles were catapulted into worldwide fame, John increasingly found himself battling a deep-rooted range of emotional and psychological issues. The greater The Beatles grew into a global phenomenon, the greater John's uncertainties about his own talent and the greater his abrasiveness and volatility. Perhaps it was just a coincidence on the part of the film's screenwriter, or insight into John's belligerence, that while in *Yellow Submarine* the character of Ringo is presented as a typical local Liverpool lad, George as an Indian mystic aficionado and Paul as a self-assured musical hall performer, John is introduced as Frankenstein's monster!

The Making of John Lennon traces the restrictive conformity of John's Aunt Mimi's narrow-mindedness and its clashes with John's pathological aversion to authority. It examines his inner turmoil and salvation through art, as well as the complexity of values found in his childhood that would aggravate him and hurl him towards inhabiting a self-contradictory persona.

John's life is too often airbrushed. Some accounts have been distorted with a view to making the Lennon 'story' acceptable to the reader, presenting a saintly, refined version of John at which he would have balked. *The Making of John Lennon* challenges the 'Beatle version' of John that has become mainstream.

An obvious example of these contradictory, standard versions of The John Lennon Story is in John's place of birth: Liverpool. Outside The Cavern Club in Mathew Street, where The Beatles played 292 times, is a life-size bronze statue of John, resplendent in his heavy leather boots, standing with one foot hooked behind the other, leather trousers, leather jacket and... a Beatle haircut. Fine; except that the Beatle haircut is normally associated with the Pierre Cardin 'bum freezer', 'Beatle suits' and tens of thousands of screaming fans: not leather, definitely not leather. But when this statue was first unveiled, it had a DA Teddy Boy slicked-back hairstyle – just like The Beatles had when they played Hamburg, when they wore leather suits. Those responsible for the statue's commission, upon viewing this accurate depiction of Lennon at a particular time in his development, decided that this wasn't what they wanted. History was rewritten, and, despite the statue being modelled on a photograph taken in Hamburg which was later to become the cover for his 1974 *Rock 'n' Roll* album, the 'greaser' look head was removed and replaced by the more familiar 'mop top' image.

This book is a challenge to such obvious historical rewrites. As the only writer on John Lennon to have spent all his life in Liverpool, I am uniquely placed to challenge orthodox versions of the 'Lennon Story'. *The Making of John Lennon* presents a journey into the confusion and pain that lay behind one of popular music's most researched – yet most misunderstood – geniuses. What follows is how John Lennon came to be *John Lennon, musical genius*. And it all starts in Liverpool.

CHAPTER ONE

1800s

City of Outsiders

JOHN LENNON WAS born in 1940 in wartime Liverpool. His music, his persona and his beliefs were formed through the varying influences of his home city and its port, people and culture. The city represents the single most powerful influence on John's life. Indeed, after the break-up of The Beatles, having moved to New York's Dakota building, John still kept a sea trunk inscribed with 'Liverpool' which was full of mementos from his city of birth. His feelings for Liverpool were often ambiguous and, at certain periods of his career, the city's deep-seated blue collar ethos became an obstacle and a source of friction to his later musical success. Nevertheless, Liverpool was passionately championed by its favourite son.

It is only by coming to understand the impact of his home city on John, the place in which his (paternal) Lennon and (maternal) Stanley families were born and nurtured, that it becomes possible to gain a valuable appreciation of one of the 20th century's greatest musical talents. The thread of passion for Liverpool's culture, music and people would run throughout John's life. He came to love the edginess of a seaport with a workforce more comfortable in Barranquilla, Boston and Buenos Aires than Bolton, Bury or Blackburn. In some ways, though, the influence of the city could be a double-edged sword. Much of his personality and strength came from his affinity with Liverpool's Irish culture. The most obvious characteristics of this culture that John embodied were humour and accent, but also the Irish tendency towards defiance and argumentativeness, together with a healthy irreverence for authority and cant. His own view of his hometown was candid and revealed the depth of feeling for what would be the prime mover in shaping his life and music:

> It was going poor, a very poor city, and tough. But people have a sense of humour because they are in so much pain, so they are always cracking jokes. They are very witty, and it's an Irish place. It is where the Irish came when they ran out of potatoes, and it's where black

25

people were left or worked as slaves or whatever. It is cosmopolitan, and it's where the sailors would come home with the blues records from America on the ships.[1]

John was fully aware of the unique nature of his hometown. Liverpool's influence on John and the rest of The Beatles is self-evident, not just in their accent but in their outlook, spirit and stoic determination to survive. The sense of being an outsider, of mutual support and the ability to laugh at one another was drawn from the city; it was this that kept them together in the whirlwind of Beatlemania and beyond. Liverpool was 'a transitional place looking out over the Irish Sea and the Atlantic Ocean while turning its back on the rest of the country'.[2]

It was in 1699 that the *Liverpool Merchant* became the port's first slave ship to sail for Africa, docking in Barbados with 220 Africans before making its return trip to Liverpool. In 1799, ships sailing out of Liverpool transported 45,000 Africans into bondage. The commercial success story of Liverpool and its relationship with the slave trade saw a rapid growth in port-related activities. This matched the growth of the British Industrial Revolution, in which the demand for imports and exports seemed insatiable on the back of that slave trade. At this time of mercantile expansion, Liverpool sailors were soon gaining a particular reputation and character. Indeed, novelist and sailor Joseph Conrad would comment: 'That crew of Liverpool hard cases had in them the right stuff. It's my experience they always have'.[3]

This growing development of trade routes to and from the port meant that large numbers of sailors were drawn to the city from all corners of the globe. This encouraged the opening of numerous pubs and gin houses, lodging houses and brothels. Seafarers began to be seen as an important mainstay of the port's industry. Liverpool had become the first capitalist commercial boom town, as novelist Herman Melville observed in his novel *Redburn*:

> Of all the sea-ports in the world, Liverpool, perhaps, most abounds in all the varieties of land-sharks, land-rats and other vermin, which make the hapless mariners their prey. In the shape of landlords, bar-keepers, clothiers, crimps and boarding-house loungers, the land-sharks devour him, limb by limb; whilst the land-rats and mice constantly nibble at his purse.[4]

The importance of the port and port-based activities would constitute the main driving force behind Liverpool's economic development for two and a half centuries. The city's function as a port turned it into a commercial rather than an industrial centre, the capital invested there making it the major distribution centre and importer of raw material. Liverpool's confidence in itself and sense for innovation was such that it pioneered the world's first electrically powered overhead railway system, stretching seven miles along the dockland zones, which both New York and Chicago later emulated.

Trade with the Americas proved to be a huge attraction, for those not just in Britain, but all over Europe. The city and port were booming. But while Liverpool was generating itself into a boomtown, across the Irish Sea a disaster of biblical proportions was taking place:

> As far as the Famine goes, we are dealing with the most important episode of Modern Irish history and the greatest social disaster of the nineteenth century in Europe...[5]

When the 1847–49 potato famine hit in Ireland, the exodus of Irish emigrants towards the city, in terms of its social fabric, was enormous. In 1847 alone, 300,000 people crossed the Irish Sea, fleeing the famine to live in England, with many starting a new life around the port. By 1851, 25 per cent of Liverpool's population was Irish-born. An alternative set of values, beliefs and religion was developing, and the Catholic enclaves along the north end and south end dockland zones were becoming a city within a city.

The steady expansion of the city and its Irish contingent meant that by the 1890s, Liverpool had become the largest Roman Catholic diocese in England with over 400,000 Catholic citizens, one fifth of the total Catholic population of Britain. Between 1851 and 1911, the city also witnessed the arrival of 20,000 people in each decade from Wales. The 'Celtic nations' were never so well represented in one city. These Irish and mercantile influences on Liverpool have played a major role in defining its literature arts, music, culture and social fabric. Indeed, in the case of The Beatles, John, Paul and George shared Irish ancestry. The Beatles' backgrounds were also inherently tied to the port, with John and George's fathers being seafarers and Paul's father working in the cotton industry, which relied on the port for shipping.

Liverpool had become a terminal for people, not just goods, and had established itself as the port *par excellence* for the mass movement for those seeking a better life – particularly for emigrants to Northern and Western Europe and the Americas. Between 1830 and 1930, some nine million emigrants sailed from the Mersey into the Atlantic. In 1886, *London Illustrated News* described Liverpool as 'the New York of Europe; a world city rather than merely a British provincial'.

At beginning of the 20th century, Liverpool was at the peak of its commercial power and was considered the world's first global city. In response to this, it celebrated and declared its position as second city of the world's largest empire. The mercantile elite decided to create what would later be known as the 'Three Graces' – the Royal Liver Building, the Cunard Building and the Port of Liverpool Building – set on the Pier Head looking out to the Mersey Bar and Irish Sea. Tipping their hats towards the port in their film *Yellow Submarine*, we see The Beatles sailing off for their series of adventures in the Sea of Dreams, departing from their home city's Pier Head.

The vibrancy and cut and thrust of a large seaport like Liverpool was to have a profound effect on John, as would his family life, which had its own Celtic roots to add to the influence of the city's own home-grown Irish culture. The influence on his music, however, has to a large extent been overlooked. John's rebellious nature has been attributed to the early absence of his parents and the death of his mother, Julia. But if one looks at the history of rebellion in the city, we find that this particular character is rooted in the port and the mix of blue collar workers, large numbers of Afro-Caribbean people (the largest community in the UK) and a Chinese community, the oldest in Europe. The influx of Irish immigrants, Welsh and Scots seeking work in the port, as well as African and Chinese seamen, lead to an eclectic cultural community. The word Scouse, for example, comes from the word *lobscouse*, a Scandinavian stew. John's Aunt Mimi was to take particular exception to John's adoption of a Scouse accent upon forming The Beatles. To many, the garrulous, sharp-natured 'Scouser' can on the surface be seen as caustic or delivering a certain truculence, but this is not the full story. It is no coincidence that Liverpool, Naples, New York and Kingston have always had much more in common with each other than their own particular country. They are populated by outsiders fully aware of their sense of otherness.

The cultural makeup of the city encouraged a particular tendency to puncture pretension and defy authority, while its internationalism and multiplicity created an accent tailored to support the case: *dese* for these, *dat* for that, *giz* for give us, *youse* as a plural for you, all of this interchangeable with the accent of Brooklyn or New York. The transatlantic shipping lines between Liverpool and New York conveyed not just people, but cultural and social discourse.

The nature of both dock work and seafaring demanded team work and good communication skills. In factory jobs, the noise of the shop floor or the gaze of the foreman limited socialising via the spoken word. With seafaring, however, signing on for a trip meant bringing to the job the ability to compromise, and an understanding of the needs of others. This was especially true on a deep sea trip, where there was a more intensive need to communicate, to give and take, gain acceptance and generally get on. This centred on dialogue concerning common values and interests. In order to gain acceptance, maintain a shipmate's welfare and aim for a 'good trip', there needed to be a sense of comradeship. It was this ability to 'rub along' that formed a seafarer's profile. And these traits were transferred over to land jobs, when gangs were formed on the docks. From this casual type of work and the Celtic fondness for the *craic* emanated the image of the Scouser.

As a suburban teenager, John's first ventures into inner-city Liverpool would have been one of intrigue and awe at the unfamiliarity of the terms and the machine gun delivery of dialogue. To John, this was a different country. This provoked clashes with his Aunt Mimi over, amongst others things, his previous Received Pronunciation sliding into Scouse. But when The Beatles achieved world fame, John declared:

> The first thing we did was to proclaim our 'Liverpoolness' to the world, and say, 'It's all right to come from Liverpool and talk like this'. Before, anybody from Liverpool who made it... had to lose their accent to get on the BBC... After The Beatles came on the scene, everyone started putting on a Liverpudlian accent.[6]

John's father Freddie recalls ringing up from dockside Southampton when John was five years old: 'He spoke lovely English,' Freddie enthused. 'When I heard his Scouse accent years later, I was sure it must be a gimmick'.[7] It wasn't a gimmick – to John it was much more important than that. It was a matter of survival.

Having nailed the accent, John was quick to pick up on the 'Scouse attitude', seen at times as a split personality of argumentativeness and extreme *bonhomie*. The Liverpool accent, it must be remembered, was in many ways the product of influxes to a port city, much like its far-flung sister port, New York. Turn of the century Liverpool and New York essentially grew up together, their working-class culture resembling each other more than they would of the English Home Counties or the oil fields of Texas. Playwright Eugene O'Neill's work dramatically reveals this closeness, most notably in his 1939 play *The Iceman Cometh*. Here is Rocky Pioggi, speaking in a downtown West Side dive: 'De old anarchist wise guy dat knows all de answers! Dat's you, huh?', or 'Why ain't he out dere stickin' by her?'.[8]

This is Scouse set in a New York bar; an accent and demeanour that ran through both cities' histories like a thread.

John's view of his hometown was that 'it was less hick than somewhere in the English Midlands, like the American Midwest or whatever you call it'.[9] In the same interview with *Rolling Stone* founding editor Jann Wenner, John 'regrets profoundly' that he wasn't born in New York. It gave further resonance to the similarities, attractiveness and pulling power to John of both cities to his idea of himself. Due to its seafaring internationalism, Liverpool was open to exotic, non-English ideas, to the extent that the Mersey was paradoxically viewed as an inland extension of the Irish Sea. As a port of world status, it had the confidence to 'choose' its own nation state. It wasn't only England. Although young John was not a Scouse in the true sense of the word, he readily threw himself into a world of poverty, sheebeens and communities of sharp-tongued, hard-faced, generous, quick-witted and quick-tempered people. A world that was sensitive to injustice, a rowdy, rock 'n' roll world, the world of dockland Liverpool. This was the life he wanted. It was not what his aunt wanted for him, which couldn't have been further from rock 'n' roll: listening to the sound of the establishment in the shape of the BBC Light Programme, being in bed by 12 o'clock, with a bookcase full of *Just William* and Mimi's *Encyclopaedia Britannica* beside him for company.

It was time to move on, and he had the perfect place on his doorstep. John was confronted with fast-speaking young men his own age 'talking with their hands' and fashioning new language patterns around themselves, pounding the ears of the listener with a language of street slang and ruthless mickey-taking; and this was the world for him. The verbal street corner duals must have amazed him, encouraging him to listen and learn, to add to his own armoury and develop speech as a weapon to beat an opponent. If he was going to lead this group called The Beatles and provide a platform for his musical goals, he needed to have the audacity to step up to another level of wit and guile. This was demanded in inner-city Liverpool: fight not only with fists, but with verbal putdowns, with cunning and, above all, the ability to get one over while outflanking your opponent.

Throughout his life, John used Liverpool as an anchor to give stability to the maelstrom of Beatlemania, the persistent mental health and drug problems and the final break-up of the group. What mattered to him was his identification with music and this first came with his own burst of independence, as a teenager on the streets of Liverpool. His creative, artistic flourish was nurtured against the backdrop of the edginess of a bustling multi-cultural seaport.

The whole notion of being an outcast in a city full of outcasts – located in a last refuge seaport, no less – nurtured a sense of otherness that appealed to John. In the year of his Aunt Mimi's birth in 1906, the City Council Health Committee revealed that:

> there was not a city in this country, nay in Europe, which could produce anything like the squalor that... officials found in some of Liverpool's backstreets.[10]

Like the 'Famine Irish', another group of peoples that faced impossible suffering at that period were Afro-Americans. Like the Irish, Afro-Americans were also inclined to develop an aspect of their culture that was derived from prejudice and derision and reflect this defensively in their language. Afro-American writer Stanley Crouch argues that:

> Negro Americans are not predisposed to follow people. They aren't. That's why there's always a certain element of chaos in the Negro world, because... from slavery onward, we didn't like to listen. No.[11]

If we draw a comparison between Crouch's understanding of black resistance and that of the history of the Irish, who suffered and died of hunger by the million and who were subject to extreme social prejudice in England and America, one gets an insight into the outlook of the 'belligerent', non-compliant Liverpool-Irish identity from which John derived his character.

The link between Crouch's Afro-Americans and the Irish of Liverpool is the sense of shared oppression and the innate need for respect through independence and nonconformity. Crouch continues:

> So someone telling you over and over you gotta do this, you know… I'm not doing that, *just because you said so*. 'Yes but it's right.' I don't care if it's right, I ain't doing it anyway. Why am I not doing it? For the same reason that Dostoevsky said 'I'm not gonna do it', so that I can tell you that *I exist*. I'm just gonna mess your stuff up.

If conforming and being like everybody else supports and validates the whole system of oppression, don't conform. The influence of Liverpool on John was to follow this advice, protecting his individuality by using his music and art to challenge; to 'mess your stuff up'.

CHAPTER TWO

1900s

Toxteth Park

AT THE TURN OF the 19th century, Liverpool was still a vibrant port and an integral part of the British Empire. It was a bustling city of 750,000 people and rising, and it was in this environment that John Lennon's parents, Freddie and Julia, were born – a city culture that was in the north of England but in many ways not of it.

Freddie and Julia had a stormy relationship of 14 years, during which they expressed a love of life and a rejection of society's norms, set against the fraught backdrop of the Great Depression and the Second World War. It was a marriage that took place despite opposition and interference from both families.

Meanwhile, the cultural influence of Ireland that infused the city was now joined by an American one in which thousands of cargo ships and hundreds of liners annually crisscrossed the Atlantic to and from the United States. What entered the Port of Liverpool was a multitude of fresh ideas, innovative music and challenging attitudes, which then fanned out into the city.

But the new century heralded little change with regards to the poverty, squalor and adversity of many people in the city. As is often the case when groups of people are faced with injustice, there developed a strong sense of solidarity and in 1911 the city saw a series of strikes and industrial action, climaxing in a general strike by 70,000 transport workers in and around the port. This involved carters, railwaymen, dockers and seafarers, and lasted 72 days. Tens of thousands of troops were called and barracked on the city's outskirts. The conflict which followed between the strikers and the police and military resulted in two strikers being shot dead. The then Home Secretary Winston Churchill ordered gunboats into the Mersey and stated that:

> You need not attach great importance to the rioting in Liverpool last
> night. It took place in an area where disorder is a chronic feature.[1]

Such bias was deeply ingrained, nurtured by a long-standing xenophobia towards the Irish immigrant community. Indeed, in 1866 *The Anthropological Review and Journal* claimed that the 'Gaelic man' was characterised by:

> his bulging jaw and lower part of the face, retreating chin and forehead, large mouth and thick lips, great distance between nose and mouth, upturned nose, prominent cheekbones, sunken eyes, projecting eyebrows, narrow elongated skull and protruding ears.

Scientific xenophobia was common in the 19th century, directed not just towards the large immigrant Irish population but also towards Jewish and African people. *Punch* magazine was not averse to portraying the Irish in cartoon form as Neanderthals dragging their knuckles along the floor. The bias against those who made up a significant part of the Irish Diaspora only served to firm the sense of otherness of those within the city. The fact that the city was the only one in Britain to elect a representative (T. P. O'Connor, 1848–1929) to the Houses of Parliament who was a member of the Irish National Party, which supported Home Rule for Ireland, only furthered the notion that Liverpool was a law unto itself. The communion with Ireland meant that Liverpool was to endure a degree of negativity and discrimination not seen by other English cities. But then again, Liverpool wasn't just another 'English city'.

The discrimination against Liverpool found an easy target in the city's distinctive accent. But during Beatlemania, it seemed that half the teenagers living within a 30-mile radius of Liverpool spoke with a 'plastic' Scouse accent in emulation of their idols. This became a complete turnaround from previous views on Liverpool people's accents. Cilla Black made the point that:

> People hated us because of the way we spoke, especially the fellas, who were very guttural. If you asked for a drink in a pub in Blackpool or North Wales, they'd throw you out.[2]

As a teenager, John was aware of this prejudice and fought a constant battle with his aunt in his attempt to declare his independence by adopting a local Scouse accent. To him, speaking in a distinct Liverpool accent was a badge of rebellion and freedom. Paul McCartney was also conscious of his accent and has expressed this sense of otherness:

Liverpool has its own identity. It's even got its own accent with about
a ten-mile radius. Once you go outside that ten miles its deep Lancashire, lad. I think you do feel that apartness, growing up there.[3]

Paul became one of the three most important people in John's life. He
impacted upon him as a friend and as a musician. Other major influences
on his formative outlook and beliefs were his Aunt Mimi and his mother
Julia. They were all Liverpool born and bred. Yoko Ono certainly influenced John later in his life, but by the time they met, he was already a
blend of his hometown's history and character.

John's Aunt Mimi (christened Mary Stanley), was born in Head Street
in the Toxteth area of Liverpool, where the influence of Catholicism surrounded the non-Catholic Stanley family. At the top of the street stood
Saint Patrick's Mission Church, home to the largest parish in the south
end of the city and Mother church to half a dozen other Catholic churches
in the area. At the other end of Head Street stood the Dexter Street
Laundry, one of 300 or so whose main purpose was to service the transatlantic liner trade. They cleaned tablecloths, bed linen and a whole host
of other items for recently docked liners. A liner in port for an overhaul
could well employ 2,000 people for over a month. The Stanley family's
home in Head Street was thus sandwiched between the two most
influential of dynamics of the city – the Irish and the sea.

Mimi's parents, George (known as Pop) and Annie, had Irish and Welsh
ancestry. The couple had five daughters, Mimi being the first, born in
1906, followed by Elizabeth (nicknamed Mater), Anne and Julia, who
was six years younger than her eldest sister and sometimes known as Judy.
Finally there was Harriet. The Stanley family had been left an endowment
by a well-off aunt in Wales. The money was invested in the purchase of
half a dozen small properties around the area of the Anglican Cathedral.
Pop Stanley was a sail maker by trade, and the nature of his job entailed
accompanying ships around the world. With the decline in the shipping
industry, he later took employment at home, working between the Mersey
and Irish Sea with the London, Liverpool and Glasgow Salvage Company,
which specialised in the salvage of submarines. His position meant status.
When Pop spoke, people were expected to listen. He addressed work sub-
ordinates using their surnames, while he in turn expected to be addressed
as 'Sir' or 'Mr Stanley'. In the workplace, Pop was a skilled and influential
artisan; in the home he could be a hurtful and spiteful head of house.

Being the oldest daughter, Mimi developed a close relationship with her father. She was given the major responsibility of looking after her four younger sisters. This mother model developed a strong air of the disciplinarian in her which carried over when she became John's 'new mother'.

The area where Mimi and Julia lived was essentially solid upper-working-class/lower-middle-class. As a rule of thumb, the further you lived up and away from the river and the docks, the better the housing and status of the area; dock workers, on the other hand, needed to be near their place of work. The casual nature of such work meant a precarious living based on being selected for a gang from a 'pen' of men seeking work. This humiliating act of selection is vividly captured by Marlon Brando's Terry Malloy in the Brooklyn-set film *On the Waterfront*. Some of the 'lucky' chosen dock workers owed their selection to buying a drink for the foreman in the pub, commonly known as the 'blue eye system', while those unfortunate enough not to be picked would go home and later return to the pen for the afternoon selection, hence the importance to live as near as possible to the riverfront.

The four-mile stretch from the Pier Head that made up the north end and south end dockland zones contained at this time 250,000 people, the most densely populated area in either Europe or America.

Pop was intimately familiar with the dockland neighbourhoods. He regularly made his way through the narrow walkways and dismal courts on his way to work, an experience that instilled in him a desire to provide a better standard of living for his own family. No daughter of his was going to work in a seed cake mill, margarine factory, or as a sack maker or soap wrapper. Mimi, as the eldest daughter, would be fully indoctrinated by Pop into being self-regarding, status-conscious, thrifty and thick-skinned. She learned, as second mother to her sisters, to make certain she would better herself as soon as possible and move up. Whereas Mimi was thus constantly looking to climb the social ladder, Julia was content to pick up the new wisecracks of Mae West in her latest movie at the local picture house.

The conditions of housing in Toxteth made living 'cheek-by-jowl' the norm, and John's parents were both living in these conditions in streets that were less than a ten-minute walk from each other. But this short distance represented the difference between the free and easy casualness of the Lennons in Copperfield Street and the skilled disciplinarian atmosphere found in Head Street. Alf Lennon (more commonly known as Freddie) was six years younger than Mimi and lived with his brothers and sister at the family home at 27 Copperfield Street. The red-bricked terraced houses were built to accommodate skilled and semi-skilled workers mainly from the port-related industries, such as shipyard, marine engineering or transport workers. From Copperfield Street, where Freddie lived, it was a short walk to Head Street down the district's main thoroughfare of Park Road, named after the path taken to King John's medieval royal hunting ground of Toxteth Park. This is also the walk Freddie's Irish-born dad would have taken to the Flat Iron pub, which sat in front of Head Street at the Junction of Mill Street and St James Place. Here, not 25 yards from where Julia lived, John's grandfather Jack, the vaudeville minstrel reputed to have toured America, would regularly give a song and dance routine for the benefit of his friends and pub regulars.

When Jack died of liver damage, Freddie was seven years old. Shortly afterwards, he was placed with his sister in an orphanage. Freddie was in some ways lucky insomuch that the children's home turned out to be the local charitable Blue Coat School, which was well considered and had a good standing, being located in the Wavertree suburb of Liverpool – less than half a mile from Penny Lane.

While Freddie and Julia grew up, the pressures to find work increased as the recession of the 1930s continued. Freddie was at a distinct disadvantage here, having suffered from rickets as a child. This condition forced him into wearing callipers, which resulted in stunted growth (5ft 4in) and bandy legs. But any physical disadvantages were more than made up for by an exuberant personality and the ability to perform a song at the drop of a hat. This came together with a strong sense of humour and wit. As a youngster he would give Saturday 'shows'. This would consist of taking in a few pennies from friends for a performance which included songs and imitations of Charlie Chaplin and the latest hits, which he played on his harmonica.

While at Blue Coat School, Freddie, with his older brother Sidney, visited the local Empire Theatre to see the children's spectacular Will Murray's Gang. He was immediately bitten by the showbiz bug. Backstage after the show, Freddie approached Will Murray with the less than subtle declaration of 'I'm better than your leading boy'.[4] Taken in with the young Freddie's confidence and smart Blue Coat School uniform, Murray offered him a place in the troupe. His delight was shattered when he was told in no uncertain terms by the headmaster that this would not happen. Undeterred, the rebel in Freddie made him decide to write his mother a farewell letter and make his own way to Glasgow – the next venue for the show. Within a few days, Freddie's world collapsed. Blue Coat's headmaster turned up at the Glasgow venue and escorted him by train back home. Worse was to follow when the same headmaster ridiculed him in a full assembly at the school. He derided and goaded him with such comments as: 'You thought you were going to be a star', and 'Which part were they going to give you, Tom Thumb or perhaps one of the Seven Dwarfs?'.[5] The assembled boys laughed on cue.

If this was an effort to break Freddie's spirit and make him conform, it failed. He determined to make his own rebellious and unorthodox way in life and turned a deaf ear to those who criticised him. The showbiz bug in Freddie was to find inspiration in two places. The first was the opportunities that a life in the Merchant Navy could offer and the chance to give a 'turn' to both the ship's crew and passengers. Freddie would spend many hours down at the Pier Head gazing enviously at the cargo ships and liners passing through the mouth of the Mersey, making journeys to places such as Valparaiso, Cape Town and Shanghai. A local journalist at the time described the Pier Head as 'a threshold to the ends of the earth'.[6] The second source of inspiration turned out to be the free spirited – and some might say the slightly eccentric – Julia Stanley. The problem for Freddie was simple: life at sea and being with Julia weren't compatible.

Julia Stanley was a nonconformist during a time of mass unemployment and political uncertainty, a period when one couldn't really afford to be as unconventional as she was. The 1930s were witness to unprecedented economic depression and extreme austerity, but she did not worry. The vagaries of trade for the port left it particularly vulnerable to high unemployment. The largest area of work for women in the city, and still a reflection of the wealth, was domestic service. Thousands of household servants found employment in the richer sections of the city. The attitude of a nonconformist like Julia to a position 'in service' as a parlour maid or scullery girl was incredulity and disdain. At her first job in a printer's shop in the city centre, she lasted only a week before being sacked due to her indulgence in horseplay and practical jokes. Freddie's own first job, by coincidence, was as a bellboy at the Adelphi Hotel, the same hotel that was to employ Julia's common law husband, Bobby Dykins, as wine waiter.

While Julia was in many ways an easy-going type of person, often described as happy-go-lucky and good company, Mimi was assertive and aggressive. The sisters could not have been more opposite. Mimi looked towards social mobility and the skills she had gathered in her role as 'second mother'. This brought authority and obedience over her younger sisters. Mimi was all for pulling oneself up by the boot straps. She was a social climber of the first order. She lived by a code in which accent was one of the first indicators as to how she would treat a person.

These values would be exercised on the young John Lennon in later years at Mendips. The effects of the 'Hungry '30s' increasingly moulded in Mimi's already powerful personality a burning need for status, career and a comfortable niche in life. Julia's reaction towards a career, by contrast, was not to have one. Because she liked films, she instead found herself a job in the local cinema as an usherette. Mimi, meanwhile, moved from the discipline of dealing with her siblings to the discipline of dealing with patients: she became a trainee sister in the Woolton Convalescent Home, situated in an affluent suburb of Liverpool. She was also personal assistant to an industrial magnate who made his fortune in biscuits in Manchester. Mr Vickers invited Mimi to become a personal secretary at the family home in Betws-y-Coed on the North Wales coast. Here she enjoyed the life she craved. She was treated as one of the family with trips on Vickers' yacht around the coast. For reasons that remain unclear, this position was to last only a year.

While Mimi had her goals of self-advancement, Freddie found his size and frame disqualified him from the manual work of the docks, but his education at a well-respected school led him to the position as bellboy at the Adelphi. Eventually, when the Great Depression hit really hard and unemployment in the city reached 30 per cent, Freddie found work as a ship's steward. Julia, much to the concern of her family, was content to continue work as a shop girl or usherette.

One escape from the gloom of the depression was the cinema. Cinema was glamorous, warm and cheap, while working-class homes were in the main cold, damp, overcrowded and uncomfortable. Just as people had their local pub, so many neighbourhoods had a network of cinemas in the 1930s; they were geared to accommodate just how far the person could afford to travel to their 'local Pally' (Palace). A network of neighbourhood cinemas existed in Liverpool and other major cities, and Picture Palaces were in walking distance for most city dwellers. American films of the period depicting hardnosed, wise cracking Irish-American actors such as Spencer Tracy, Pat O'Brien and James Cagney were much preferred to those featuring their English counterparts: Basil Rathbone types, decked out with a pair of brogues and a three-piece Harris Tweed suit, who solved and explained mysteries in oak-panelled drawing rooms with a clipped Oxbridge accent. But the Liverpool audiences could identify with streetwise people like Cagney as 'one of us'. Cagney's persona of tough guy, underdog and cynical wisecracker showed what could be achieved by a second generation Irish family. The previous decade of Celtic influence in Liverpool gave way and morphed into an Irish-American perception of how the world should be run. The sense of apartness from England and of being connected to Ireland was, perhaps, finally on the wane. But, if anything, the severity of the Depression and lack of government support in the 1930s gave cities like Liverpool an added insularity, something that persisted into the 1950s, 1960s and beyond.

In the dockland area where the Stanleys lived, an integral part of community life was the ability to get on with one's neighbours. This was essentially the ability to live and let live. The proximity of living and working arrangements called for, if not a public spirit, then insight into the importance of some sort of very basic, intertwined collective network – a community. You either got on with those in the community or, if you had the funds, got out. The Stanleys got out. Nearby, neighbours who were stokers, carters, porters and dock labourers were not seen as part of a community the Stanleys wanted to be involved with. In the case of the slow middle-class drift from the centre of Liverpool, the Stanleys' move was to take them further up and away from the river to upmarket Berkley Street, running adjacent to the premier location of Princes Avenue. Here the 'bookends' of Saint Patrick's Mission Church and Dexter Street Laundry were replaced by Saint Nicholas Greek Orthodox Church and the Welsh Presbyterian Church, nicknamed 'the Welsh Cathedral'. This was a church modelled on St Theodore's in Constantinople, the second only of its type in Britain and a symbol of the cosmopolitan nature of the city.

At Berkley Street, the Stanleys could take satisfaction in the traditional Sunday morning walk along the boulevard of merchants, cotton brokers and ship owners who occupied the four-storey red brick townhouses complete with servants' quarters. This was an affluent area where, as locals would say, 'a man wouldn't be seen outside without his hat'. To accommodate the religious needs of Liverpool's elite, grandly designed churches and places of worship were spaced along the avenue, designed to promote the wealth and status of the captains of industry and commerce that funded them. Jewish, Greek and Congregational churches were all part of this rich fabric.

Freddie and Julia would eventually meet and begin their courtship when he was 16 and she 14 at Sefton Park Boating Lake, which lay to the south of the city, a few miles from each other's homes. On Sunday afternoons, families would take their children there to feed the ducks. Young men and women would dress up in their best clothes and parade themselves for each other's approval in the hope of finding a date. In Liverpool parlance, Freddie and Julia 'copped off' in an unusual way. Although small, Freddie was handsome, with jet black hair and the gift of the gab. He spotted Julia as she sat on a park bench, and the attraction was easy to see – she could have been mistaken for the movie star Ginger Rogers, petite in size and with a mane of flaming red hair.

Julia had noticed what seemed to be a small 'boy' wearing a black bowler set at a jaunty angle, a cigarette holder in his hand. The 'boy' was Freddie. As suavely as he could, he asked Julia if she may be so kind as to permit him to sit on the bench with her. Julia turned slowly, studied the bandy-legged, bowler-hatted Freddie and screamed with laughter. She told him to take his hat off, for he looked daft. Instead of taking umbrage, as most young men would, Freddie did as he was told and skimmed the hat across the boating lake, nearly decapitating a duck. This act of going against the grain, spontaneity and zaniness instantly endeared him to Julia.

Their relationship immediately ran into problems with the total lack of approval and contempt of Freddie from Pop and Mimi. That Freddie was a bellboy, and came from a 'less acceptable part of town', had been in an orphanage and was stunted in size, left Pop and Mimi in no doubt that he would not be welcome over the Stanleys' doorstep. 'I knew he was no good to anyone, certainly not [for] our Julia',[7] judged Mimi. Freddie's family view of the courtship was that of a seven-day wonder, just like his dreams of showbiz stardom.

Over their long period of courtship, Julia was constantly discouraged by her family from having anything to do with Freddie. On Freddie's side, his older brother Sidney regularly cast aspersions as to the strength and 'sense' of the relationship. Such was Pop's antagonism against the young Freddie Lennon that he conspired with Mater's husband, his son-in-law Captain Charles Parkes, to arrange a two-year trip for him on a whaling ship. Sometime later, Pop had to be restrained by Julia from beating up the pint-sized Freddie for the crime of knocking over a radio speaker.

After a long and sometimes tortuous courtship, Freddie and Julia were married on 3 December 1938 at the Liverpool Registry Office, Mount Pleasant. They did so without informing any members of their respective families. After a desperate search for a witness for Freddie, a last minute call was made to his elder brother, Sidney. Their honeymoon consisted of going to the Forum Cinema in the city centre, where they bought tickets to watch *The Boy from Barnardo's*, starring Mickey Rooney. This was followed by a return to their respective family homes. Within the week, Freddie shipped out on a liner for a three-month trip to the West Indies. If Freddie couldn't believe his luck in obtaining such a good post, it was because it wasn't luck. It was Pop Stanley again, who had worked behind the scenes with Charles Parkes to arrange Freddie's absence. Even when married, Freddie was to be kept as far away as possible from his daughter.

If Freddie and Julia felt that their courtship was beset with pitfalls and emotional hardships, then Freddie being 'lost at sea' and the arrival of a baby in war-torn Liverpool would test their love for each other to breaking point.

CHAPTER THREE

1940–45
Salvation Army Hospital

THE MARRIAGE OF FREDDIE and Julia was followed a year later by the outbreak of war. The initial period of the conflict in Britain was named 'The Phoney War' – phoney inasmuch as, unlike mainland Europe, life in Britain for the large majority remained much the same as before. The Battle of the Atlantic, in which Freddie was involved with the Merchant Navy, however, was to be the longest conflict between allied and German forces within the whole of the Second World War.

From the start of the hostilities, the transatlantic crossing of vessels manned by merchant sailors like Freddie soon became a lifeline for those in Britain. Such work was not without its dangers, though. Thirty-six thousand merchant sailors lost their lives during the period 1939–1945, of which 8,000 were from Liverpool alone. And although the Stanley family criticised Freddie for not sending Julia money home while he was away at sea, they did not realise he went AWOL in 1943, with his pay stopped immediately.

The Port of Liverpool was responsible for the bulk of shipping coming in and out of war-torn Britain. The Western Approaches HQ was the command post for the entire British Fleet and Merchant Navy Head-quarters, based in Liverpool's city centre. It lay half a mile from the Mersey and directed the supply of foodstuffs and armaments for tens of millions of Britons.

Just two weeks before the outbreak of war in September 1939 and after a protracted courtship, Mimi married George Smith. Their marriage was to bear no offspring. Later on, Mimi's view of being childless was that she had already been a mother to her four sisters. Furthermore, at 34 years of age, she was getting to a point where having children was becoming less likely. George's family was relatively wealthy and owned land in Woolton, along with a dairy farm. This is how Mimi and George came to meet, when he made the deliveries to Mimi's place of work in Woolton Military Convalescent Home. The agreement to get married began with a formal shake of the hands by the couple: 'Farmers always shake hands on a bargain',[1] George was to declare. Not long after they married, George's father committed suicide by drowning himself in a local pond. The resulting will was shattering. Instead of leaving the bulk of the estate to George, the eldest son, his father gave it to his younger brother Frank. George was given a small cottage next to the main farmhouse. Both George and Mimi took this decision hard. Having been financially overlooked, Mimi especially became very bitter.

Julia Baird (the eldest daughter of John 'Bobby' Albert Dykins and Julia Lennon, and half-sister of John Lennon) recollects how Mendips, the home where John spent most of his early life, came to Mimi and George in what can only be described as an unusual and unlawful way.[2] The house, whose name came from the previous owner's fondness of walking on the Mendip Hills, was separated from Mimi's previous home at the rear by a fenced garden. The new house was located in a prestigious position on the prominent boulevard of Menlove Avenue. When Mimi noticed that the neighbours were moving out of Mendips, she quickly collected all her furniture in her back garden then proceeded to pile it over to her neighbour's garden.

Breaking into the empty but secured house, she claimed squatter's rights – even though she and George had a perfectly good home just yards away. In Liverpool parlance, this was 'hard faced'. The owners of Mendips had intended to sell the house when the previous tenants left, now they were left trying to negotiate with 'sitting tenants'. The outcome was that Mimi claimed possession as being nine-tenths of the law. She drove a hard bargain in the price she paid for the house. This was to be one of many examples of how what Mimi wanted, she eventually got... including John.

While Mimi's 'house moving' was taking place, Freddie's time was spent in the Merchant Navy, whose Liverpool-based transatlantic convoys were to supply the bulk of Britain's war supplies. Freddie's discharge book reveals that during four years at war, he had only three months' leave at home. The major problem with Freddie and Julia's marriage was that the words 'Freddie', 'dependable' and 'sensible' couldn't be used in the same sentence. Freddie's time away from Liverpool became a catalogue of misfortune, naivety and downright dullness.

In addition to attacking Liverpool's docks and the war materials coming through its port, there were also grain silos, power stations and gas works for the Luftwaffe to target. It made Liverpool Hitler's number one British target, outside of the capital. The effects of the war really started in earnest for the civilian population of Liverpool (and many other big cities) with the German Luftwaffe bombings in 1940. Twelve months after hostilities started, Liverpool (and the nearby Bootle docks and Birkenhead shipyards across the river) were to suffer shocking devastation and terrible civilian casualties. 3,875 people were killed during the Blitz; 7,144 seriously injured and huge swathes of the city destroyed. Out of 282,000 homes, 10,840 were completely destroyed along with considerably more damaged. This devastation resulted in tens of thousands of people being made homeless.

On 9 October 1940, during one of the worst periods of air raids, Julia gave birth to a boy, later christened as John. He was born in the city's Oxford Street Maternity Hospital. Mimi was to recall in vivid detail:

> I was dodging in doorways [in] between running as fast as my legs would carry me... There was shrapnel falling and gunfire, and when there was a little lull: I ran into the hospital ward and there was this beautiful little baby.[3]

Later, according to a relative of Mimi's who lived nearby, 'there were 56 people blown to pieces in an air raid shelter',[4] while Mimi had to grapple with a number of incendiary bombs that constantly dropped into her garden, tossing wet blankets on the bombs then and stamping them out. This version of events was intended to paint Mimi as a determined, brave and lovable surrogate mother. These certainly weren't the first efforts to muddy the waters of the true role she was to play in John's life. The account of the night's bombing offers up Mimi as a cross between Wonder Woman and Mrs Doubtfire. It is ludicrous and untrue. There were no German bombing raids on Liverpool the night John was born. Although the city was bombed no fewer than 60 times that year between September and December, no raids occurred during the day or night that Mimi gives her account. It seems somewhat perverse that she should want to paint this scene of 'heroic' selflessness against a backdrop of real heroics, suffering and deprivation by those in the inner city.

During the air raids on Liverpool, the bombs fell mostly on the docks and industrial areas of the city. This is where the very people whom Mimi had come to look down on lived, the people who stoically bore the brunt of the raids. Mimi's account of her role during the birth of John and the Liverpool air raid is one that she gave not once, but on a number of occasions. It was not just a case of a single recollection. If it was a straightforward recollection, inasmuch as there were bombs falling when John was born, leaving out the misinformation of her 'deadly dash' five miles across bomb-strewn Liverpool, then this could be accepted. It was neither, though, and as Julie Baird points out, 'Mimi lived 11 years after John had died. And in that time, Mimi reinvented herself. With John gone, she could say anything she liked, without anyone to contradict her'.[5] Mimi set out to rewrite John's history at Mendips. Her account of John's life became a familiar pattern of fabrication and misleading statements. The story of his upbringing at her hands is riddled with inconsistencies.

Freddie's service on the *Empress of Canada*, which started on 30 July, only ended on 1 November and he missed John's birth by some three weeks. Initially, Julia and baby John had moved from Newcastle Road to the cottage owned by Mimi's husband George. The problem with this move was that while Newcastle Road was ideally placed for transport and shops, the cottage was out in the sticks. It made for long spells of isolation. For Julia it made for greater pressure to get out and about, and out and about is what Julia did. When home, Freddie would accompany Julia to the local dance halls. He was not a dancer himself, but he would be content to watch her dancing with a string of different men. Aware of the pressures on his young wife, stuck at home with a baby, Freddie's 'instructions' to Julia when he sailed away was to 'go out and enjoy yourself'.

The following year in New York, he shipped out on a short voyage as the Chief Steward only to discover he was to be demoted to Assistant Steward. Instead of the short trip, he would be transporting arms and ammunition to the Far East. He consequently jumped ship, hid out in New York City and waited for a liner directly back to Liverpool. Days later he was arrested under suspicion of breaking into a cargo of whisky, locked in the ship's brig and then jailed at Ellis Island. Released two weeks later, he waited another month before being allocated on the *Sammex*, which was bound for the Far East again. This time Freddie found himself set up by another crew member on a charge for stealing whisky and cigarettes from the ship's hold. He was placed for another two weeks in a cell on Ellis Island and then for three months in an army prison camp in Malta. After 18 months away, Freddie made his way back home. What would be waiting there would surprise even him.

With little contact with her husband and even less money, Julia did not sit at home and mope. Instead she decided to 'live a little'. Returning to Liverpool as part of a convoy in 1943, Freddie stayed at the cottage with Julia and John. One Saturday night this pleasant family scene was interrupted by the sound of knocking on the front door. When it opened, Freddie was surprised to discover a sailor in full uniform with a platinum blonde on his arm. They were both in high spirits, asking for Julia. The couple had come to take Julia out for a drink. Freddie was shattered and begged Julia not to go. His wife was having none of it. 'I hardly ever go out,' was her response to Freddie's pleas. Freddie slammed the front door and barred it against Julia leaving. For her part, Julia took her high heels off, climbed on the kitchen sink and out of the window, and proceeded to run down the road, shoes in hand, to catch up with the sailor and his blonde girlfriend.

Freddie's wartime service in the Merchant Navy was characterised by a complex series of cock-ups and incompetence. The highlight of this odyssey was Freddie giving a 'star turn' to wildly appreciative servicemen in a New York bar. He was then carried shoulder high down Broadway to Jack Dempsey's bar, where he continued with his show.

Freddie came home to find his young wife pregnant, but obviously not by him. Instead, the father turned out to be a young Welsh soldier called Taffy Williams. At first, Julia claimed that she had been raped. After Freddie confronted the soldier, it was discovered that this wasn't the case. Taffy offered to marry Julia. She laughed in his face. Freddie offered to accept the child into the family, but Julia refused and instead she entered a Salvation Army Hospital in the Mossley Hill area, where she went full term and gave birth to a girl. As previously arranged with the hospital, after six weeks the baby – named Victoria – was eventually given up for adoption to a Norwegian sea captain and his Liverpool wife.

Julia would now return to Pop at Newcastle Road. Further conflict was to follow when Freddie, returning from another trip, discovered his wife had been having a six-month affair with Bobby Dykins, who was two years her junior. During this period, Mimi was to make her move for John. When Mimi was interviewed by Hunter Davies 'She claimed Julia wasn't caring for him properly'[6] and informed Freddie that John had walked from Newcastle Road to her house at Mendips. This was in all likelihood untrue. That an unaccompanied four-year-old would be in a position to navigate two major dual carriageways and make his way along the mile and half route past a police station seems extreme in the least. Why would

Mimi say this? It was the beginning of a long campaign of false accusations, half-truths and lies against Julia and Freddie to gain permanent access to John.

On Freddie's next return home to Newcastle Road, he was shocked to find Julia in a steady, long-term relationship, now living with Bobby Dykins. Julia hadn't heard from Freddie for 18 months and took it upon herself to find another man. Freddie must have known this was the end of the marriage. He asked to see John and was informed that he'd spent the last two weeks in Mendips. When he called to see him, Mimi demanded £20 for John's 'keep'. This was a month's wages.

Mimi was critical of Julia for bringing shame on the family with her relationship with Dykins. She seemed to be unusually supportive towards Freddie's position. What was later to transpire was that Mimi and Pop had been in collusion. Julia's mother had died in 1941, and since then Pop had been looking to snare one of his daughters to take the place of his wife-cum-housekeeper. At 71 years of age, Pop was becoming incapable of looking after himself. He desperately needed a carer and, as all of his other daughters were unavailable, Julia was the one he chose. Mimi, on the other hand, wanted a child, and she was determined it would be John. The plan was to give Julia a home in Newcastle Road along with Bobby (but if possible without him) and in return she would give up John to Mimi.

Before Freddie finally bowed out of the Stanley family, there was the sad spectacle of him taking John to his brother Sidney's home in Blackpool. The intention was for them both to emigrate to New Zealand. John's prospective antipodean adventure with his father ended when Freddie was located by Julia and Bobby. John, just five years old, was presented with the traumatic choice of who he would like to live with: his mother or his father. John's first choice was his father Freddie, followed by a quick reversal. He ran into his mother's arms. For such a young child, his first few years had been stressful in the extreme. Sadly, things weren't going to get better.

Following on from Blackpool, Mimi was to argue continually that John would be better off with her at Mendips where a 'stable environment' could be provided. Julia vehemently refused. There then followed a campaign by Pop and Mimi to ensure that they both got their way. Julia, much to the chagrin of Mimi, was allowed to stay with Pop at Newcastle Road together with Bobby Dykins. 'Living in sin' was anathema to Mimi. Such a state of affairs brought shame on the family, but perhaps there was method to Pop's madness. Bit by bit, pressure was applied to Julia to relinquish John into Mimi's care. She and Bobby could stay and take care of Pop. The pressure to give in was so intense that Julia, John and Bobby moved out of Newcastle Road and into a small flat in nearby Gateacre. This was the chance Mimi had been waiting for. With Pop in attendance, Mimi paid an unannounced visit to the flat. Both declared that it was an unfit place for John to live and Mimi demanded he be placed with her. A campaign of harassment against Julia was to pay dividends. 'She saw a window of opportunity, and if she'd have let that go, there wouldn't be another chance,' states Julia Baird (née Dykins):

> The first time she came round to collect John, my father put her out. The second time she came with a social worker who said – or rather told – Mimi that she could find nothing wrong with John's staying with his mother. Mimi then probably appealed to the Director of Public Services. She was determined. He asked where John slept. There was only one bedroom and my parents weren't married. He agreed with Pop and Mimi that John should go and live with George and Mimi at Mendips.[7]

Mimi's belief was that John living in the same house as his mother's common law husband was enough to get him away from his mother. Refusing to take no for an answer, she went to the Head of Liverpool's Public Services. The Director sided with Mimi. The result was that five-year-old John was removed by order of the Public Services from Julia, just one summer after he had lost contact with his father.

Mimi would say later that 'Julia had met somebody else with whom she had a chance of happiness, and no man wants another man's child'.[8] But Bobby Dykins showed strong intent to take John on as his own son. He was willing to set up home with Julia and John. If Freddie could be tracked down and agree to a divorce, it was highly likely the couple would marry. And as for 'no man wants another man's child', where did this leave George Smith, in whose home John would be living? 'Mimi changed John's school to Dovedale from Mosspits, and took over running his life. Or should that be ruining his life?' Julia Baird comments. She continues:

> It was obvious that Julia and Bobby needed a bigger place, where John would have his own bedroom. Julia and Bobby moved back with Pop

at Newcastle Road, where John could have his own room. That would solve the problem, so Julia went to Mimi to get John back. Mimi turned her away at the door.[9]

Mimi had acquired John as she has acquired Mendips: by stealth and subterfuge. Her appetite for self-advancement included the 'ideal family', which of course included a child. John was to be the final part of Mimi's transformation into a post-war, *Woman's Own* accomplished suburban matriarch. John had now been subject to a tug of war between his parents, having to choose between his mother and father, the introduction of social workers in the battle for his custody between his mother and his aunt, and the introduction of a regimented and cold regime at Mendips. It's no wonder that he sought solitude in his writing and art.

'Hypocrite to the core. Flawed. Unbelievable what she put my mother through,' concludes Julia Baird. '[Mimi] had set her heart on having John, no matter what the price to pay, no matter what my mother thought. Mimi just battled away. This was her opportunity to have a child'.[10]

CHAPTER FOUR

1946–50

Wandsworth Jail

JOHN'S NEW HOME was now 251 Menlove Avenue, a three bedroom, bay windowed, pebble-dashed semi-detached house, complete with lead glassed quarter light windows and the name plate of 'Mendips'. John's bedroom was the small box room over the vestibule. He would stay there throughout his childhood and into early adulthood.

Mendips was a sign to Mimi of having 'made it' – no more living next to butcher shops, drapers or costermongers. Here at Mendips, Mimi could look over a golf course a hundred yards away and was surrounded by a variety of mansions built by the great and good, whose money had been made in trade from the port. Woolton should have been an ideal place to bring up a child with its woods, green spaces, its golfers and a village with a history going back to the Vikings. For post-war Liverpool families living with their bomb-damaged houses, cluttered inner cities and decrepit housing stock, Mendips was a dream. For five-year-old John, it would be anything but.

The post-war world of Britain in which the young John was brought up was in a period of social revolution. A war-weary population was demanding a better way of life to the deprivation suffered during the 1930s. The 1945 General Election produced a shock at the polls in the shape of a landslide victory for the Labour Party, which ran on a mandate of addressing issues of poverty, social class and the fairer distribution of wealth. The formation of the Welfare State was to be the vehicle for this change.

The 1945 General Election radically changed the country's political landscape, with newly elected Labour MPs singing 'The Red Flag' on the first day of Parliament, which caused more than a hint of concern to the British Establishment. The General Election result was seen by many as a kick in the teeth to the Conservative Leader, Winston Churchill. His supporters were amazed that the electorate should see fit to jettison the nation's wartime leader. Upon hearing the election result, Arthur Marwick relates how an upper-class supporter of the Tory party announced: 'But this is terrible – they've elected a Labour Government and the country will never stand for that'.[1]

The Welfare State was to provide a clear divide between those of in favour of the 'pull yourself up by your bootstraps' ideology and those in favour of collective support. The Welfare State was to deliver cradle-to-grave provision of social care. This included the need for decent housing. Many, like Mimi and her family, had already followed the route of the 'respectable working classes' in moving steadily further afield from inner-city Liverpool. Indeed, not long after Mimi took John to Mendips, the following item appeared in the *Liverpool Echo* regarding a home in Mimi's old neighbourhood, Head Street: 'A Beaufort Street family were awakened at one in the morning by a loud crash to find a hole five foot square [in diameter] had opened in the side of their home'.[2] The reporter concluded with the view that this was not an uncommon incident.

Berkley Street in Toxteth, where the Stanley family had moved, was sliding towards decline just as the family moved further afield again to Newcastle Road, in Wavertree. Sociologist J.B. Mays' research into the once prestigious Princess Road area of Toxteth area noted that:

> It is significant that Negroes serving in the United States Forces stationed in the Merseyside area find their way to the Berkley Street region in search of recreation and companionship. There is little doubt that one reason for the visitation of coloured and white men is the attraction of certain dubious clubs where illegal pleasures may be bought. According to reliable information, there were a great number of brothels in the area during the war years...[3]

Liverpool's Berkley Street was the area where Stanley Crouch's 'Negro chaos' met 'Scouse chaos' and Lindy Hopped the night away. Like many factors of life, housing and where you lived in Liverpool could be a seen as a badge of honour or shame. Liverpool's rented housing stock always had a history of being extremely poor in quality. In 1954 the National Building Association estimated that Liverpool had around 88,000 unfit dwellings which housed approximately 90,000 families. This meant almost a third of the city's population had to live in slum housing.

> When John commented on where he lived, he insisted it was not: the poor kind of slummy image that was projected in all The Beatle stories. In the class system, it was about half a class higher than Paul, George or Ringo, who lived in government subsidised houses.[4]

He was fully aware how distinctly housing differentiated people. This was why the council estates where Paul and George lived brought out all the snobbery in Mimi. During John's time under her 'mentorship' there would be frequent and varied references to both Paul and George as 'scruffs' and 'common types'. Indeed, when a young Paul McCartney came calling for John, he was made to wait by the side entrance of Mendips and, after being given a slow, deliberate once-over by Mimi, she would call to her nephew, 'John, your little friend's here!' Paul noted:

> She'd smile. I'd know what she'd done. She'd know what she'd done. I would ignore it. It was very patronising... she was very aware that John's friends were lower class. John mixed with the lower classes, I'm afraid, you see. She was the kind of woman who would put you down with the glint of an eye.[5]

'Common' and 'lower' seemed to be her regular terms of reference, and Paul McCartney was aware of this clash of cultures from very early on:

> John, because of his upbringing and his unstable family life, had to be hard, witty, always ready for the cover up, ready for the riposte, ready for the sharp little witticism. Whereas with my rather comfortable upbringing – a lot of family, lots of people, very northern, 'Cup of tea, love?' – my surface grew to be easy-going...[6]

Social hierarchies and the shifts they were subject to were certainly significant at this time. A Gallup Poll commissioned in the early 1950s asked 'What do you think [the] Labour [Party] stands for?' Responses included: 'more money for less work'. A headmaster's wife: 'Giving the working classes power they are not fitted to use.' A commercial traveller: 'They say social security but I think class war.' A solicitor's wife: 'Pampering the working man.' A dentist: 'Class hatred.' An engineering technician: 'Revenge and grab.' A butcher's wife: 'To keep down the people with money.' The same set of interviews revealed the views of a housewife who believed that 'the chief value of the middle classes is that their way of life represents a standard which the working class can emulate'.[7]

Many of those at the bottom of the social hierarchy that the Labour Party sought to help lived in poor housing and welcomed the demolition of the slums, which were to be replaced by central government supported council house estates. But in post-war Britain, Mimi and many others felt under attack by the Welfare State's New Jerusalem. The issue of financially supporting social, educational and economic provision in the country at large became a battleground for left and right. Mimi saw herself as a 'get up and go' type of person and believed that giving people state money only made them 'soft'.

The consensus of the post-war period in many ways hid a build-up of resentment on both sides of Britain's class divide, with the upper and middle classes resenting the 'uppity' working class for not recognising their betters, and the working class equally resentful for not having their part in the recent World War recognised or being provided with sufficient provision for a decent quality of life.

Woolton was where Mimi's husband George was born and brought up. Such a village existence – quiet, slow-paced and seemingly unchanging – may have contributed to George's laid back approach to life. It could be argued that inner-city Liverpool had much more in common with New York than it did with Woolton. Mimi's courtship with the man who was to be father to John for ten years began with him delivering milk from atop horse and cart from his family's dairy business to Woolton Convalescence Home, where Mimi worked as a nurse. Though George was well thought of, he liked a drink and a bet with his friends. He was good looking, six feet tall, and his constant requests for a date were rebuffed. Eventually, after years of George's overtures, Mimi agreed to go out with him.

During their dating, mild-mannered George fared no better than Freddie in being bullied and harassed by Pop. In Berkley Street, Pop had a habit of bursting into the front room where Mimi and George held their courtship nights and demanding that polite, middle-aged George leave. *Now!* Even Mimi was to comment that Pop 'was a bit of a bully'. She was to learn from this, though.

George had by this point suggested marriage to Mimi many times, but she stalled. Mimi's view of George was that he was no more than a stop gap or fall back – when someone let her down, she'd call George. According to Mimi, she had already been engaged to a doctor at the hospital who died from an infection that he caught from a patient. Then she was engaged to a doctor who left for Kenya and finally she had a relationship with a RAF fighter pilot who later died in the War. Mimi's accounts of these Mills and Boon romantic interludes made the role of a milkman's wife less than attractive. But there was the not insubstantial matter of George's intended inheritance of the farm, surrounding land and its buildings. Mimi was 32 years old; George ten years older. Mimi was in danger of becoming what her father Pop cruelly labelled his youngest daughter Harriet – 'an old maid'.

With war looming and a man shortage on the horizon, Mimi had a choice of George or continuing employment as a spinster in Woolton Convalescence Home. Finally, after another delivery of milk, George proposed once more and Mimi accepted. To him it was a marriage of respectability. To Mimi it was a marriage of convenience.

Pop's support of Mimi was based around the notion of getting Julia to move back in at Newcastle Road and take care of him. When approached, Julia refused. She wouldn't move in without Bobby. The birth of Victoria, whose father was Taffy Williams, along with the constant pressure by her family not to keep the child, left her in a depressed and debilitated state. She spent almost the entire pregnancy indoors. Bobby was her only means of emotional support and refuge. She wasn't going to leave him just to provide Pop with a housekeeper. Pop's old age and physical frailty had made him reconsider his previous righteous indignation and rants. Julia and Bobby moved in with him.

When Julia and Bobby arrived at Mendips and attempted to get John to come and live with them at Pop's home at Newcastle Road, it ended in crushing defeat for his mother, who was categorically told that John would not be leaving. John's older cousin, Leila Harvey, witnessed Mimi flinging John behind her and screaming at Julia: 'You are not fit to be this boy's mother!'.[8] A combination of postnatal depression, the loss of Freddie and her new dependence on Pop for the roof over her head all led to Julia becoming an emotional shell. She was finally worn out by the uncertainties of life. This included Freddie's seagoing escapades. The birth of John without her husband's support, the pressures and judgement that surrounded the illegitimate birth of Victoria and the almost immediate demands for her to be adopted had left Julia no match for Mimi, whom Julia Baird describes as a 'Rottweiler' and a 'bulldog'.[9]

As part of the 'deal' for John living at Mendips, he was brought to Pop's by Mimi to visit his mother only on a Saturday afternoon. Mimi refused to let Julia call at Mendips. It is also worth noting that, had Mimi really wanted to, she could well have adopted Julia's daughter, Victoria. Why didn't she? She didn't want a newborn baby for adoption, even in the shape of her own niece. Newborn babies are a full-time, high maintenance job.

Mimi, it seems, wanted one off the shelf, one already 'housebroken'. Her complex psychological makeup reveals a permanent clash between her extreme, independent, confident and narrow outlook to life and her unquestionable deference and admiration for those she saw as her betters.

A curious aspect of Mimi's attitude towards Julia's 'stain of shame' and the dishonourable shadow this cast over the Stanley household is that she was herself an illegitimate child. Mary Elizabeth Stanley was born on 24 April 1906; her parents married in a Liverpool parish church on 19 November 1906. Perhaps the child Julia gave birth to in a Salvation Army Hospital would be, if the child remained inside the family, a reminder to her oldest sister, Mimi – a sister who spent the best part of her life moralising, and who was herself born out of wedlock.

Regardless of her motives, Mimi had emerged triumphant over Julia. All that remained was to eliminate the unwanted input or presence of Freddie. Freddie's particular lifestyle made it easy for Mimi to do this. It was the simple matter of a threat. When John started school, seafaring Freddie found himself docked in London, eager at the prospect of travelling to Liverpool to see his son for the first time in nearly 18 months. 'He was immensely excited at the prospect of being united with his son,' Freddie's second wife Pauline recalled, but couldn't face the idea of meeting Julia in the home she shared with Bobby and in order to gain some 'courage' for the forthcoming visit proceeded to go a massive bender with five of his shipmates.[10]

The group ended up on a central London street admiring the expensive gowns in an exclusive women's clothing store late at night. Before anyone could utter 'it wasn't me, guv', a shop window was smashed. His shipmates 'legged it'. With typical Freddie logic, he stepped inside the store, withdrew a mannequin off its stand and proceeded to dance around with it in the middle of Bond Street. The same Freddie, who wouldn't dance with his own wife to save his life and had stared blankly at Julia as she entertained a stream of new dance partners at the local dance hall, now plucked up the (Dutch) courage to engage in a quick foxtrot down the streets of the West End. As with most of Freddie's escapades, it ended in tears, or, to be more accurate, in his arrest by two passing policemen. He was sentenced to six months in Wandsworth Prison.

But behind the farce there were severe repercussions for John. Not only would he not see his father again until he was an adult, but Freddie compounded his arrest by making the fatal mistake of writing a letter to Mimi, with the intention of seeking her advice with regards to his time behind bars and how best to get out. Mimi's view of her brother-in-law had always been coloured by embarrassment and contempt. On his marriage to Julia, Mimi's view was blunt and unambiguous: 'Why she picked him I'll never know. I couldn't believe she ended up with a seaman. He was a good for nothing'.[11] But Freddie wasn't to know the extremely low opinion that his sister-in-law held for him; he also wasn't fully aware of the role Mimi had played in taking John from his mother. Now in Wandsworth Prison, he had made it game, set and match as to where John was to spend the next 17 years of his life. Mimi's return letter to the prison told Freddie exactly where he stood – that he had better start a new life well outside of Liverpool, unless he wanted John to find out his father was a jailbird. Essentially, Freddie was blackmailed out of his son's life.

Julia had originally placed John in Mosspits Infant School near Newcastle Road. When Mimi took John away from his mother, she placed him in Dovedale Infant School, which was nearer to Mendips, and further away from Julia. The move was not, as some have stated, due to John's bad behaviour, but was intended to isolate John further from his mother and to make him more dependent on Mimi. This ruse backfired when the generation gap between those mothers of John's fellow classmates and Mimi became a barrier to friendship or networking.

A major problem in trying to untangle what really went on in John's childhood is that most information on John's early years relies almost entirely on Mimi's own recollection. Yet the exaggerated accounts of John being surrounded by the love and affection of a mother figure, with his education and all his leisure and social needs addressed, are largely fabricated. The reason behind Mimi's rose-tinted view of John's time at Mendips was to mask the reality of what happened with Julia and the destabilising and emotionally harmful upbringing that John received. Mimi prided herself as the standard bearer of a puritanical discipline whose rallying cry to any of young John's protests would be 'it's for your own good'. Mimi herself stated: 'I had no time to go playing ducks in the bath with him'.[12] This in many ways speaks volumes about her, the message seemingly being that not only was she indifferent to the needs of her young nephew, but she was a *busy woman*. That was in spite of the fact that Mimi had one child to look after, a husband, whom she would make sure looked after himself, and no full- or part-time job of her own. Such unwillingness to take voluntary or paid employment, along with Mimi's own misanthropic attitude, left her socially isolated and John gradually became an unnatural focus of her attention.

Mimi lacked maternal instincts, but had the confidence to fake it. It was Uncle George who came to John's rescue – he understood the confusion and emotional turmoil that, at such a young age, John had gone through. It was Uncle George who spent endless hours teaching the young John to read, starting with the headlines of the local paper and then helping him all the way through to picture books. This eventually grew to classic children's books such as *The Wind in the Willows*, *Swallows and Amazons* and the *Just William* series. It was George who played the parental role. With studied indifference to the effects of the absence of other family members on young John, Mimi would declare: 'George would see him to bed with a smile most nights'.[13]

John's older cousin Leila recalled that, notwithstanding George's night-time security job, 'he took us all to the pictures [and] to the park', and he allowed the children to have a picnic in the garden shed.[14] George loved John in a way that Mimi could never dream of. Maybe it was George's own insight into Mimi's destructiveness that gave him some semblance of understanding towards what young John Winston Lennon had to endure.

Mimi had always had herself at the forefront of her thoughts. She may have developed this attitude from having to take on the responsibly of looking after her four younger sisters, demanding deference and obedience from them.

Mimi needed the reassurance of acceptance from those she felt were her peers, those who were professionals, self-employed, those of independent means – the cultivated and university educated. Those who fell outside this circle were 'common'. In essence, Mimi was a snob. After George Harrison's first visit to Mendips, Mimi was to comment that: 'You always do go for the low-class types, don't you, John?'.[15] She needed John to gain acceptance into the magic circle of friends who she saw as the better half of society. The problem was that she had gained serious black marks on her venture into middle-class suburbia. She had made herself and George look like a pair of common house breakers with Mimi's hunger for a better and more prestigious house. The sight of the pair spending hours humping furniture over a backyard fence from one house to the other must have proved a shocking scene for those who viewed it – think a 1940s version of *The Beverly Hillbillies*, minus the humour. Because of her greed for the house, Mimi didn't consider how she and her husband might have looked to others. She never considered the housing shortage of war-torn Liverpool.

Mimi's lack of acceptance from her neighbours also came in the shape of her husband George. He was a quiet and decent man, liked by all who met him. But he was also a functioning alcoholic and compulsive gambler. George, still a relatively young and attractive man when he married Mimi, had at that time some degree of standing in the community. He had a pleasant personality and was deemed a gentleman by those around him. He was presented with an inscribed tankard by the landlord and patrons of his local pub, such was his sociability. But a pleasant personality was not enough to hide his reputation as a hard drinker. Mimi wasn't fully aware that his twin diseases were public knowledge before they married. In Mimi's eyes, George now became 'damaged goods', which goes some way towards explaining her constant putdowns of him. The final nail in the coffin for George's credibility was his failed effort to become an entre-preneur, in the shape of independent bookmaker, a venture carried out from the confines of Mendips. Historian Ross McKibbin has described the area of George's 'employment' as

> a large and sophisticated industry [which] was constructed to meet the demands of the small better. A press with a huge circulation told him (more rarely her) what he needed to know to make an informed bet; an army of tipsters was at hand to assist him further; and, above all, in most pubs and clubs, in nearly every factory or workshop and on the streets of every working-class community, there was a book-maker with whom he could make that bet. There was only one problem: it was illegal.[16]

Illegal bookmaking was made possible in working-class areas due to a team of 'bookies' runners', a lookout or two, a safe place (usually a crowded pub) for the bookie to operate from and the safety of being surrounded by a supply of gamblers provided by the densely populated area. But George's bookmakers in Woolton, which operated out of his own home of Mendips, stuck out like a sore thumb.

A major factor in Mimi's permission for Mendips' use as a bookies shop was greed. Her student lodgers complained of 'paying over the odds' for their rent, at least by comparison to similar student digs. Cynthia Lennon, who lived with Mimi after she and John were married, believed that 'Mimi loved three things: money, Lennon and her cats, in that order'.[17]

Essentially Mimi married a man whom she could dominate, and with the added promise of a hefty inheritance. When this didn't materialise, she was prepared to risk the negative and criminal consequences of running a bookmakers at home. Even with her background in nursing, at a time of labour shortages and plentiful opportunities for people with her experience, she never worked in paid employment when she was married. For women in her position, it wasn't the thing to do. She would rather witness a stream of dubious strangers make a beeline to her front door, but not before furtively glancing around for plainclothes policemen or nosy neighbours, than go out to work herself. The *Beverly Hillbillies* nature of Mimi's arrival at Mendips, her marriage to a known chronic alcoholic and gambler, and their use of Mendips as a substitute for Royal Ascot led to the total ostracism of Mimi by her neighbours. Her cold manner didn't help to persuade her neighbours that she should be given a second chance.

Mrs Bushell, a neighbour who shared a common garden fence, would have an occasional chat, but in the ten years as her neighbour, Mimi was never invited in for a cup of tea. Mrs Bushell described her as 'unfriendly'. According to Mrs Bushell, the neighbours' views of Mimi and George were that they were merely 'working-class folk', a view that was reaffirmed by George's job as night watchman in a factory. What Mimi needed was a remedy to this outcast situation. She believed she had found it in the shape of John.

Mimi would always maintain that she needed to bring John up due to the need to save the boy from the shameless lifestyle his mother was leading. Indeed, she would later refer to Mendips as 'The House of Correction' and her sister's and Bobby's house as the 'House of Sin'. Mimi had a penchant for theatrics, but behind this hyperbole was the cruel and stark assumption that John's mother was nothing short of a 'fallen woman' and his father a 'good for nothing'. John was constantly told by Mimi he was wanted by her, but not by his mother, and that she was 'the parent of last resort'. *She deserved John.*

John's move to Mendips should have provided him with the stability that was missing from his life with Julia and Freddie. Instead, he was faced with a bitter matriarch who tried to mould him in her own image.

This would cause internal conflicts that would last John a lifetime. At her home in Toxteth and, to a lesser extent, Newcastle Road, it was enough for Mimi to play the part of acting like 'a person of quality'. Her place in Woolton Convalescence Home helped support her view that she was a solid member of the middle class. With the addition of John, she was able to demonstrate to 'those that mattered' in the Woolton community that she was committed to traditional family values by taking care of her nephew and removing him from the influence of his dysfunctional parents.

Mimi's view that you only get out of life what you deserve was motivated by what she wanted and by what she didn't want to be. She had lived in the inner city and knew its problems of poverty and poor housing – she wanted better. She was not a subscriber to the view of George Bernard Shaw that 'if you don't get want you like, like what you get'. Indeed, she would constantly refer to Paul and George as 'those scruffs'. Anyone talking in a local Scouse accent was seen as being on the lowest social rungs: 'I had high hopes for [him] and I knew you didn't get anywhere if you spoke like a ruffian,' remarked Mimi of John. Emphasising her view on the role of Queen's English, she revealed:

> I remember once he came home from town on the bus and he'd heard these Liverpudlians talking to each other – Scouse, you know. And he was shocked he couldn't understand what they were talking about... I told him he should avoid people like that. He was a country boy... he would never meet [them] except if anyone came to the house to mend something.[18]

Some insightful points come out of Mimi's comments. Firstly, her reference to 'these Liverpudlians' suggests that Mimi considered herself and John as being outside of this culture. Then there's the label of 'country boy' for John. This conjures up images of John with straw in his hair taking the family cow to Lime Street Market and coming back with five magic beans. The top and bottom of Mimi's problems were that she was a puritanical snob and wasn't a contented person. Despite the husband and the semi-detached house and the child, she wasn't acknowledged by those from whom she most wanted acceptance – her suburban community, her neighbours. Whatever ideals she had towards being 'a lady of the manor' at Mendips slowly dissipated as the *real* middle classes ignored the upstart from Liverpool 8 who was married to a drunken ex-milkman. The doctors and teachers that Mimi so desperately wanted validation from turned their backs on her the moment she started her life as a squatter. Her visions of an idyllic, middle-class life were finished before they had even begun.

John's arrival at his new school half-way through the school year only served to further distance Mimi. The introduction of John was intended to provide Mimi with the much-needed legitimacy of family values, her entry into the network of parents waiting outside the school gates of the infant and junior schools. But these friendships had already been formed at the school, starting early in September. The arrival of Mimi and John did not take place until April – a not insignificant gap – and with Mimi at this time being 38 years old, she was too old to be seen as a credible friend and confidante of those mothers who were a decade or so younger than her. The next ten years of picking up John consisted of curt nods to other mothers along with a doorman's smile, which hid a murderous desire for a lightning bolt to come down and strike this gaggle of unfriendly modern mums. George would fare no better. Being nearly 50 years old, he was in the 'grandparent range' and his appearance at the school gates with his shock of white hair and security guard uniform would only confirm what the mothers at the school gate would have already known – too old, not our 'type'. In the terminology of the day, Mimi was in a pickle. John was no use to her and she couldn't give him back without making a complete and utter fool of herself, so she was left with having to grin and bear it.

CHAPTER FIVE

1950–55

Gladstone Hall

THE WARTIME AGE of austerity was coming to a close, employment and consumerism were on the march, and the Port of Liverpool was buoyant in its trade with the Americas and the Empire. The Port shipped in and out more cargo than the next eight ports combined. The city's population stood at nearly 800,000, almost half of these crammed into the dockland zones and the city centre. The housing stock within the city was as bad as ever. The rapid rise of the port in the 19th century had left in its wake a swathe of jerry-built slum housing; a legacy of heavy immigration.

In the early post-war years, the Ministry of Housing identified 26,959 unfit houses in Liverpool, with conditions deemed so bad that they were marked for demolition. A further 61,724 required major repairs, making a total of 88,683 substandard dwellings. This, together with demobilisation and the consequent return home of thousands of servicemen, a high birth rate caused by the post-war 'baby boom' and a scarcity of construction materials all contributed to a severe post-war housing shortage. In 1949, John's mother and Bobby (who now had two daughters, Julia and Jackie), were more than fortunate to gain a three bedroom, front and back garden semi of their own, just a few miles from Newcastle Road. After Pop died in 1949, the owner of Newcastle Road had offered Julia and Bobby the opportunity to buy the house. Financially, the couple weren't in a position to take up the offer. Instead, they were provided with a new home by Liverpool Corporation in the Allerton area of the city at 1 Blomfield Road.

As post-war Britain progressed into the 1950s, it reverted to Tory rule with Winston Churchill becoming Prime Minister once again. The developing Cold War blanket of suspicion and fear divided many of those in Britain into those who supported the established order and hoped to maintain Britain's colonies, and those against, who were deemed unpatriotic. This divide slowly grew, and, as a further blow to national pride came the realisation that there were now two world super powers, and

Britain wasn't one of them. The cultural impact of such radical changes led to a reaffirmed belief in and commitment to pre-war family values. Any behaviour seen to be challenging the conventional wisdom of the established order, especially by the young, was anathema to those in authority and to trenchant parents alike – those brought up on a diet of King, Empire and Class. American influence on British culture, meanwhile, was deemed vulgar and shallow.

But the Allies' victory in Europe meant not just a change in power relations, but also to the development of a post-war USA bringing cultural hegemony to much of Western Europe. The UK in particular witnessed the arrival of American culture, from fashion to cinema and in language and music. Ten miles from Liverpool stood RAF Burtonwood, the largest American air force base in Europe, where 12,000 American servicemen lived only a short ride from the city. At an age when teenagers were expected to be mini replicas of their parents with regards to fashion, music and outlook, the sharply dressed, 'Hollywood talking' American GIS became an instant hit with the teenagers of the city. Tied to this was the presence of the 'Cunard Yanks', the thousands of Liverpool seamen who manned the great transatlantic liners.

Liverpool was a great attraction to the GIS and became a welcome alternative to the staid environment of barrack life at Burtonwood. The Toxteth district of the city in particular, with its large immigrant population, provided a variety of (illicit) night clubs, dodgy characters and music spots which presented a 'safe haven' – an exciting night out for many Afro-American GIS, especially given that these men enlisted in the war on racially-segregated lines in terms of the units they belonged to. Figures by the Colonial Office and League of Coloured People at this time reveal that a third of Britain's 'coloured' population were packed into the decaying Georgian and Victorian town houses of the city's south end.

Mendips was not immune to such shifting cultural perceptions. Philip Norman reveals that, of all the British comics (such as *The Victor, The Lion, The Commando and The Tiger*), Mimi only allowed *The Eagle* comic into Mendips. According to Norman, 'Mimi had forbidden [John] comics, except perhaps the high-minded *Eagle*',[1] which was edited by a clergyman. American comics with what Mimi deemed to be their lurid and sensational storylines were banned outright. *The Eagle* though was the only one to escape her censorship. 'Moral seriousness made *The Eagle* stand out from the silly high jinks of its American rivals, but it did not dent its appeal,' Dominic Sandbrook pointed out. Indeed, *The Eagle*:

> was a good example of the way in which old notions of patriotic duty and Christian service were reinvigorated rather than abandoned after the war; although Dan Dare's adventures take place in the far future, he retains the services of a batman and the International Space Fleet is identifiably a British hierarchical organisation.[2]

The battle was not just for the hearts and minds of children, but for the broader values of British culture, the concern for which would stretch to debates in the House of Commons. Motions were put down which sought to ban the sale of American comics, supported by the National Union of Teachers convention. But to children like John, who were oblivious to such events, being brought up in Britain during this period was to be brought up in what many saw as the golden age of childhood. With the war finally over and rationing gradually phasing out (although it took until 1954 for the end of sugar rationing and therefore sweets and chocolate to be made freely available), many children of this generation looked back to an idyllic time of their lives.

Removal from his mother, followed immediately by a change of school, had begun a confusing and distressing time for the five-year-old John. The effects of the absence of both parents came to the surface in the playground and classroom, where belligerent and hurtful behaviour began to emerge. This attitude would ebb and flow throughout John's whole life. From very early on, John was at war with the world and at war with himself. He recalled later:

> I did fight all the way through Dovedale, winning by psychological means if ever anyone looked bigger than me. I threatened them in a strong enough way that I would beat them or they thought I could.[3]

An interesting comment of John's gave an unintended insight into his own childhood in a throwaway remark he made about Ringo, who spent much of his childhood in hospital. It appears in Michael Braun's *The Beatles*, the first book to be written on the group:

AUTHOR 'We talked about Liverpool.'

PAUL 'There is a certain awareness about some people in Liverpool. Like Ringo; he's never been to school except two days. Three times they told his mum he was going to die.'

'Anyway,' said John, looking at Ringo, 'to be so aware with so little education is rather unnerving to someone who's been to school since he was fucking two onwards'.[4]

On first reading it seems that John is insulting Ringo but it's quite the opposite. He's criticising *his* own extensive education process and admiring Ringo's street smartness and lack of schooling.

During his time at Dovedale School, John found a fellow malcontent in the shape – somewhat ironically – of a policeman's son, Pete Shotton. They became fast friends, bonded by their commitment to refuse education. The two 'refuseniks' came across to their schoolmates as a double act. They delivered comic relief, the latest rude words and pranks, all sprinkled with a generous smattering of kicks to the shin, Chinese burns and forearm smashes. The bully in John was helped by his being upwards of 11 months older than some of the other pupils in his year. Pete lived close to Mendips and the two became inseparable. Pete's limited acceptance by Mimi was no doubt entirely due to the position of his father as a high-ranking officer in the local police force.

In post-war Mendips, Mimi continued her commitment to a lifestyle of listening to *Woman's Hour* and *Mrs Dale's Diary* on the radio. This alternated with broadcasts of classical music and her reading of 'quality fiction'. Cynthia Lennon recalls that:

Early on it became apparent to me that Mimi was something of a snob: she was faux middle-class with upper-class aspirations and one of her favourite words was 'common'.[5]

But for all her attempts to bolster what she saw as cultured, suburban living, she had forgotten one key factor in achieving upward social mobility – acceptance from the community.

Mimi, still seething from her failed attempt at further social mobility, fell back on her rigid values and opinions, an attitude of bitterness and resentment which would, after a time, seep into the mindset of young John. This sowed the seed of many of his destructive perceptions in his teenage and adult life. John would later talk of having a 'chip on the shoulder'. 'But on the other hand,' he continued, 'I want to be loved and accepted. That's why I'm on stage, like a performing flea. Because I would like to belong'.[6] Life in Mendips didn't equip John to be comfortable within himself. Compassion wasn't in great supply at 251 Menlove Avenue. Mimi built up a strong sense of dependency in John, stemming from her own deep insecurities, and she cajoled, intimidated and bribed him into following the 'right path'.

John spent most of his time between school and his small bedroom. The emotionless environment in which John found himself forced him to suppress his feelings for fear of further rejection. He sought security in an imaginary world of *The Wind in the Willows*, *Alice in Wonderland* and *Jabberwocky*: a world created and maintained through the nurturing of his precious reading, writing stories and poetry. The birth of John's creative genius lies here, in this refuge of his imagination.

Up to the beginning of secondary school, John was limited in his involvement with other children outside of school. There was a radio in Mendips that could have helped pass the time, but Mimi had forbidden John to use it. He was later to recall:

> In our family the radio was hardly ever on, so I got to pop later: not like Paul and George, who'd been groomed in pop music coming over the radio all the time. I only heard it at other people's homes.[7]

Uncle George would play board games with John, but his night shifts limited the amount of time he could spend with his nephew. The cinema could have been used as a treat and escape from Mendips, but Mimi regarded the cinema as 'vulgar', only allowing John a trip to the Picturedrome (as she called it) twice a year, taken by Uncle George at Easter and Christmas to catch a Disney feature. Mimi's view of the local picture house was perhaps coloured by her own upbringing. Neighbourhood cinemas were home to a frequently boisterous audience whose behaviour contravened and undermined the culture of the day with their mocking of authority figures such as the clergy, police and politicians. In essence, John's access to the local cinema was blocked due to the legacy of it being seen as an arena which was 'dark and dangerous'. The only resource left to combat this isolation and his own internalised loss of his mother and father was a young boy's creativity and imagination.

In the absence of cinema, radio and friends outside of the school playground, John continued with his ferocious love of books. He particularly cherished his 'comics', through which, like his hero William and his gang of Outlaws, he could emulate William with his own gang. He soon began writing his own stories, many of which featured himself as the hero, enjoying similar escapades to those as his fictional heroes. With Uncle George's support and encouragement, he ploughed through *Swallows and Amazons, Biggles, The Famous Five* adventures and *Doctor Dolittle*. When visiting John, a teenaged Paul McCartney discovered fully-laden bookcases, one of which included the complete works of Sir Winston Churchill, gold inlaid and leather bound. Paul was suitably impressed. It was this love and wonderment of the world of stories and words in which John would immerse himself. Later, it would form the basis for much of his songwriting and art. John's unhappiness led him towards an inner world of fantasy in which emotional satisfaction was gained by escapism. By engrossing himself in the creative world of the written word, he sought to protect himself from what the stern and flinty figure of Mimi.

At Dovedale, meanwhile, John's interest in learning continued to be minimal, and it was only after threats from Mimi that he applied himself to prepare for the 'Eleven Plus' exam, the determinant of whether a child went to a grammar school or one of the newly instituted comprehensive schools or technical colleges. John passed his exam and gained a place at Quarry Bank, located a mile from Mendips. Grammar school, with its rigid practices and competitive measured outputs, didn't necessarily help matters. Far better for him emotionally, perhaps, had he failed the exam and found a place at a local comprehensive or technical college, with its progressive emphasis on the individual student's progress rather than exam results. Indeed, arguments raged throughout the 1950s with regards to the impact of this educational selection process. Labour MP Wilfred Fienberg argued in the *New Statesman* that:

> It is socially pernicious. Taking the Grammar school cap is a more potent emblem of privilege than the old school tie. Public school snobbery affects a few children. The snobbery of the local Grammar school sets the tone in every city and country.[8]

If it wasn't hard enough for John to be rejected by his parents and find himself being brought up in a dispassionate household, now he had to be forced into a pressure cooker of continuous grading and have his behaviour and manners measured by masters in gowns who wished to ape the public school system.

Pete Shotton, John's 'partner-in-crime', also passed the Eleven Plus and they found themselves once again as classmates at Quarry Bank. Both carried on where they left off at Dovedale: causing havoc. John and Pete rekindled their 'adventures' outside of school hours too, with Pete becoming a kind of Millhouse to John's Bart. The reason behind John's behaviour is simple. Any serious attempt at his lessons could end in disappointment, and due to the corrosive attitude of Mimi, he was already a 'reject' and therefore a failure. John's older cousin Stanley Parkes recalled that 'John was afraid of Aunt Mimi, as she'd tear into him if he didn't behave'.[9] As Mimi wasn't into physical punishment, this 'tearing' into John was on a psychological level.

John's now deeply entrenched insecurity meant that he wasn't going to set himself up for another fall. It was better to be punished at school for not trying, using the smokescreen of bad behaviour, than to go through the mental turmoil of academic failure. John was torn between what was expected of him by school and Mimi, and rebelling against what a young boy perceived as the unfairness of it all. The conflict and contradictions in John's life at this time are reflected by the fact that as well as being a fighter, petty pilferer and bully, he was also a church-going choir boy and (like his hero *Just William*) a boy scout. In every area of every town, there were rogues like young John. It was rebellion, suburban style.

After John's move to senior school, there began first a trickle and then a flood of mixing with other children outside of school hours. It was at this time that John discovered his mother's address, not 20 minutes away from Mendips – a discovery that was to cause a further radical change to his outlook. Visits to his mother's house were barred by Mimi – Blomfield Road was strictly off limits. Mimi successfully rewrote John's childhood with comments like:

> Of course things couldn't have worked out better if we'd have planned it because George and I loved him madly and every day Julia would come over and play with him, so really he has two mothers in a way.[10]

Stanley Parkes, John's older cousin by six years, remembers it differently. Stanley lived in Scotland and would travel down to Liverpool for the summer holidays, and in many ways he acted as a big brother to John, taking him and his cousin Leila on trips to the park and days out to New Brighton beach. All in all a good egg, he looked out for his younger cousin, who had already been through so much. Stanley asked on John's behalf if they could visit Julia, a request which Mimi refused. Stanley then used subterfuge. Asking Mimi if he would be allowed to take John and Leila to his Aunt Harriet's, Mimi agreed. Stanley risked the wrath of Mimi by 'smuggling' John on a visit to his mother's house. Stanley recalls:

> John tolerated Aunt Mimi. She was a bit of tyrant. She kept a tight rein on his activities, but he would rebel against her.[11]

Len Garry, John's friend at this time, goes further:

> Mimi was a cat lover… She loved her cats more than she loved kids, that's for sure. She was a frightening woman. She wasn't homely, she was more like a headmistress, librarian type person. And you were scared to knock on the door.[12]

Little wonder that as John grew up he would gravitate towards Blomfield Road.

At various times in his life, John would give the general impression that all was fine with his childhood. Occasionally, though, he would provide insights into a somewhat different opinion of his time at Mendips. His comments of a happy childhood and his own inner turmoil could be compared to a duck sailing along a pond – all peace and calm while underneath the paddling feet creating turbulence and purpose invisible to those above. While at Rishikesh in a search for inner peace John reflected that:

> When you're born, you're in the pram and you smile when you feel like smiling. But the first game that you learn is to smile before you get touched. Most mothers actually torture the kid in the pram – make it smile when it doesn't want to: smile and you get fed.[13]

The important term of reference here from John is 'most mothers'. This could be a subconscious term intended to deflect directly from Mimi and couch the cry for help and understanding by denial of the emotional distress he was going through.

Child Psychologist Alice Miller's research showed that:

> … repressed pain blocks emotional life and leads to physical symptoms. And the worst thing is that, although the feelings of the abused child have been at the point of origin, that is, in the presence of those who caused the pain, they find their voice when the battered child has children of his own.[14]

John's confused childhood entered a new phase when, at the age of ten, he had to live with total strangers. These strangers were Mimi's lodgers – local university students who rented out the spare rooms at Mendips. Mimi moved her and George's bedroom into the downstairs living room, which left John upstairs in his box room flanked by a yearly change of students. An interview for the *Liverpool Echo* by one of Mimi's old lodgers revealed that she 'targeted' male students from the Veterinary Department of the University. This particular department was chosen so that free, professional pet care could be doled out to her three cats and John's dog, Sally. Not only were the students expected to provide free pet care but they had to endure 'greasy breakfasts, sometimes with cat hairs floating in them'.[15]

Julia Baird remembers the young John being taught 'The Dirty Alphabet' by one of these student lodgers which entailed 'A is for Arse, B is for...' Well, you get the idea. What other introductions made towards the adult world of sex by this conveyor belt of students is anyone's guess. In Hunter Davies' authorised biography, *The Beatles*, he reveals nothing at all of John having an annual round of new faces to share his home with. There was certainly no mention of one of the very early students from Yorkshire, Michael Fishwick, a student of biochemistry who would later return to Mendips while completing his PhD.

The introduction of these lodgers may have served Mimi well, providing additional monies and free pet care, but for John, beside the issues of his privacy and sheer uneasiness of the situation, he was constantly reminded by these young men of the educational path he was expected to take: O Levels, A Levels and then university, like many other pupils at Quarry Bank. The pressure of a grammar school education was compounded by the constant reminder at Mendips to apply and adapt to the homilies of 'getting on' in life by 'building character' and 'a need to learn right from wrong'.

After the release of the double 'A' side *Penny Lane/Strawberry Fields*, fans were interested as to where Strawberry Fields was or if indeed it actually existed. It's interesting to note that John's response to questions on Strawberry Field(s) is tied to a boys' reformatory. There were two famous houses in Woolton, John has stated:

> One was owned by Gladstone: a reformatory for boys, which I could see out my window, and Strawberry Field, just around the corner from that, [which was] an old Victorian house converted for Salvation Army orphans.[16]

His cousin Stanley mentions this other establishment as well: 'the Bad Boys borstal... intrigued us'.[17] This particular borstal was a remand centre for youngsters mainly from the inner city, comprising of boys as young as a seven years old who had been convicted of theft, ill-discipline or truancy – the types whose parents couldn't control them, or didn't want to. It's not too hard to imagine John gazing out his box bedroom and catching sight of one of these unhappy, unloved and rejected kids staring back from a barred window and unconsciously recognising a fellow traveller, no matter how wide the distance in background between them. In his 15 years at Mendips (a stone's throw away from the front entrance of Gladstone House), it is likely that John would catch sight of boys leaving in their course grey uniforms accompanied by a member of staff, youth officer or even a policeman. It wasn't just the visual influence of Gladstone House that mattered – it was the physical impact as well. The former Merchant's Mansion had been converted into a borstal (officially known as the more inviting 'Woolton Country School for Boys') and was home to three dozen boys. Due to the nature of the construction of Menlove Avenue, the pavement actually ran under Gladstone House. This meant a vestibule entrance encroached onto the full pavement of Menlove Avenue, and pedestrians like John had to walk through the vestibule. The *Liverpool Post and Mercury* reported:

> the excavation was made under the billiard room... To see the four-storey school rising over sheer over the edge of the pavements and pedestrians underneath is one of the most interesting not on that avenue but on any modern road.[18]

John must have walked through this entrance to the 'young boys prison' hundreds, if not a thousand, times or more.

Moving to and from school, John had to pass under the portcullis and come within yards of the doorway which contained and hid the misery of dozens of children his own age. Despite her recollections in later years about her taking John to the Strawberry Field Fête, Cousin Stanley recalls a different view of Mimi's attitude with him and John climbing over a fence then playing and talking to the girls at Strawberry Field only to be told by Mimi that: 'we should not mix with "those kind of children"'.[19] So, if young orphan girls where condemned, it's easy to imagine what Mimi's views were of Gladstone House.

One wonders, when the initial brief for a childhood theme was decided for the *Sergeant Pepper* album, why write about a field? Why not another part of his childhood, perhaps at a later date, like Paul's 'Penny Lane' which is full of movement, evocative images and teenage smut? Because up until the age of almost 12, John had only really left the house for visits to the cinema twice a year, no days out with Mimi, no friends outside of school, only leaving Mendips for school, and a few weeks when his cousin Stanley came for visits from Scotland – this was his sum contact with the outside world. In John's mind, Strawberry Field was associated with escape, going so far as to say 'Strawberry Fields was psychoanalysis set to music really'.[20]

As a picture of John's childhood emerges, there is little wonder that John (when not providing a sanitised version of his upbringing) had such a jaundiced, and at times terrifying, outlook of his childhood:

> Some people cannot see that their parents are still torturing them, even when they are in their forties and fifties... They still have that stranglehold over them, their thoughts and their minds. I never had that fear of, and adulation for, parents.[21]

John's use of the word 'torture' in this instance is arguably extreme; he is not using hyperbole, however, but expressing his mental state at the time. John's major problem with dealing with the psychological abuse he encountered is in common with a lot of other victims of similar types of mistreatment: denial. He hid behind the absence of parents of Julia and Freddie as the cause of his mental distress. Nobody knew what was happening except himself and Mimi. Uncle George probably knew to some extent, but he couldn't bear witness. Julia perhaps had some idea, but with her own health problems and a young family to raise, she was not in a position to intervene. She thereby offered passive consent. Mimi never missed an opportunity to self-publicise herself as a caring mother substitute – 'firm but fair'.

Mimi's explanation for taking John with the aid of social workers from Julia centred on the 'love' she had for him the instant she saw him. This follows Mimi's fairytale 'mad dash through German bombs'. In her mind she had no competition in writing the history of John and Mendips. In all the interviews she gave, she never once mentions spending time with John as a baby or toddler. Not one word of buying baby John clothes, a pushchair or toys. Not one word of going on days out with toddler John or trips to the park or cinema, *nothing*. These omissions are strange when one considers the complete 'accuracy' Mimi gave to every little detail she had in John's upbringing from birth to adulthood. Only when John was taken to Mendips was there any recollection of her involvement with the child. The story of Mimi being besotted with John as a newborn baby appears to have been essentially a smokescreen for what she would carry out with the aid of Liverpool Corporation Welfare Department five years later. Mimi took Julia's child not for any altruistic means, but because she wanted to and she could. The manipulation, threats and total insensitivity to the needs of young John would ultimately leave him psychologically scarred. Later, John would recall that he had a 'subconscious urge to get above people or out of a rut'[22] and in terms of his childhood, 'nothing would drive me through all that if I was normal'.[23] John's reflection of his childhood was honest and heart rending:

> The worse pain is that of not being wanted of realising your parents do not need you in the way you need them… When I was a child I had experience of not wanting to see the ugliness, not wanting to see not being wanted. This lack of love went into my mind and into my eyes.[24]

John was plainly aware of how the perceived absence of love in his life tainted his perception of the world. A double blow for John was that he was conditioned to judge and dislike his parents and hence be dependent on Mimi, who in turn left him in emotional turmoil. John's feelings for Julia and Freddie became increasingly complex and confused. Cynthia Lennon, a first-hand observer of Mimi and John's relationship, commented that:

> She loved to fuel the image of the stern but loving aunt who provided the secure backdrop to John's success. But that wasn't the Mimi I knew. She battered away at John's self-confidence and left him angry and hurt.[25]

Hunter Davies explains what happened when Mimi insisted he sent her a draft copy of *The Beatles*:

> … she had hysterics. The manuscript came back with almost every paragraph which concerned John's childhood heavily crossed out or amended. In the margins she had written beside John's own quotes such things as 'Rubbish', 'Never!'. She denied so many of John's own

memories of his childhood, especially if they contradicted her memories of the same people or events.[26]

As John slowly developed a capacity for self-reliance, his arguments with Mimi grew. There were painful consequences. John's emerging self-assurance was closely matched to his confidence in his writing, but this would often be frustrated and criticised by Mimi:

> I used to say, 'Don't you destroy my papers.' I'd come home when I was 14 and she'd rooted through all my things and threw all away my poetry out. I was saying, 'One day I'll be famous and you're going to regret it'.[27]

Mimi went to even greater lengths to curb this sense of independence. At a time when John was forming a stronger relationship with his mother, his visits to Blomfield Road having significantly increased, Mimi stepped up her opposition. Continuous quarrels developed over these visits, which Mimi venomously opposed. One weekend stay turned into a particularly hurtful episode after John threatened to stay with his mother. When John returned to Mendips a couple of days later, he found that Mimi had had his dog Sally, who he had owned since Junior School, destroyed. Mimi's excuse was that 14-year-old John had threatened not to return and she wasn't going to walk *his* dog. So, in the space of a weekend, she had no choice but to have the dog put down. John's life-long friend Pete Shotton recalls that it was 'one of the few times [he] ever saw John cry, after he returned home from Julia's house and found Sally missing'.[28] John's 'big brother', cousin Stanley, believed that the dog's fate, 'which he adored', dramatically affected him. His feeling towards Mimi changed, hardened and 'he never forgave her for that'.

The story of John's childhood has largely been told through the narratives of Mimi. Major 'players' such as Julia, Freddie and the Stanleys have been silenced, discredited or been persuaded to accept Mimi's version of events. John's sister, Julia Baird, has stood out amongst those writers on John's history in her attempt to bear witness for their mother, and has sought to reveal a more accurate picture of John's life. She argues that:

> Mimi lived for 11 years after John and she continued to rewrite her story. She said, 'I knew I wanted John from the moment I first saw him.' We all like our sister's children, but she made all that up. Give her another 50 years and she'd have claimed she had John herself.[29]

John used his creativity to help stem the tides of such unhappiness. 'It was all imagining I was *Just William*, really'.[30] John's life though wasn't like his hero's childhood with William getting up to comic scrapes along with his gang the Outlaws in a mythical corner of England. In fact, the adult John recalls how 'the first thing I remember is a nightmare'.[31]

CHAPTER SIX

1955–57
Town and Country

THE FATE OF HIS dog Sally was just the spur John needed to find justification for spending more time with his mother. At Blomfield Road, the house was always alive with Julia's two daughters, Jackie and Julia, then five and seven years old respectively, and their friends; Julia's neighbours would also often pop in for a cuppa and a chat. The difference to Mendips in terms of warmth and vibrancy could not be more apparent. The only problem John had with Blomfield was Julia's husband Bobby. 'I met her new bloke', John recalled later, 'I didn't think much of him.'[1] If Bobby and Julia were 'officially' married, it might have made a difference, but the problem was that, although the couple wanted to marry, it was assumed that Freddie wouldn't agree to a divorce. And that was on the basis that Freddie could be found – which he couldn't.

His family had last heard of him 'down south', working in the hotel trade. The Stanley sisters felt the same barely concealed contempt towards Bobby as they had towards Freddie. Bobby's pencil thin moustache and his ability to gain access to such items as chocolate and nylons, neither of which were easily available on the open market, earned him the name 'The Spiv'.

Generally, though, it seemed the partnership between Julia and Bobby was like that of most other couples of the 1950s; getting on with things as best they could. Bobby still worked at the Adelphi Hotel, which gave a sense of security and balanced out any misgivings of neighbours who were concerned about Bobby and Julia living 'over the brush'. The chances are that no matter whom Julia lived with, married or not, John would have had issues with her partner, but with Julia and Bobby unmarried, sharing the same bed and having two children of their own, well, it was just a matter time as to how these issues would manifest themselves.

John's somewhat cruel nickname for Bobby was 'Twitchy', due to the nervous facial tics he sometimes produced when talking. But the fact that Julia's partner had such a 'poncy' job as head wine waiter gave John further ammunition to look down on his stepfather – it's highly likely that John's dislike for Bobby was the product of the social snobbery cultivated in Mendips. Julia's response to her early 'setbacks' – a failed marriage, a child born out of wedlock and then given up for adoption, interweaved with postnatal depression – was to not take things too seriously any more. In actual fact, she was just as much, if not more, of a rebel as was John. 'I can remember her walking up the road with us one day wearing an old pair of spectacles with no lenses in them,' Pete Shotton recollects. 'Whenever she happened to run into someone from the neighbourhood she would casually slip her finger through the glasses and rub her eyes. Meanwhile, we would all be falling about in the bushes, pissing ourselves with laughter'.[2]

Julia's quirkiness might have been acceptable in certain avant-garde circles, but on a council estate in Liverpool it was 'daft', 'crackers' or 'a good laugh'. Pete recalls his first visit to Blomfield Road, having been told what a great mother Julia was by John:

> I hardly expected, when he first invited me to accompany him to Allerton, to be greeted with squeals of girlish laughter by a slim attractive woman dancing through the doorway with a pair of old woollen knickers wrapped around her head.[3]

It's easy to imagine John grinning, proud as punch at the audacity of this mother of four and almost shouting to Pete Shotton, 'That's my mum, *my real mum*. She's great, isn't she!'

Regardless of her popularity with the youngsters, though, Julia's past meant that she was viewed as a pariah by her sisters. But when John came to call at Blomfield Road, all those misfortunes and pangs of guilt faded. John had grown into a tall, handsome young man, full of vitality and love of life, in spite of Mimi's influence. Just as John's reaction to the break-up of his parents was to rebel, so Julia's safety valve to losing John was to 'not take things seriously,' or to 'have a laugh'. So in an effort to compensate for not being in a position to resist Mimi, Julia would enthusiastically indulge and encourage him in all his interests, especially music. John was relaxed around his mother, seeing her as a 'big sister'. She was in tune with him in his *Goon Show* humour and love of all things musical. Learning the banjo from her grandfather, she taught John the basic chords of the instrument. Pete Shotton reflects that Julia was a:

kindred spirit who told us all the things we desperately wanted to hear. She made us feel welcome and always encouraged John to try and go as far as he could with his music. We loved her because she did everything for laughs. To her, nothing was really serious, except maybe having a good time.[4]

It's easy to imagine Julia alone in Blomfield Road casting her mind back to that young carefree girl who met Freddie on that summer's day in Sefton Park, moving towards a marriage to a husband whose seafaring odysseys left Julia unsure whether he was dead, captured or in jail, then giving birth to John at a time when Goering's Luftwaffe aimed to raze her city to the ground. Any respite found in a wartime romance with Bobby Dykins seemed permanently damaged due to a child being born to Julia by a 'one night stand'. All this combined to break her spirit and send her into the depths of depression. In a few short years, Julia suffered the pain of losing two of her four children. If John was to have a relationship with his mother at Blomfield Road, it wasn't going to be centred around reprimand and criticism. She would leave that for Mimi. Julia had been given a 'bum deal'. Now was a chance to put right the love and affection which should have been given to John as a child.

When Julia moved into Blomfield Road, she found herself in a dilemma. She desperately wanted John back, but the pressures of bringing up two children and John's attitude towards Bobby affected her. The problems inside Blomfield would have proved to be too much for all concerned. Knowing Mimi as she did, Julia was justifiably concerned that Mimi would threaten her with a return visit from the social services, this time with the added fear that Jackie and young Julia could also be taken into care. The very idea was an emotional minefield, just too much to handle – better to see John when she could, and the older he got, the more she saw him. These early visits must have generated a great deal of joy for John, but in his adult years it hurt tremendously to reflect how much he had missed out in his earlier years. Julia Baird would recall the many occasions her mother would cry uncontrollably at the loss of her son. The loss of a childhood that could have been at Blomfield Road would forever burden John, and this manifested itself as a permanent pattern of melancholy and frustration in his music and outlook on life.

John's time at Quarry Bank, meanwhile, meandered along in much the same way – conflict and dumb insolence in the classroom, fighting and bullying in the playground. He'd progressively moved from an A stream class to a B stream and then finally a C stream, sinking to 20th out of a class of 20. It's easy to imagine John deciding the world was against him. An outlet for this frustration and adolescent anger came from the years John had spent 'locked away' in his bedroom writing poetry, verse and doodling cartoons – all these came together in his production of the *Daily Howl*. This was John's home-made magazine – personal jokes and caricatures, comic strips and cartoons of teachers, TV and radio stars and other well-known personalities.

John's gift for drawing took on a dark side, with his focus on those with special education needs and physical disabilities, or, as he termed them, 'cripples'. Why John should develop such prejudices is uncertain. It perhaps stemmed from his own plea for validation and acceptance, a feeling of insecurity that was not helped when, from the age of 11, he was required to wear prescription glasses. This fed towards his perception of himself as an outsider and loser in which he felt 'really ashamed',[5] which could only be compensated by 'mind reading' the negative thoughts of others towards himself and then bashing them up. Essentially, John spent a large part of his life disliking people for no other reason than his self-worth was so low that he believed they disliked him. A case of get your retaliation in first.

Cousin Stanley was fully aware of the play-acting behind John's tough image: 'John was rebellious all through his schooldays... However, John was a coward. If you faced up to him and stood your ground, he quickly backed down'.[6] John certainly acknowledged as much himself, later stating:

> I used to dress tough like a Teddy boy, but if I went into the tough districts and came across other Teddy boys, I was in danger. At school it was easier because I could control it with my head; they thought I was tougher than I was. It was a game. I mean, we used to shoplift and all those things, but nothing really heavy. Liverpool's quite a tough city.[7]

Stanley also reveals that John's time spent outside of Liverpool revealed a kinder nature. During summer holiday visits to Edinburgh, Stanley would take John for days out in the countryside, salmon fishing and shooting rabbits – far removed from the contrived image that John was to assume in the near future of Teddy Boy *bête noir*.

While John was in Scotland on one of his visits to Stanley, Uncle George suffered a liver haemorrhage at Mendips. An ambulance was called, but George died a short time later at Smithdown General Hospital. He was 52 years old. As fate would have it, George was found collapsed on the floor by Mimi's lodger Michael Fishwick. On returning home, John's reaction to this news was to fall about in pleats of laughter in his bedroom with his cousin Leila. His reaction was clearly a defensive, nervous response in coming to terms with being confronted with a sudden death – the two young cousins using the only way they knew to deal with the new emotional challenge of this bereavement.

John's childhood and growing up was conditioned by a female family clan in the shape of the Stanley sisters. Later John described his aunts as 'Amazons', due to their domineering and forceful manner. So the loss of his uncle would have further tipped the balance towards a female-dominant extended family, but maybe John's notion of Amazon-like women could have been misplaced with regards to their natural independence, in that, quite simply, the men in the Stanley sisters' lives were notably passive. This is especially so with George Smith who was very possibly gay.

If we look at John's Uncle George's background and his relationship with Mimi we see that he was late in getting married at 37 years old – this was unusual. From a woman's point of view he was a good catch, tall, good looking and he had a respectable position in the community. He didn't meet Mimi in the usual way, through friends or in a pub but in a formal business way collecting money on his milk round at Mimi's place of work. It is possible that Mimi knew George was gay long before the relationship began. She would have been alerted by the fact that he was still single and she probably quizzed him on his personal life and used her ability to root out information about George from the hospital staff, many of whom would have lived and drunk in the pubs of Woolton where George was brought up. This had echoes of John's 'gift' for spotting weakness in others. Mimi herself states she didn't really 'rate him' as a potential husband – her view of George was to use him whenever she saw fit, calling him up 'whenever I was hungry or stuck in town'. For Mimi, being a spinster wasn't an option. She knew, as did George, that the marriage was to be one of convenience. The marriage being unconsummated confirms this. Mimi's dominant personality would also protect George from any raised eyebrows with regards to him being a single man approaching 40 years of age.

George may have had other 'covers' for his sexuality, but these were at a cost. In his local pub George was 'one of the lads'. He wanted to be liked, which was why he was presented with an inscribed tankard from his local in recognition of his likable nature. But it is possible that this cover resulted in him becoming an alcoholic which was to eventually kill him. He was also a gambling addict – such vices may have been used by George to help him cope with the fear and shame of being found to be a homosexual in 1950s Britain.

George's father had committed suicide by drowning himself in a local pond. George's brother, a teacher at Paul's Liverpool Institute, was nicknamed by the pupils 'Sissy Smith' for his effete manner and dress. It could well be the case that George's father took his own life out of shame. This is borne out in his father's will, in which George was overlooked in favour of his younger brother Frank (Sissy), a decision which made Mimi bitter for years.

That George was possibly gay and married is, in itself, not so unusual, but it was significant because of the impact it had on John's life at Mendips. He was good looking, well liked, had a decent job with the prospect of inheriting the family business and, most important of all, he was malleable to Mimi's whims, 'I used to give him a look and he'd know all right if he'd upset me. Just give him *The Look* and he'd know'.[8] The subtext to Mimi's comment was not so much a case of 'he'd know' more a case of '*I knew*'. That they wouldn't have sex (as revealed by Michael Fishwick to Julia Baird) was just a small price that Mimi was prepared to pay. At the end of her life Mimi found herself in a nursing home and Lynn Varcoe, an auxiliary nurse, spent two years looking after her – Mimi was willing to speak freely to her about John, The Beatles and Yoko, but when asked about her husband, 'Mimi really did not talk about George. When asked she always changed the subject'.[9] But how did all this affect John? The male role model that most boys of John's age looked towards did not materialise at Mendips.

What John experienced was his uncle being dominated by his aunt. To have a dominant mother figure in the household is no bad thing in itself. However, the male figure, in the shape of George, was a role reversal of what many expected the paternal figure to be in the shape of a caring, understanding, supportive and compassionate guardian. This attitude of George may have been a natural disposition – or it could have been developed as his own role of underdog, being gay and aware of John's misfortune not only losing his mother and father, but also given over to Mimi. It's likely that Mimi made life hard for George when married. The forfeit of the 'family fortune' to George's younger brother compounded this loss.

When George died, Mimi found a replacement in the form of Michael Fishwick, who had returned to Mendips to complete a PhD at the University of Liverpool. With George now gone and John almost always out the house with friends or at Blomfield Road, Mimi and her young student lodger began an affair. Mimi shaved some years off her age and claimed to be 46 years old rather than the 50 that she was – twice his age, not only easily old enough to be Fishwick's mother, but she also claimed that she was a virgin. Now the morals she so reviled at Blomfield Road were replicated at Mendips, as she embarked on a non-marital sexual relationship.

When Julia Baird first got wind of Mimi's secret lover through the family, she initially thought it was the neighbour, Mr Caplan. Mr Caplan and his wife had recently built a bungalow next to Mendips. Julia Baird reveals that Mimi didn't like Mrs Caplan:

> but Mimi was not a woman's woman. She didn't like the female race. You see Mimi didn't go out. She didn't go anywhere.[10]

Julia's observation is revealing. Indeed, Mimi was not a 'woman's woman': 'I liked the company of men. But I didn't fancy being tied to a kitchen or sink'.[11] Julia Baird's second observation, that 'Mimi didn't go out', further evinces her isolation within the Woolton community. Mimi didn't go out because she didn't have friends, or a job. She didn't like people. She was left to rattle around Mendips, suffering the 'slings and arrows' of misfortune that she herself had created.

It's uncertain as to whether John was aware of this liaison between his aunt and her lodger. But if he was, by that time he wasn't bothered. He had his own goals in the shape of Lonnie Donegan and skiffle. Skiffle hit the UK as a teenage craze in the mid-1950s, fired by the ease with which skiffle could be learned (just like Punk Rock 20 years later). All a group needed was a guitar, three chords, a tea chest bass and washboard, and of course the confidence to just get up and 'do it'. John had the confidence. Leading a skiffle group to John was a natural extension of leading his gang. 'I always had a group of three or four or five guys around with me who would play various roles in my life,' recalled John. 'Supportive and sub-servient in general, me being the bully boy. The Beatles became my new gang'.[12] His ability to coerce, bribe and cajole others in his neighbour-hood gang would serve him well in his attempt to form a skiffle group.

The skiffle craze was the first national declaration of rebellion by Britain's youngsters. It was led by Lonnie Donegan, the son of a profes-sional violinist, who sang about trouble in the Cumberland Gap and smuggled pig iron on the Rock Island Line. It was not actually a precursor to the later images of Brian Wilson's sun, surf and girls, but attractive enough to improve the annual sales of guitars bought between 1950 and 1955 from 5,000 to 250,000 by would-be skiffle stars. In 1957, the young John Lennon was at the front of the queue, or, to be more precise, his mother Julia was.

> It was just before the time rock and roll started getting big in Britain. I think I was around 15, so it would be 1955. Everyone was crazy about skiffle, which was a kind of American folk music, and it sort of went like *ging ging-a-ging, ging ging-a-ging*, using washboards. And all the kids who were 15 and 16 used to have these groups, and so I formed one at school.[13]

For John, skiffle was to become a unification of his first love – that of words, with the new lifeline of music. Although his later musical genius is not in doubt, it is his literary acumen and love of the written word that sits at the forefront of John's creativity: 'When I was 15,' he recalled, 'my ambition was to write *Alice in Wonderland*'.[14] While writing satisfied his creative needs within the seclusion and isolation of the cheerless Mendips, music and its group dynamic addressed his longing for being wanted. But it wasn't a total push over for skiffle as John's headmaster, Mr Pobjoy, recalls:

> I asked him to write out for me what were his principle interests in order and he began with salmon fishing. Now sometimes people think it's a joke, but no, his aunt enabled him to go up to Scotland and fish for salmon and he liked that very much. Then he was keen on poster designing. He was very keen on painting, he was keen on writing poetry, and then in the middle of the second line came skiffle.[15]

Had the skiffle bug failed to capture the young John, perhaps he would have conformed: accepted the obligatory white collar job suitable for a grammar school boy without qualifications, and become a wax-jacketed, fly fishing, would-be poet...

Coming closely on the tail of skiffle was the appearance of the Teddy Boys. Initially taking root in London in the early 1950s, the Teddy Boy began as a celebration by working-class teenagers of their differences from their parents and society at large. Eventually it grew, spread and morphed into being associated with rock 'n' roll, toughness and violence. Cinema seats being ripped up at the showing of *Blackboard Jungle* made newspaper headlines. The term 'Moral Panic' could have been invented just for them. John was quick to adopt the dress code of the 'Ted' – skin-tight trousers, drainpipes or drainees, DA (duck's arse) hair style, 'brothel creepers' or winklepicker shoes and loud shirts. Julia's role in this was one of encouragement: 'She gave me my first coloured shirt,' John recalled.[16]

For John the combination of rock 'n' roll and Teddy Boys breached the wall of staid, crooning '50s music and it was to pave the way for what was to really grab John by the scruff of the neck – rock n' roll. In 1955, Bill Haley and his Comets hit the charts in the UK, with huge hits like 'Rock Around the Clock' and 'Shake, Rattle and Roll' becoming the scourge of parents and the emblem of teenagers. But if 30-year-old Bill Haley gave parents a fright, what was to come next across the Atlantic would scare them witless. It came in the shape of 21-year-old Elvis Aaron Presley. If tartan-coated, kiss-curled, moon-faced, bum-shuffling Haley was from another culture, then Presley, with his dyed hair, makeup, gold lamé jacket, white patent leather shoes and rubber legs, was from another planet. After hearing 'Heartbreak Hotel', John solemnly declared that 'before Elvis, there was nothing'.[17] Tied in with the rise of Elvis had been the 'supporting acts' of James Dean and Marlon Brando. For John, it was bit by bit starting to come together.

Rock 'n' roll was the perfect foil to his love of writing and was a vehicle of expression for his rebellion and discontent. Just as writing and poetry provided an insecure young man with sense of security, in music John confirmed his own sense of worth and purpose. He was good at it, maybe not the actual chords and chord changes, but the delivery. Here he excelled – his confidence developed via a 'plastic hard case', a schoolboy tough and suburban gang leader led to a natural confidence in which whatever he did on stage was alright... with him, which was great, just great. He had finally found his shield against Mimi's cutting comments.

Back at school, nothing changed other than the enormous effort he was making to being an academic failure: 'I wouldn't study at school'.[18] The result of this attitude pointing towards impending examination meltdown, it took a lot of skill and dogged determination to achieve so little in the face of such determination from the education system. In an effort to escape this academic drudgery, John redoubled his efforts in music and writing. As a defence against any criticism of these pursuits, he would develop the already bellicose, and at times cruel, side of his personality.

He chose, from Julia's music catalogue, a Gallotone guitar (delivered to Blomfield Road, to save the hassle had it been sent to Mendips), and she then taught him a clutch of banjo-converted guitar chords. He began listening relentlessly to 78 RPM records of skiffle and rock 'n' roll. Together with his cronies and school pals, John and The Quarrymen (previously named The Blackjacks) were ready to go. The first appearance of the band was in aid of the 750 year celebration of Liverpool's founding. The location was Rosebery Street, off Princes Road in Toxteth, which sat in the heart of the area that J.B. Mays described as:

> Liverpool's Chinatown and Harlem... a strikingly cosmopolitan district compared to the north end of the city. The presence of many old and decayed mansions has made it possible for lodging housing clubs, brothels and sheebeens to be set up to attract their regular clientele.[19]

The fact that they were playing outside on a flat-bed coal truck in a tough part of Toxteth belies a tremendous amount of self-assurance for a 15-year old with limited musical ability, and especially for one who was accompanied by a band with even less. But John's confidence in the delivery of his small collection of rock 'n' roll songs appealed to the knots of young girls gathered around the sides of the truck. This wasn't lost on a local gang of youths – *real hard cases*, the type that would tear your leg off and hit you with the soggy end! When The Quarrymen's set was completed, there followed a chase which foreshadowed the beginning of *A Hard Day's Night*, only this time, the girls were replaced by a pack of teenagers with murder in mind who wanted to show John what he could *really do* with his Spanish steel-stringed flamenco guitar. Sanctuary was found in the nearby house of drummer Colin Hanton's auntie.

In the view of John and his sidekicks, if they could get away with performing to a street crowd in Toxteth, everything else would be a piece of cake. For John, the future was rock 'n' roll. The future was freedom. The members of The Quarrymen, like most young bands of the time, were in a state of constant flux. Owning an instrument (usually a guitar) was a help in joining. Knowing how to play it improved your chances ever more. Unfortunately, though, John's determination to master his newly found art form was not always matched by the other Quarrymen. His role as leader was characterised by arguments and difficulties. It was also responsible for the high turnover in band members – John gave a subtle clue to Pete Shotton that his services would no longer be required by smashing a washboard over his head. But John finally met his match at a local summer fête on 6 July 1957, when The Quarrymen found themselves in the company of the Liverpool Police Dogs Display and the Band of the Cheshire Yeomanry at the nearby Saint Peter's Church. 'We all went – Nanny, everybody but Mimi,' Julia Baird recalls.

> She didn't go, and I don't know why. She was probably disgusted with them playing in public or something like that. But we all went; my mother, my dog, and everybody. That was the day that John and Paul met.[20]

That was the day the world of rock 'n' roll slowed and stopped – just for a second. It could be said that it was a case of the Master meets Apprentice – but who was whom? In the 12-year musical partnership of John and Paul, the roles of principal and junior partner would, at times, ebb and flow imperceptibly.

Paul McCartney had recently moved from the south end council estate of Speke to a house in the highly sought after council estate of Allerton. It was a mile or so long walk across the golf course from his home to Mendips. Paul was bright – very bright. He was diplomatic, well-disciplined and courteous – in short, everything John wasn't. Moreover, Paul attended the Liverpool Institute, arguably the best grammar school in the city (it even produced Charles Glover Barkla, a Nobel Prize winner). Paul was confident in all he did or set out to do. When he was asked to go to Saint Peter's fête to watch The Quarrymen by a mutual friend of John and Paul's, Ivan Vaughan, he went along with more than a hint of interest and also to pick up girls, kitted out in his white sports jacket (threaded with metallic strips to make it sparkle) and black drainpipe trousers. Paul was impressed by John's ability to stand up in front of a crowd of people and sing a series of mangled versions of almost all the songs he had in his locker.

The unabashed self-assurance of John's public performance was matched after the show by baby-faced Paul's supreme confidence as an accomplished guitar player, turning out a perfect rendition of Eddie Cochran's 'Twenty Flight Rock'. Not content with this, 14-year-old Paul dove into a medley of Little Richard's 'Long Tall Sally', 'Tutti Frutti' and 'Good Golly Miss Molly'. Both teenagers were now circling each other, trying to find chinks in one another's armour, trying to find out who was the best guitar player, best singer, sharpest dresser! Eventually, the deal was clinched when Paul delivered his *coup de grâce* of cool, revealing to those all around that he knew how to tune a guitar.

John needed Paul, and Paul knew this. John had taken his band as far as he could – he needed fresh ideas and momentum. His concern was how long he would be leader with Paul in the band. The 18 month age difference between him and Paul might matter now, but later on it would lose most of its significance. John's psyche meant he *had* to be leader. There could be no other way. His dilemma was whether to improve the band with Paul to the point of achieving the fame he craved, at the potential expense of his control and leadership as John would reveal later:

> I had a group, I was the singer and the leader; I met Paul and I made a decision whether to have him in group: was it better to have a guy who was better than the people I had in, or not? To make the group stronger or let me be stronger? The decision was to let Paul in and make the group stronger.[21]

As Pete Shotton, who was there when they first met, pointed out, 'Paul had made a huge impression on John. In a way, his ability underscored all John's [musical] shortcomings'.[22] Not all the band was taken in by Paul's musicianship – Quarryman Nigel Whalley felt that 'he was a bit big-headed'. The band's drummer, Colin Hanton, remembers Paul 'always telling me what to do: "Can't you play it this way?"'.[23] What Paul lacked in age, he made up with his natural ability for guitar and drums, but as The Beatles progressed to world fame, his exceptional musical talents would, for John, become a poisoned chalice.

Paul was unconcerned about how his 'audition' went – he had confidence by the bucketful. After all, he was a head boy at the prestigious Liverpool Institute, studious, polite and academic: a reverse image of John, Ying and Yang. Paul received the response he wanted: a week after the summer fête, he bumped into Pete Shotton, who passed him the message, 'John wants you to join the band'. What should be remembered with John and Paul is that they were two rock 'n' rollers who became friends, not two friends who became rock 'n' rollers. The music was the glue of their friendship and, in later years, when their musical differences became too wide, the fragility of this friendship was to fracture and split.

Before Paul could make a debut with the band, there was the little matter of a summer break in Butlin's Holiday Camp in Yorkshire, and later missing The Quarrymen's first gig due to the fact that he and Michael were attending a Boy Scout weekend in the Peak District. Paul's background was distinctly at odds with John's. A telling aspect of their early meeting is Paul's comment about John's insecurities when he revealed that John used to brag about his family owning half of Woolton and shooting rabbits and fishing; he also mentioned that there was a dentist in the family along with an uncle who was an English teacher in Paul's school. But it was Paul, whose mother had died when he was 14, leaving his office worker father to look after himself and his younger brother Michael in their corporation house, who declared to have had a comfortable upbringing. Although Paul wasn't raised Catholic, his mother was and so were her sisters and brothers. The resulting family christenings, first holy communions, weddings, and funerals supplied Paul with access to a stream of informal and formal gatherings – these provided ample opportunities for him to develop his social skills. The result was that Paul was comfortable within the areas of music, song, banter and humour. Mimi's Calvinistic approach to life did not offer John the same opportunities to mix.

John's involvement in music helped in that it gave him a reason to stay out of Mendips and distract himself from its cheerless atmosphere. This absence helped to a degree, but his dress sense, his Tony Curtis hairstyle and his all-encompassing interest in rock 'n' roll gave Mimi further opportunity to criticise and discourage. In all of her interviews concerning her nephew, even when the group John led became Masters of the Universe, she very rarely gave a crumb of praise to John or The Beatles; instead, a series of negative asides characterised her judgement of John, bragging that when she found that John was playing in The Cavern, 'I want to pull him off stage by his ear',[24] this at a time when John was a young man, 21 years of age. George Harrison's mother gladly owned to having watched her son perform with the group 47 times, even travelling to Dublin to see them, but Mimi was parsimonious in her praise. Why would she go on record to pour cold water on his achievements? Perhaps she didn't like the attention drawn to Mendips and reporters asking who Mimi was, *how did she come to raise John*? Mimi wanted a quiet life, far removed from Julia and the manner in which she came to raise her son.

Regardless of Mimi's feelings on the matter, John's ability to master the guitar grew with the help of Paul and the trips to friends' houses to learn new chords and listen to new records. His musical talent grew in inverse proportion to his academic performance. He reached a new low when he was put in for nine General Certificates of Education (GCSEs/O Levels) and succeeded in gaining none, not even in art! John saw himself as a 'hopeless failure'. Fortunately, his headteacher, Mr Pobjoy, was prepared to go that extra yard for him. Whether this was because he knew something of his background or whether he'd had dealings with Mimi (giving him an insight in the Mendips regime), he was willing to help.

John's failure to secure any qualifications whatsoever resulted in Mr Pobjoy calling a meeting with John and Mimi. He proposed that he would write a letter to the local art college pleading for John's entrance, despite his lack of qualifications. In return, Mr Pobjoy wanted John to be on his best behaviour for the rest of his duration at Quarry Bank. With no other educational establishments willing to take him, and with his one-time partner in crime Pete Shotton taking a place on a police cadet course, John had no choice but to agree to keep his head down. He knew that without art college, he'd have to find a job, the thought of which brought him out in a cold sweat.

True to form, Mimi undermined the idea of John as a capable young adult. She insisted on accompanying him to the interview at the art college, which was based in the city centre:

> Otherwise, he'd never have been able to find it. He'd only ever been into Liverpool on the one sort of bus, to the shop opposite the bus stop where he used to buy his Dinky cars.[25]

Mimi made John fully aware of how much he cost her in money and her 'poverty' was often thrown in John's face. The fact that she had to pay his first year's college tuitions fees and give John an allowance didn't go unremarked to those who she spoke to. What did go largely unremarked, however, was a property worth £10,000, which had been left to her by a relative in New Zealand. This would be approximately £400,000 by today's values. Mimi's ongoing relationship with Michael Fishwick developed into a plan which entailed both of them emigrating to New Zealand after he had been offered a three-year research grant to study there. Philip Norman reports Fishwick informed him that: 'If it hadn't been for Julia's death, she'd have been gone by the end of '58'.[26] As it was, the relationship fizzled out.

As much as John wanted to dismiss the importance of academic qualifications, he was always aware of his failure, especially when measuring himself against those of his school friends and the future that was mapped out for them, in advanced level study at Quarry Bank and then possibly university. Not only had he spent four years loathing the high pressure academic environment in which he found himself at school, but he'd also spent longer than that listening to the university undergraduates at Mendips drone on about seminars, tutorials, end of term exams and forthcoming job prospects. Every time he looked around, he saw failure and sadness. The challenges that were put forward for him were the challenges he didn't want.

But now another challenge awaited him – Liverpool College of Art, with its 'proper' students, older students, mature students, some even with beards, no doubt liking jazz, which John hated, sensible students in duffel coats with Ban the Bomb badges. No home here for Little Richard, Larry Williams or Fats Domino, but he'd give it a try. After all, there were female students as well, lots of pubs nearby and just around the corner was the Liverpool Institute, where Paul and George Harrison, Paul's little Scouse mate, were studying. *We'll see, give it a chance...*

CHAPTER SEVEN

1957–60
Hope Street

DUE TO MR POBJOY's supporting letter and Mimi's insistence, John found himself with a choice of his Sunday best, or worse still, his school uniform, and kitted out accordingly, he turned up for his art college interview. Mimi was of course in tow, and after a confident pitch from her that John had been 'misunderstood' at Quarry Bank, he was offered a place at the college on the two year diploma course. Many of the students at the college intended to take a further 12-week teacher training course, followed by a career at the chalkboard. John wasn't there to entertain the idea of teacher training courses and *more school*. For John, art college was just a convenient port in a storm. His own expectations were limited and totally wide of the mark: 'I went to Liverpool College of Art with an idea of drawing gorgeous girls for toothpaste ads'.[1]

On his way to his interview with the Principal, John would no doubt have noticed the contents of the students' bulletin board and its display of CND posters, along with those offering Jazz Nights, advertisements for theatre productions and requests for drama players, political debates with titles such as 'Why Socialism is an Infantile Disorder', and meeting times for the Vegetarianism Society. John probably would pause, reflect, take all these offers in and think, 'Not a soddin' dog's chance!' John was in college for three very distinct reasons: first, it kept him out of Mendips; second, it kept him out of a job; thirdly, and most importantly, it gave him more time to develop his skills as a rock 'n' roller.

To John, his first day at art college was something akin to being in the trenches and going over the top. He was dressed in his 'Teddy Boy Best', ready to shock, intimidate and cause wonder. That he refused to wear his glasses, as he had done since first being prescribed them, meant he gave an impression of staring hard at those within three yards of him. His hunched posture and head that stuck out beyond his coat collar like a myopic tortoise popping its head out of its shell didn't help matters. This adopted pose of macho hard case couldn't help but counsel his student colleagues that the best option when seeing him coming was to duck down an alleyway, the labels of 'nark', 'trouble maker' and 'nuisance' given by fellow students would be worn later as badges of honour.

The site of the college also appealed to John – located in Hope Street, it ran alongside the 331 feet high, still incomplete, gothic Anglican Cathedral, with the impressive Georgian and Victorian mansions that faced it. The original port-enriched owners of these mansions had made a steady drift away from the city, first to London and then, following the opening of the Mersey Tunnel in 1934, to the greenery of the Wirral countryside just a ten minute car ride from the port. Now the houses had been converted into multi-occupancy flats and bedsits. John would discover that students at the art college lived as tenants in these bedsits and flats and he himself would in turn stay there before heading off to the seaport of Hamburg. Indeed, John lived for a brief time at Gambier Terrace, a parade of extravagant but faded town houses that sat behind the cathedral.

The bohemian quarter which so attracted John, and where he would spend the next two years, was previously 'base camp' for 19th century Liverpool's opulent mercantile dynasties. Liverpool at that time created more millionaires than any city outside London, but the legacy of these sad, dilapidated mansions was to be handed over to struggling immigrants, students and those seeking an alternative or cheap lifestyle. The idea that art college would give a channel to John's aggression and waywardness was totally misplaced by Mr Pobjoy and Mimi. If anything, going to Hope Street was like adding fuel to the fire.

At Quarry Bank, the staff had been expected to discipline the students. At college, the students were expected to discipline themselves, which in John's case was a futile hope. The lack of commitment to college made it easy for John to cast around for things to rail against. After all, most of the staff was of a middle-class, left of centre politics; the caring sharing middle class that John would later come to love and hate in equal measure. John's own political philosophy developed and morphed until it become a form of anarchist conservatism and, while the students and staff took themselves seriously in their political stance, he looked to the absurd for guidance.

The student body was generally well educated and well meaning, whereas John stuck out on both counts. Students and staff were fully dedicated to the subtleties of their art – for the young Lennon, if it wasn't in your face, raw rock 'n' roll, then he wasn't bothered. That John now came up against the liberal avant-garde who claimed to 'suffer for their art', combined with a fair mix of students from outside Liverpool, meant he could have a dry run at his role as a macho Scouser. The aggressive, flippant and contemptuous attitude he developed acted as an antidote to the fear, uncertainty and anxiety that he'd had to live with for as long as he could remember. In a sense he had to gamble going for broke as the archetypal rock 'n' roll star or risk playing in bog standard 'pop' bands around Liverpool and being remembered as 'that daft fella who used to be at art college'.

Between '57 and '59, John's musical obsession proved to far outweigh his interest in pen-lettering and still life painting. The Liverpool Institute being but a stone's throw away provided convenient access for the band to practice in the college's student common room, along with the essential exchange of information on the latest 45s and local band gossip. The idea that college staff expected a degree of mature responsibility from students was lost on John. Tutors at the college who came into contact with John – and his surly refusal to conform mixed in with a large dose of bloody-mindedness – could well have been forgiven for speculating 'we must have been short on applicants that year'.

College tutor Arthur Ballard tried to understand and support John and guessed, rightly, that the young student largely bluffed his blasé attitude when the truth was the opposite. Arthur knew that John didn't read up or take any interest at all in his lessons and concluded, with hyperbole, that 'John Lennon had never read anything except a comic in his life. He was totally uninformed in every kind of way'.[2] Nevertheless, Arthur Ballard took John under his wing and also invited him to Ye Cracke, a local pub to the rear of the college, where he held many drink-fuelled tutorials with a coterie of students. Arthur guessed that what was seen as a tough guy attitude could partly be put down to John being a fish out of water whose way of coping was to be dismissive about the whole process – he needed a 'front' to achieve this. As Arthur points out: 'I think Lennon put it on. He had a posh accent at the time, by Liverpool standards'.[3] An interesting later connection to John concerning Arthur Ballard is that of the renowned Liverpool artist and Communist Party activist, Arthur Dooley, a devoted Catholic and as argumentative as John. Dooley was a janitor at the art college during the time that John was a student and on one occasion found himself engaged in an argument with Arthur Ballard; both men had been good amateur boxers in their younger days, and a fight ensued with Arthur Ballard being knocked out. Dooley went on to complete the circle of his Beatle connection by giving homage to the band in the 'Four Boys That Shook the World' brass sculpture, which now hangs in Mathew Street facing The Cavern.

For John to 'get on' with his studies would be an acceptance of the status quo – the same status quo that existed in Quarry Bank High School, a status quo that kept him disillusioned and dissatisfied, and would only perpetuate a way of life which had kept him unhappy since childhood. College tutor Philip Hartas remembers him as being:

> like a fellow who'd been born without brakes. His objective was some-
> where over there, that nobody else could see, but he was going, but
> in that process, a lot of people got run over. He never did it to me, but
> he had this very sarcastic way of talking to people – and at other
> times, he could be very charming and he would be charismatic.[4]

At college, John gravitated to like-minded people, that is, so-called 'head cases' like Geoff Mohammed, born of an Italian mother and Indian silk merchant father. Geoff, at 27 years old, was as eccentric as John. Geoff was known for picking up his grant cheque, changing it into half-crown coins then returning from the pub, going to his living room, turning the lights off and lashing the coins all around the room, with the intention that, later on in the college term, when broke, he could search for and find the coins. John and Geoff considered themselves on the same wavelength, going on regular drinking binges in Ye Cracke and generally acting daft. 'He could be very cruel at times, but he was hilarious,' recalls fellow student Rod Murray, 'everyone was dominated by him'.[5] But not everyone saw him as such. Annie Mason, another student, reflected that:

> He was quite a sight, shocking, but also ridiculous, because he was
> the *only one* in a Teddy Boy outfit. Nobody else at college was inter-
> ested in that trend... The more *in* fashion someone tried to be, the
> more *out* of it they seemed. So, after the initial impact, we didn't take
> much notice of anybody like John.[6]

One way John used to gain what he saw as credibility was to sponge off other students: 'I used to cadge all the time'.[7] His fellow students constantly complained of his whinging of being 'skint'. Yet Mimi's pocket money to John was a fairly generous £1 and 10 shillings, which in today's values would be approximately £60 per week. The notion of John bumming money for coffee or cigarettes at college was just a guise that he adopted in order to remain in character: that of the rough Teddy Boy. The chances are that he was indeed sometimes short of money, but the notion of him constantly being on the mooch was less about being broke and more about power. Power in the sense of 'demanding' others pay for *his* company, and indeed, this cadging was largely associated with the women students of the college. While many gave in due to a genuine sense of benevolence or intimidation, John interpreted it as another part of his macho persona.

College introduced John, in part, to what it was like to be a Scouser, albeit a pre-entry course – a stabilisers-on-your-bike type of introduction. The college was on the edge of town, away from industry, the docks and council houses, but near enough for John to get a taste of being 'Scouse'. He quickly picked up on the particular nature of those locals of the inner city – the slang, the expressiveness and lack of deference – and found it suited him. He also picked up on the sense of a city that was separate from the country at large, both in attitude and language. The gift of The Beatles at their early press interviews to deliver wickedly sharp and deadpan humour has its roots in a general disregard for outside authority.

Within a month or so of joining The Quarrymen, John and Paul's partnership in songwriting had begun in earnest. Most of these sessions took place in Paul's home at Forthlin Road, and Paul was to comment later that these sessions were mainly 'moon in June' type of songs, but, to their credit, around 200 compositions were created. The discipline needed to complete so many songs is a credit to their ambitions – Paul's to be a rock 'n' roll star and get the women, John's to be a rock 'n' roll star and escape Mendips. John knew the value of Paul, his ability to accommodate others, network, partner up with strangers, his flexibility; all the things John didn't have. Paul needed John for the times when smooth talking couldn't do the trick – then John would be introduced as a battering ram to smash down those barriers that blocked them from where they wanted to be.

The Quarrymen kept going into 1958, competing for gigs along with an estimated 300 other Liverpool bands in social and working men's clubs, dance halls and church halls around the area. Before Paul joined The Quarrymen, John and the rest of the band had played The Cavern, which was then a jazz club. John and The Quarrymen were accepted as a dedicated skiffle folk combination with honest intentions. This particular booking was memorable for the 'brass-balled' Lennon who, in front of a packed collection of trad jazz and folk aficionados, delivered skiffle standards such as 'Rock Island Line' and 'Cumberland Gap' almost seamlessly. But before the audience could 'jump down turn around an' pick a bail of cotton', John had the band launch into a gang buster delivery of Little Richard, Fats and Elvis songs, only to be frantically told by an incensed owner to 'cut out the bloody rock 'n' roll!'

The way in which The Cavern gig came to be booked in the first place reveals the significant social elements to the group's success. Quarryman Nigel Walley left school at 15 to become a full-time golf pro at the nearby Childwall Golf Club, and it was there that he approached club member Dr Joseph Sytner, whose son Alan owned The Cavern. Nigel pitched the idea of booking The Quarrymen at The Cavern to Dr Sytner. This middle-class network that secured the booking was to be supplemented by a working-class one, in which ex-seafarer George's dad, now the MC cum entertainment officer at his local bus drivers' social club, like Dr Synter, used his influence to win a booking for 'our George's group'.

Like John and Paul, George Harrison was truly bitten by the rock 'n' roll bug and, although he did not have their stage presence, his dedication to his craft made him, at a very early age, adept at the challenging chords, leads and rhythm changes needed to accompany the band's singer. George had lived in a terraced house in Wavertree before moving to become a 'neighbour' to Paul on the council housing estate of Speke. Like Paul, George passed his Eleven Plus and gained a place at the Liverpool Institute. On their way to and from the Liverpool Institute, George and Paul became nodding acquaintances, which was followed by tentative discussions about rock 'n' roll. From this love of music a bond was formed as firm as most brothers, but in this instance it would always be as Paul the big, and at times pushy, older brother.

Before joining The Quarrymen, George had been involved in other bands and performed at local social clubs and community halls. Like Paul, George had the benefits of a close and extended family and the community experience of living in a council housing estate. Paul's first home was in the tenement block of Sir Thomas White Gardens, in the Everton district of the city. These tenements, many of which housed up to a thousand or more tenants in a series of blocks, sprung up in the 1930s mainly to accommodate those in the dock-based workforce. The blocks consisted mainly of four storeys and shared common stairways that inevitably fostered a sense of neighbourliness and community.

As John's time at Liverpool Art College progressed, The Quarrymen's aspirations for stardom developed with unbridled enthusiasm, mainly thanks to Paul. Following the departure of John's best friend, Pete Shotton, Paul began to play a greater role in most of the band's business. One by one, the old members began to drop out or were forced to leave. Paul, ever the talent spotter, knew his little pal George could do a job for the band and put his name forward to John; the problem was if Paul was seen to be small compared to John, then George was tiny. In Liverpool parlance – *spit on him and he'd drown.* John could handle that Paul, 18 months his junior and baby-faced to boot, was balanced out by his musicianship and absolute confidence in himself. John knew that the acceptance of Little George into the band would put him in danger of looking like 'King of the Kids'. Both Paul and George would need to mount a charm offensive, which they did. After much cajoling, including George's famous note-perfect delivery of 'Raunchy' on the upper deck of a bus, he was in.

George was certainly different. What the 14-year-old lacked in size, he made up for in his outlandish dress sense. With his pink shirts, tiny tucked in ties, mandatory tight drainies and his bouffant hair, with its large, protruding centre piece precariously held in shape with a mixture of sugar, water and a sense of blind faith, all this effort aimed to elicit backward glances from strangers and the sense of awe and audacity, coming across to all intents and purposes as a miniature version of a Little Italy street crooner. Whereas John dressed as the street-wise thug and Paul as apprentice suave and sophisticated man-about-town, George's preferred the sense of otherness that the city was renowned for.

George immediately dedicated himself to becoming John's friend, but at two and a half years younger, this proved to be difficult. John was embarrassed at the age gap between them, and outside band practice or bookings, he constantly found excuses not to be around him. George, however, was undeterred and constantly called around to Mendips, only to be confronted with a po-faced Mimi who explained to young George, with his bus driver dad and part-time job as a butcher's boy, that John wasn't in. Meanwhile, John stood in the hallway listening to George's response as to whether he should 'call back later, Mrs Smith?' If Mimi saw the well-presented Paul as 'common', George's Teddy Boy haircut and dress, council house family and nasal Scouse accent were enough to make her wince.

On 12 July, John, along with Paul, George, Pete Hanton and piano player John Duff Lowe, made their way to the Kensington area of the city to 'cut a disc'. All five Quarrymen had clubbed together to record two songs at the tiny, rudimentary recording studio run by the elderly Percy Phillips, who had set up the studio in the back room of his terraced house. John was to sing vocals on Buddy Holly's 'That'll be the Day', while an 'original' McCartney/Harrison song 'Cry for a Shadow' was also recorded. Only having enough money to pay for one acetate to be cut, the boys argued on their way back to the south end of the city as to the pecking order of who was to be the first to be loaned the record. Three days later, on 15 July, John's mother was killed in a car accident.

Julia's death destroyed John. It couldn't have come at a worse time. Julia gave him hope that the parental love and companionship which he had for so long been led to believe had abandoned him, was possible. He was getting on (albeit in his own non-conformist way) at art college and The Quarrymen were making slow but steady progress on what was later to become known as the Mersey Beat scene. Julia's death confirmed to John that he was right: the entire world was against him. Julia was hit by a speeding car as she left Mendips, the car driven by an off-duty policeman without a full licence, who was accused in court of failing to brake until after hitting Julia. 'Rejected' by both mother and father, taken into care by a loveless, manipulative aunt, John rediscovered his mother then lost her under the wheels of a learner driver. If John had a chip on his shoulder before the death of his mother, following it, this chip would develop into rage against the world. If before he looked for pretence to be a rebel, after the death of Julia, he needed none.

Julia was the friend John needed. His low self-esteem and confidence masquerading as arrogance and cruelty could be addressed and righted with support and encouragement from her. Julia's death brought about a genuine response of concern from Paul. Frequently calling to Mendips in an effort to coax John out, he was aware of what he was going through, for Paul's own mother, Mary, had died in 1956; but for all Paul's efforts, John stayed indoors. This form of inaction was maybe not the best way of dealing with his grief, his already vulnerable emotional state of mind left him ill-equipped to deal, on his own, with such a loss. But Paul was, and always would be, in the eyes of John, a junior partner in their relationship and junior partners don't make the best of confidants. Whereas Paul's loss of his mother was cushioned by supportive, close and extended family, John wasn't so fortunate. His mother was the black sheep of the family, largely ostracised and reminded when needed to be of the sins of her past. John was emotionally damaged during his time at Mendips.

In interviews, John would use the term 'depression' frequently – sometimes in a passing way, and other times in a plea for help or understanding. His mental wellbeing, or lack of it, was exacerbated by this time spent with his rage, and dealing with his grief, alone in his room. The 'Black Dog' of depression had taken firmly hold and the thought patterns of the illness would last his lifetime. He expressed one of his earliest recollections of this misery:

> When I was 17 I used to think, 'I wish a fucking earthquake would happen, or a revolution'... but if they blow the world up, we're all out of our pain then. Forget it – no more problems.[8]

Such was the extremely poor state of John's depressive condition; he seems to be alluding to suicide by proxy. The loss of Julia was a devastating blow and in later years he spoke of losing her twice, with the second time being in many ways much more damaging.

On his return to college, John was faced either with comments such as, 'I'm sorry about your mother, John', or with a silence brought about by the fear of embarrassing or upsetting the already unpredictable Teddy Boy art student.

The autumn term carried on more or less where the summer one left off, the only difference being that the time with the band had ground to a halt. The thought of belting out 'That'll be the Day' a couple of months after the death of his mother would have been grotesque in the extreme. Later on, John would evoke this time at college with bitter honesty:

> I do recall at college punching through telephone box glass, you see, so it was a kind of self-destructive suicide side of me.[9]

John was to compare Julia to a big sister, but in many ways she was more, much more. Julia was the one who taught him banjo chords, who let him bring his records to her home, to play and learn them (Mimi forbade the possession of a record player at Mendips). Julia bought his first guitar and on her visits to The Quarrymen's bookings in local church halls, danced herself silly and whistled and clapped after every song. In between intervals she came across as their number one fan rather than mother of the band's leader.

On John's return to college, his skits now included not only the disabled but also Jews and those with special educational needs; the hard humour which he had honed with the *Daily Howl* and at Quarry Bank took off again with a new vengeance. Any particular 'weak or different groups' were fair game for the super-charged bitterness of the recently bereaved son. Student Helen Anderson recalls:

> If John would see anyone with a physical or mental need he would half shout, 'Some people will do anything to get out of the army'... John had a thing about Jews and loved taking the mickey out of them... But it wasn't nearly so cruel as his thing about cripples and afflicted people.[10]

Maybe these 'misfortunates' that John would ridicule almost his entire life were just a bit too close to revealing his own emotional 'differences', the drive hence to prove he wasn't like them: he would jeer, ridicule and imitate them. By his own admission, John did admit in such circumstances he was 'cruel'.

Although it wasn't easy, and many certainly sympathised with John's loss, there comes a time when sympathy crosses over to exasperation. Generally, the lower he sank, the more obnoxious he became and the more resistance he was met with; in turn he became even more obnoxious. What John needed was a distraction to help deal with his depression and circle of aggression. This came in the shape of a diminutive Scotsman – Stuart Fergusson Victor Sutcliffe. If John thought of himself as a rock 'n' roller, then Stuart knew he was an artist, and so did those around him. John's friendship with Stuart would provide a safety valve for his spiral of self-destructive behaviour, which Stuart recognised as part of the artistic temperament. He would help to control John's depression.

If Mimi could have picked an ideal friend for her nephew, then Stuart Sutcliffe would come close to ticking all her boxes. His father, Charles, was a public school boy, army officer, prominent member of the Tory Party and leading fellow of the Masons. He had entered the Civil Service, becoming an executive officer almost immediately. Stuart's mother, Millie, was privately educated, a junior school teacher and an active supporter of the Labour Party. During the war, the family transferred down to Merseyside from Edinburgh due to Charles's position in the War Office, administering the Cammell Laird shipyards munitions department in Birkenhead.

Stuart, like his father, was a talented painter and found himself drawn towards the arts. A year above John at College, he soon made a name for himself as 'one to watch out for' by staff and students alike. John really only got to know him six months after his mother died, when a mutual friend and art college student, Bill Harry, suggested setting up an arts and music magazine. The three young men met in Ye Cracke. Straight away, John found in Stuart something he wanted. Stuart was cool, calm and collected, he was liked without trying to be liked, and he had exceptional artistic talents and an inner sense of confidence. He had all the things John didn't have, but wanted.

From Stuart's point of view, his friendship with John had its roots in their shared love of rock 'n' roll, as well as the attractiveness of John's over-the-top view of life. Stuart's idol in the art world was Italian painter Amedeo Modigliani, who lived in Paris at the turn of the century. Modigliani's behaviour was extreme, even by bohemian standards – known for his numerous affairs and heavy indulgence in absinthe and hashish, he died of tubercular meningitis at the age of 36 in the arms of his nine months pregnant girlfriend, his death the personification of the tragic artist and lost soul.

Stuart's notion of suffering, Modigliani style, for your art, appealed to him and those around him, and in John's background and attitude he saw a distress not recognised by others. To everyone else, John's bouncing around the college like a boxer waiting for the bell to ring was just... well, John. But Stuart was aware of and sensitive to John's pain, seeing his behaviour as a reflection of this. Perhaps he saw in John similarities to the romantic self-destruction of his idol, Modigliani. John liked the idea of being fully genned-up in the world of art, but until his friendship with Stuart, he was too afraid to reveal his ignorance. 'It was Stuart who nurtured an interest in John to know more things than he knew,' Arthur Ballard pointed out. 'In other words, he was educating him. Lennon wouldn't have known a Dada from a donkey. He was just so ignorant'.[11]

Stuart delivered discreet and informal lessons to John on Kierkegaard,

Sartre and Kerouac, and the whole gamut of what it took to be part of the ultra-cool beatnik culture of 1950s Britain. John accepted this insight into the precursor of hippy culture with a typical affected blasé and disparaging attitude, but was nonetheless aware that Stuart could fill the role of confidant that the younger Paul McCartney could not. Still in a fury at what he saw as the unfairness of life due to the loss of Julia, he needed someone to fill the vacuum of her loss.

Stuart had culture and intellect. John picked up on his sensitivity, sense of independence and his own outsider status, all of which he wanted to cultivate in himself. The relationship with Stuart was in many ways complex – John criticised and ridiculed him publicly, while at the same time was obsessed with being his friend and defended him to the point of violence. The emotional confusion and immaturity of John forced Stu's sister Pauline to comment that, 'John's whole history speaks to a desperate kind of nurturing'.[12] The complexity of this relationship lay in the fear John felt in revealing himself as weak to others. Attacking Stuart in public was his way of saying to others 'I'm not like him', but in reality he was, and it both scared and confused him.

Quarryman Len Garry, who was a student with Paul at the Liverpool Institute, remembers:

> At lunchtime Paul and I would just whip in and see John. We met this guy called Stuart, who was a very morose, quiet sort of guy, sort of character. Very much an introvert, I would say. I never really got to know him all that well. He was really heavily into his art.[13]

John, on the other hand, played to the balcony to win validation, switching at a moment's notice from hard-knock rock 'n' roller to class clown; Stuart, by comparison, had the confidence to *be quiet, listen and hear* the insults without taking offence. He had the self-assurance to ride John's slights without being riled and John wanted to know how it was done.

At the same time as John was forming this friendship with Sutcliffe, he was also developing a relationship with fellow student Cynthia Powell. Cynthia, an attractive blonde from 'over the water' on the Wirral, was like many others at the college, making her way through the curriculum towards teacher training school and a position as an art school teacher. A relationship with any woman for John would never be straightforward. One attractive feature of Cynthia which seemed to boost John's fragile attempts at being a Scouse Macho Man was that she could be passed off as someone who was even more posh than him. She was also more likely to put up with troubles he brought to her door. John would not have got away with half the things he did with a local girl from the docklands; in Liverpool terms, *she'd have chased him*. As the relationship developed, John became more demanding and possessive, constantly 'borrowing' money off her, insisting she model herself on Brigitte Bardot (his ultimate sexual fantasy), and even being violent towards her. Cynthia's best friend at art college, Phyllis McKenzie, recalls the time she and Cynthia received a lift home from two boys after a party. Cynthia mentioned this to John. Phyllis later found Cynthia crying, a seething John having slapped her in her face for accepting the lift: 'and I thought he's a right bastard really, you don't do that to women'.[14] Phyllis concluded. This streak of jealousy that John possessed would be a recurrent theme in his life.

With the passing of time, though, the influence of Stuart and Cynthia brought some sort of respite from Julia's death. John found himself back with Paul and George, practising and looking for bookings. When the bookings dried up, George gigged around with other bands, finding a place in the Les Stewart Quartet, who held a residency at The Casbah. The Casbah Club in the West Derby area of the city was essentially a non-alcoholic club for the local teenagers, set in the basement of a large, detached 14-roomed house, run by owner Mona Best. In the summer of 1959, The Quarrymen gained a spot at The Casbah, and by then had gained a fourth guitarist in the shape of Ken Brown, but lost their drummer Colin Hanton.

Six months previously, after a gig at The Pavilion Theatre in Lodge Lane, Colin, John, Paul and Pete Shotton travelled home on a bus, and John launched into his punishing 'spastic' talk. Colin, who was older than John and worked in an upholstery shop with people from the deaf community, took exception. Colin had had enough of John's almost-constant ridicule of anyone who was different from or weaker than himself. A fight nearly broke over this issue between Colin and Paul which resulted in an angry Colin being shepherded off the bus by Pete Shotton.

A drummer less band in a rock 'n' roll mad city with hundreds of bands to choose from meant bookings were hard to find, so when the Les Stewart Quartet fell foul of the dogmatic Mona Best, George tipped John and Paul the wink for a booking at The Casbah, and after a successful one nighter, they were offered a residency. The Casbah was the lucky break the band needed to kick-start their efforts to make a mark on the local rock 'n' roll circuit. A casualty to this small but important success was the loss of Ken Brown, who, due to having a cold and not being able to play one night, was put on the door to collect the money of the hundreds of people who attended The Casbah to watch The Quarrymen. Mona, in her wisdom, decided to still pay him an equal share of the booking fee, much to the annoyance of the rest of the band, especially Paul.

Following on from the success at The Casbah, John found himself in a talent contest held at the Empire Theatre. At the audition for the contest, which was run by Carroll Levis for his TV *Star Search*, the band changed their name to Johnny and the Moondogs. The Moondogs passed the two Liverpool auditions and performed in the final at The Hippodrome Theatre in Manchester. Unfortunately, despite the band's initial triumphs, they failed to win. After gaining a place in the final, The Moondogs were asked to wait for the winners to be announced. This would have meant missing their last train back to Lime Street, so any victory was forfeited. But on the train home, some satisfaction could have been taken by John and the rest of the band for having got as far as they did, especially without a drummer; but even so, a rock group without a drummer made them look too much like a skiffle group, which was now passé.

If John couldn't find a drummer then he would have to make do with a bass player, and this came in the shape of Stuart, who until then had no inclination to play bass, no inclination to join a rock 'n' roll band and certainly no inclination to disrupt his studies. This changed when John found that he had won a prestigious art competition with a prize of £65. Stuart's fate was sealed. At the beginning of 1960 and within a month of Stuart receiving his prize money, John had persuaded him to 'invest' his windfall in a Hofner President Bass. It was a very large guitar which Stuart may well have unconsciously took into consideration with a future view to hiding behind it on stage. But as George was to comment, 'having a bass player who couldn't play was better than not having no bass player at all'.[15]

Rock 'n' roll groups without drummers were not greatly sought after, and after a poorly-marked dance card for bookings, John approached 29-year-old Allan Williams, the owner of local Beatnik coffee house cum night club The Jacaranda, to become their manager. The connection to The Jacaranda in the city centre's Slater Street came through Stuart. The

Jacaranda or 'Jac' was one of the many coffee houses, cafés and clubs that sprung up around the Duke Street area of the city, accommodating university and college students alike. Stuart and John would bunk off college to hang around The Jac, cadging coffees and cigarettes from waitresses and patrons alike, enacting their suburbanite version of living on the edge. Other 'real' rock 'n' rollers also hung out there; members of such groups as Cass and the Casanovas, Kingsize Taylor and the Dominos, and Rory Storm and the Hurricanes. Allan Williams had a lot of time for Stuart and was impressed by his demeanour and art skills and, feeling sorry for his poor financial position, he offered him the job of adding some artwork in the basement of The Jacaranda. Williams, a short, barrel-chested Welshman, was an entrepreneur of the old school, a ducker and diver into whatever could earn him a few bob, the few bob that could be earned in Liverpool at the time being from rock 'n' roll. Williams set himself up as a part-time promoter and conduit for local bands. From John's point of view, Allan Williams, with his connections to the pop world, was a man whose company was worth cultivating. Williams, for his part, had no knowledge of The Quarrymen or of John's ambitions, and when John approached him about the possibility of work, Williams response was that 'all the painting's finished, sorry, John',[16] assuming that John was after some art work in the club. After much pestering by John and Stuart, and mainly due to his fondness for Stuart, Williams agreed to let the band audition for the largest impresario in the country, Larry Parnes, who was carrying out a nationwide search for new talent.

There were two problems the band faced, one serious, the other not so serious. The not so serious issue was that most of the other local bands disliked The Quarrymen, the reason being that while the makeup of Liverpool rock 'n' roll groups consisted mostly of members who worked on building sites or in warehouses and oil mills, The Quarrymen's grammar school name suggested a degree of elitism to local inner-city rock 'n' rollers. These rock 'n' rollers viewed John and his band as interlopers and posers. This wasn't helped when Paul would, in an attempt to be clever, pretend to hold existentialist conversations with the other band members in the changing rooms of venues when other local bands would enter. This might have been a hoot in the sixth form, but it only confirmed what the local band members felt to be true – that Paul and the rest were 'pretentious tits'.

The second problem was more serious – the band did not have a drummer. Allan Williams came to the band's aid and, through Cass of Cass and the Casanovas, found a drummer named Tommy Moore. Williams even allowed the band to practise in The Jacaranda in preparation for an upcoming audition, in return for them carrying out odd jobs around the club. At times they acted as a stand-in for Williams' main resident band, The Royal Caribbean Steel Band. Now that the band had a drummer, all they had to do was pass the audition, which was for a Northern Circuit of groups featuring the headliner and major star Billy Fury, himself a former Liverpool seafarer.

The auditions were to take place at the Wyvern Social Club in Seel Street, later renamed The Blue Angel. The Quarrymen also needed to be renamed. Eventually, whether by connection to Buddy Holly's Crickets, or Stuart Sutcliffe's Beat poets, the band decided upon The Silver Beetles. While the auditions were about to start, Billy Fury entered. Alan Clayson recalls:

> John Lennon was among those approaching Billy Fury for an autograph. Paul, George and Stuart had never seen him this way before, so spellbound and humble. 'Thanks, Billy – if it's all right to call you that,' he grinned after Fury signed the proffered scrap of paper. 'I... um... I'm John. I sing with a group!' 'Keep singin', man,' replied Billy.[17]

John's humbleness could have been caused by nerves, or it was the product of his sense of total failure if he were not to pass the audition. He was approaching 20 years of age and a future without rock 'n' roll in his life seemed unthinkable. He needed a break and he was willing to do anything for it.

As the auditions progressed, it became clear that the newly named Silver Beetles' drummer was not going to make an appearance. Feeling responsible for the non-attendance of Tommy Moore, Allan Williams approached the drummer of Cass and The Casanovas, Johnny Hutchinson – a hard case, even by Liverpool's standards. 'Hutch' had no time for the posers from the art college and as a rock 'n' roll band deemed them 'not worth a carrot'. Nevertheless, as a favour to Williams, he sat in. Photographs of him at the set show him utterly bored, exhibiting the look of someone who was trying to remember if he'd left the gas on at home.

The audition had mixed fortunes. Although the band didn't succeed in securing a place on the bill of Billy Fury's Northern Circuit rock extravaganza, Larry Parnes made a note of the overall enthusiasm and musical capabilities of the 'new' Silver Beetles, and within a couple of months they would be offered a tour of Scotland which, in turn, opened the door to where many argue the band really earned the right to be called a true rock 'n' roll band – Hamburg. Another seaport, Hamburg was the biggest in Europe, and one with an insatiable demand for the cravings of the flesh and the musical lubrication which carried these cravings along – rock 'n' roll.

CHAPTER EIGHT

1960–61
The Wyvern Club

BETWEEN THE LARRY PARNES audition and the offer of a short tour of Scotland, The Silver Beetles continued to practise and picked up the odd gig around Liverpool. The Larry Parnes audition meant an increased opportunity to cuddle up to Allan Williams at The Jacaranda. Williams, ever on the lookout for a few bob, had made connections with a 'street character' from Toxteth nicknamed Lord Woodbine after the cigarettes he smoked. It was through Lord Woodbine that The Jacaranda's residential steel band came, and it was through Lord Woodbine that bookings came for The Silver Beetles at various venues in the Toxteth area of the city, which was filled with clubs such as the Nigerian Social, the Ibo Club and Caribbean Centre. These perceived 'dens of iniquity' satisfied the bohemian element of Stu's cv and John's own need for proletarian credentials.

Life at art college carried on as usual. John remained dismissive as to what it took to be a successful art student, but what was changing was his relationships with Stu and Cynthia, who both found John to be investing more and more of his time in their company. Both relationships were complex and ridden with inconstancy and aggression. With Stu, John had to navigate the important issue with Paul and George that, despite much effort, Stu's ability as a musician fell woefully short of what the band expected. In fairness to Stu, he didn't want the job in the first place, and it was only after much strong-arm tactics from John that he finally offered up his prize cheque for a guitar.

John wanted to be Stuart's friend, but was uncomfortable in being seen as such. The result of this dilemma was John going undercover with this friendship. John was in aggressive denial redressing the balance of poet and rocker with snide and caustic putdowns of Stuart in an effort to keep it in other students' minds that although he 'knocked around' with arty Stu he was still the King of the Jungle. 'I was aggressive because I wanted to be popular,' John revealed. 'I wanted to be the leader. It seemed more attractive than being one of the toffees. I wanted everybody to do what I told them to do, to laugh at my jokes and me be the boss'.[1] At this point, Stu's musicianship wasn't an issue, and anyway, why should he worry? To him it was only a hobby – his real passion was his painting.

Allan Williams, although not a rock 'n' roll fan, recognised in John a hunger and need for success. And although they lacked a regular drummer, the group did have one advantage over most other local bands – time. While other band members spent eight hours plus working on building sites and in warehouses and sugar refineries, The Silver Beetles could dedicate anything up to five or six hours a day to band practice. The art college's student union had even been talked into buying 'their college band' a PA system to use. Here, The Silver Beetles played their regular Friday night gig. Eventually, John, Paul and George (with or without a drummer) began developing into an equal match to those local groups that derided them as an 'arty farty college band', condemned by hard man Johnny Hutch, drummer to Cass and the Casanovas as 'a bunch of posers'.[2]

Larry Parnes' offer to tour Scotland reinforced the need for a drummer. Here, Alan Williams came to his rescue in persuading an 'ancient' 26-year-old Tommy Moore to take time off from his job in a bottling works to sit in and play. The Scotland tour consisted of seven dates in the north east part of the country; all were small towns, the largest being Inverness. The Silver Beetles were to back a Parnes minor hit recording star, 21-year-old Johnny Gentle, performing a half-hour set of their own preceding the 'main event'. The dates were mainly uneventful, other than an accident in the van in which Tommy Moore lost his front teeth, courtesy of a flying guitar case. It left him unable to play that night's booking. On finding this out, the irate Scottish promoter of the tour, feeling short-changed, proceeded to the hospital where Tommy was under observation and sedated, and dragged him out of bed to that night's booking. Tommy sat behind his drum kit looking pitiful, teeth missing, eyes puffed up into slits, mouth stitched, his face swollen and discoloured, while John and the band played on cheerfully as if Liverpool drummers from bottle works always looked like this.

By the end of the tour, the group had proved to themselves and to others that they could 'cut the mustard'. Allan Williams was also satisfied with the results of their performance and now kept The Silver Beetles in mind for future gigs. Even without a drummer, Williams found The Silver Beetles a number of bookings at the Grosvenor Ballroom, across the water at Liscard, then out of the blue Williams received a letter from Hamburg from his steel band informing him that they were in the city playing and had secured long-term engagements. They invited Williams over. There he met Bruno Koschmider, who owned the Kaiserkeller club where the Caribbean steel band played. Williams was amazed: 'a steel band in Hamburg is like finding a whale in the Sahara Desert'.[3] A stroke of luck for The Silver Beetles came when Larry Parnes cancelled, at short notice, long-standing bookings for two of Williams' bands, Derry Wilkie and the Seniors and Cass and the Casanovas, after the band members had booked time off from their jobs. The fuming and threatening band members went looking for Williams and, in turn, Williams went down to London looking for Larry Parnes.

While in London, Williams bumped into Bruno Koschmider, who was looking for bands willing to come to the booming nightclub scene in Hamburg. Williams pitched the band Derry and the Seniors to the former Panzer tank driver, and they were immediately booked. A couple of months later, after the successful arrival of Derry and the Seniors, Koschmider opened a new club and wrote to Allan Williams asking him if he had any groups he could send over. At first Williams contacted Rory Storm and the Hurricanes, but they were already committed to a summer season at a holiday camp. Next, he spoke to Gerry Marsden of Gerry and the Pacemakers, who didn't fancy working abroad. The only group Williams could find that was available and willing was The Silver Beetles, so he offered them the gig – *if* they could find a drummer. On hearing the news that 'a bum group' like The Silver Beetles would be arriving in Hamburg, Derry of Derry and the Seniors complained that 'they'd ruin the scene'.[4]

But before they could set off to Hamburg, the band needed a drummer. Pete Best was born in Madras, India and came to Liverpool when he was four years old, passing the Eleven Plus and attending Liverpool Collegiate. Pete, tall and athletically built, represented his school at judo, boxing and track events. John knew Pete through The Quarrymen's booking at Pete's mother's club The Casbah. As with the vast majority of teenagers in Britain, Pete was taken in by the notion of a rock 'n' roll lifestyle, and decided on getting there via a drum kit. Pete had already formed his own band, but fortunately for The Silver Beetles, they split up. With two days to go before they were to head off to Hamburg, John approached Pete with the offer to be their drummer. This came with the cheeky proviso of

Pete carrying out an audition. Pete passed the audition and was in. Just prior to leaving Liverpool for Hamburg, the group decided to have a name change, in which they dropped the 'Silver' and became simply 'The Beatles'.

There's been much debate regards how The Beatles came to settle on this as their name and it is in all likelihood that it was Stu who came up with the title The Beatles, although many have assumed it was John. After ditching the name The Quarrymen, the names that followed included: Johnny and the Moondogs, The Beatals, the Silver Beats and the Silver Beetles before finally John took the plunge and settled on The Beatles. This evolution began with the introduction of Stuart – it was his fascination and dedication to The Beats which he transferred to John and proposed a homage to these alternative artists that struck a chord with him, but John would never admit Stuart's part in the decision, for in John's mind, he would be made to seem weak to take *his* band name off a friend. The name also smacked of Beatnik, and John disliked Beatniks and all they stood for.

Once more we see in The Beatles' story subterfuge and red herrings as to the history of the name, where explanations range from the influence of Buddy Holly and the Crickets, to Marlon Brando's 1953 film *The Wild One*, in which clearly seen on the backs of his motorcycle gang is their name – The Beetles. The problem with this explanation is that the film did not receive a general release in Britain until 1960, after the Beatles name began. John provides his version of the name's genesis in an article in *Mersey Beat*, in which a man appears in a flaming pie and announces, 'from this day on you will be known as The Beatles with an A'. Naturally John would have claimed as much, for to admit to the rough and tumble collection of fans, other local bands and promoters that they were named after gay, drug taking poets and writers wasn't going to increase their street-cred in 1960s Liverpool. It's no surprise that John unveiled 'his' new band name and named it 'The Beat(le)s' within the comparative safety of Hamburg, away from the predicted puzzled questions of their hometown.

The newly named Beatles made their way to Hamburg via the port of Harwich in a green and white Austin camper van, with Allan Williams driving. Also travelling with The Beatles was Lord Woodbine and Williams' wife Beryl. While the other parents of the band supported their sons' musical ambitions, if somewhat reluctantly and with a certain amount of parental worry, Mimi was horrified. Unlike John, Paul and George could

argue to their parents that if Hamburg failed, they at least had job experience to fall back on. Paul had recently been an armature winder for the
local firm of Massey Ferguson, and when this interfered with his lunchtime
Cavern gig, he moved to a morning 'Van Lad' job, helping the driver for a
large department store make household deliveries. George was an apprentice electrician at a city centre department store for a brief six weeks. As
for John, Mimi didn't even know he was in a band! John had kept it secret
and covered any tracks of the band's bookings by explaining to Mimi that
he was going out with friends. It is a measure of the influence that Mimi
had on John that, as a young man approaching 20 years of age, he found
it impossible to let her know he played in a band. When John revealed his
'guilty secret', the response was one of shock and horror, followed by
vigorous attempts to block John's opportunity to travel to Hamburg. Only
after many efforts to talk her around, followed by constant cajoling and even
threats to go anyway did Mimi very reluctantly agree. Having first wanted
John as a child then not wanted him, and having lost Michael Fishwick,
Mimi renewed her desire for John to become her lifelong companion.

John's relationship with Cynthia, meanwhile, had steadily developed.
They were in love, although John was unlikely to admit it to anyone other
than Cynthia. The relationship and competition that Cynthia presented
terrified Mimi, and her fear of loneliness was the source of the argument
that took place when Cynthia and her mother were invited for tea at Mendips.
Mimi accused Cynthia of distracting John from his studies. This soon
developed into a personal argument between Mimi and Cynthia's mother.
From this, Cynthia gained an insight into the real relationship between
John and Mimi:

> When she was openly critical of me it hurt and humiliated John, but
> she didn't even notice or didn't care because she carried on. Time after
> time I saw her upset him with negative remarks about him or someone
> he cared about. John would become angry and embarrassed then run.[5]

Although John had spent some time in other students' flats around art
college, now he was away in Hamburg on a three-month engagement. The
sense of excitement over the trip would have been intense for the entire
band, but it would have been especially felt by John, *his* group going to
play abroad, nearly 1,000 miles from Mendips. At last, he was free.

It could be argued that after Liverpool, Hamburg was the city that most influenced The Beatles. London and New York, by sheer size alone, not to mention their expansive reservoirs of culture and art, played important roles in the career of the band, but from a perspective of their formative years, a time of radical change, then the impact of Hamburg must rank second only to Liverpool. The two cities had much in common – both ports, albeit Hamburg an inland port on the River Elbe, both suffering during wartime air raids, both seen as cities of an independent nature.

The Reeperbahn ('reeper' is low German for rope-maker), a main road which ran down St Pauli district, had a history of being a point of gathering for sailors who docked in the port. St Pauli was easily comparable to that of 'outsider inner-city Liverpool' with its Celtic heritage in that it too was a city of outsiders: gamblers, prostitutes, artists, Catholics, Jews and atheists all existed here. Both cities also faced extreme hardship during the war, Liverpool being the second most bombed city outside London, while the carpet bombing of Hamburg was to destroy eight square miles of the city and claim in excess of 43,000 lives. And behind the city wall was the Indra, where The Beatles would play for up to seven hours a night, seven days a week, in the street named *Grosse Freiheit* – The Great Freedom.

Like many ports, Hamburg prided itself on being different, on breaking from convention, and nothing could have been more unconventional in the 1930s than belonging to the *Swingjugend* (Swing Youth), which was a sort of loosely stitched together anti-Hitler Youth, made up of rebellious teenagers whose love of jazz led them to non-violent resistance to Nazi orthodoxy. Beatnik-styled youths with uncut hair and the British flag pinned to the back of their coats, the *Swingjugend* would be ever present in St Pauli's nightlife during the 1930s. That is, until the growing Fascist authorities banned their appearance. It was this Hamburg generation that would produce the Existentialists (Exis), such as art students Astrid Kirchherr and Kurt Volmer, whose group visited the Indra and became enamoured with The Beatles and their outlook on life. This group of 'Exis' not only became an unofficial fan club for The Beatles – these regular visits to the club and meetings outside would eventually result in a meeting of minds between Astrid and Stu, and their falling in love. In many ways it could be argued that the *Swingjugend* had a direct lineage to The Beatles via their children's 1960s Exis fashion sense, a combination of black denim and leather, jackets, trousers and straight hair combed across their foreheads.

The Beatles, along with Allan Williams, his wife and Lord Woodbine, arrived in the city on 17 August. They started work the very next day, and began to play 58 nights straight, being paid the paltry sum of 30 DM per show. The sheer scale of the nightlife and sex trade in the city arguably made it the 'Sin Capital' of the western world. In Liverpool there was Paradise Street, which was so named by recently arrived American sailors not for its religious connections, but due to the dozens of ale houses, brothels and gin palaces. But that was in the 18th century – Hamburg was modern-day sin and sleaze, and on an industrial scale. The band's accommodation comprised two rooms behind the Bambi-Filmkunsttheater, where they had to make do with the cinema's bathroom and toilet. There were no cooking facilities, so they frequently found themselves at the British Sailors Society, cadging or being given meals by the manager, Mr Hawks.

Like the rest of the band, John was to revel in the casual sex, free drink and living on the edge type of existence which Hamburg offered. It provided, moreover, the opportunity for John to reinvent himself, once and for all stepping off the path that Mimi had set out for him. John had moved from schoolyard bully to suburban gang leader to skiffle man and now a fully-fledged rock 'n' roller. The sex, drink and handfuls of phenmetrazine (Preludin), a German slimming pill that acted in the same way as an amphetamine, all drove the motor of change towards the new John. But what John wasn't aware of was just what this new 'John' was to look like. He was only certain that the old model was redundant. And it wasn't just John who changed, but the whole band. In Liverpool they were 'youngsters' performing in youth clubs or social clubs, 'doing a turn' before the main event (the bingo). But now, in Hamburg, for six or seven hours a night they had the major responsibility for entertaining hundreds of drunken adults out for a good time. The Beatles accommodated these needs to a backdrop of Little Richard, Carl Perkins and Chuck Berry. Fuelled by drink themselves, they looked down on an audience of sailors, gangsters, prostitutes, and a smattering of tourists and young people pulled in by the club's pavement barker. An audience all pie-eyed, windblown and rubber-legged, an audience engaged in a courtship dance that wouldn't have looked out of place in a Hieronymus Bosch painting. The Beatles may have wondered who was entertaining whom.

The days of playing two 30-minute sets were now long gone – weekdays 8pm until 2am with two one-hour breaks in-between their sets, Saturdays

7pm until 3am. Sunday was an even earlier start, from 5pm to 12.30am. Back breaking. The two half hour sets of the Stanley Abattoir Social Club and Wilson Hall were quickly jettisoned. 'When you think about it sensibly, our sound really stems from Germany,' George pointed out. 'We learned to work for hours and hours on end and keep on working at full peak even when we reckoned our legs and arms were about ready to drop off'.[6]

Besides having to learn to stretch out the numbers, they had to quickly learn new ones to fill in the mind boggling timescale of their sets. The band had to pick up on who else was doing what and see what they could learn (pinch) from other bands: 'We were nicking right, left and centre off other bands there,' Paul noted. 'We'd see something that we'd like and after they left Hamburg we'd put it in our set.'[7] One of those acts was Tony Sheridan and his own band, The Jets. Sheridan, a minor but talented rock 'n' roller back in Britain, became friends with The Beatles. Paul was to recall that, ''cos he was a little bit of the generation above us, he used to play some blues – real moody stuff'. Sheridan would later use The Beatles to back him in the recording studio, with world famous Bert Kaempfert as the producer of the recording.

John wanted to use his time at Hamburg in the same way as William Burroughs set out to use drugs with his declaration of wanting: 'to shit away all my Midwestern values with heroin'.[8] John wanted to eliminate any remaining aspects of his upbringing through the excesses of the flesh. And yet, for all his outrageous behaviour while in Hamburg, John still found time to write to Cynthia. The letters, some as much as ten pages in length, contained declarations of love, poems and lewd suggestions. Many of the pages were decorated in cartoons and kisses. In one letter, John wrote about the pair of leather pants he had bought for her. Cynthia delighted at the thought of showing off these trousers at college. But when John's next package arrived, an eager Cynthia opened it 'imagining how cool I'd look in them at college'[9] only to find the contents were a pair of tiny leather knickers.

The Beatles continued much as they had begun – an exhausting six to seven hour stint, then being woken up by the noise of the first film showing in the Bambi, followed by a recount of the previous night's (sometimes) horror stories over a cup of tea and a bite to eat. This was maybe followed by a wander around the town, then back to work on a replenishment of their catalogue of songs, then back on the stage once more. But a change was to take place. Due to complaints of noise by a resident, Koschmider had to resort to bringing the club back to what it was originally used for – a strip joint. So after their marathon stint of consecutive nights on stage at the Indra, The Beatles moved to Koschmider's much larger Kaiserkeller, down the road at 36 Grosse Freiheit. Here the group alternated with a second band that Allan Williams had sent over three days previously, Rory Storm and the Hurricanes. Rory Storm, real name Alan Caldwell, had the idea of naming each individual band member himself in an American rock 'n' roll/showbiz theme and so his drummer Richard Starkey became Ringo Starr.

The nearby Top Ten Club also hosted Allan Williams' Liverpool bands, and, not surprisingly, The Beatles became regular visitors, on occasion jamming with the likes of Gerry and the Pacemakers and Rory Storm and the Hurricanes. They also became friendly with the club's young owner, Peter Eckhorn, who offered the group residency at the club if they ever needed a change from The Kaiserkeller. The offer of playing the much plusher and larger Top Ten appealed to The Beatles. When he found out about Eckhorn's offer, Koschmider was incensed at the thought of losing *his* group to his competitor's club. Koschmider's spiteful response was to inform the authorities that George was under 18 years of age, making it illegal for him to work in the country. George found himself being deported. Koschmider also cancelled the band's guaranteed work – now they were in the precarious situation of working in a foreign country, drawing down their earnings on a night to night basis.

So on 1 November, 17-year-old George was escorted by Jurgen and Astrid to the train station, where he could begin his journey back to England. Besides losing their lead guitarist, George being forced to go was a psychological blow for the band. John, as the leader of the band, must have felt acutely sensitive to their growing misfortune. Wasn't it he who had persuaded Stu to part with his prize money for a guitar he couldn't play and didn't want? Wasn't it John who gave Pete two days' notice to come to Hamburg and had the cheek to sit there as he undertook an audition? So now John had to lead, because to all intents and purposes they were drowning, not waving, Luckily enough, John and the band had built up an informal network of support in the shape of Tony Sheridan and his band, Astrid and her Exis friends and other Mersey Beat bands. John and the remainder of The Beatles could go to these and – rightly –

gripe about their treatment, make future plans, swap information for future bookings and generally develop a thicker layer of skin.

The move from the Indra to The Kaiserkeller meant a much larger stage for The Beatles to perform on, and while the relatively small stage of the Indra left little else to do but play, The Kaiserkeller's stage on the other hand was too large to just stand and run through their set. It wasn't an option just to play; they had to move or risk looking stiff. So under Koschmider's instructions, they had to *mach shau* (make show). This was when the band could fight back and scream at Koschmider's customers. First it was verbal: 'Everyone who's a Nazi put your fuckin' hand up!' Then to the visual: toilet seats around the head, eating and drinking on stage while playing in underpants, and wearing gumboots. Essentially doing what they could to piss Koschmider off.

As for Koschmider, John wasn't willing to bend the knee, panzer division or no panzer division. John's game plan was to bide his time and get the band to the Top Ten club, a better club by far than The Kaiserkeller. While Pete Eckhorn was making arrangements for new digs and a long-term booking at the Top Ten, disaster struck again and again in the shape of Koschmider. Getting wind of the band's move to a rival club, Koschmider found that on taking their meagre belongings from the rear of the Bambi, Paul and Pete had set fire to a condom. On finding out, Koschmider immediately went to the police and accused Paul and Pete of trying to burn the cinema. Paul and Pete were arrested and taken to the nearby *Davidwache* (police station). As with George, they were sent back to England, and the opportunity of playing the Top Ten was lost, all for setting fire to a condom that was pinned to the wall. As John was to comment later, 'it wasn't as though Bruno was wearing it at the time'.[10]

On 1 December, Paul and Pete arrived back home. John stayed another week with Stuart at Astrid's impressive home. Stu's relationship with Astrid had now blossomed into full-blown love and he had already taken steps towards enrolling in college in the city. Stu was moving towards leading the life of bohemian painter in a foreign land that John could only dream of. In addition, Stu had a girlfriend whom John would want for himself. The wealth, security and status that Astrid had inherited from her grandfather and his pre-war fruit machine factory meant she represented all those material values which John had been brought up to respect. His first reaction to Astrid and the Exis was one of resentment and contempt; these were the ultra 'toffees' he'd learnt so hard to hate and now their lifestyle, of which he wanted to be a part, was taking away the only person to whom he could relate. The five days it eventually took John to get home from Hamburg must have seemed like a lifetime, home to a predictable string of 'I told you so' and 'change your clothes and get a haircut' from Mimi on his arrival. This, combined with a 'walk of shame' through college, made worse by the questions as to Stu's success, contrasted with John's failure.

For five days, John locked himself in his room: the depression that so affected him when Julia died was back. John eventually dug deep to fight off his despair and called Paul. A gig was hastily arranged at The Casbah, with a stand-in bass player from Pete's former group The Black Jacks. This was followed by a Christmas Eve booking with Derry and the Seniors.

Three days later came the famous Litherland Town Hall booking, where they were advertised as hailing 'direct from Hamburg'. Such was the anonymity of the band then that the audience assumed they were from Germany, commenting to John and the others that 'Ya don't half speak friggin' good English, don't ya, lar?' John and his band were back.

The time in Hamburg had good and bad points for John. On the plus side, the whole experience of coping with the marathon shifts on stage meant a musical apprenticeship almost unique in its time. It toughened them up physically and mentally. On the downside, the jaundiced view of people that Mimi had drummed into John looked justified by the sights witnessed in the Reeperbahn. The constant sleaze and immorality seemed totally at odds with his sensibilities. His previous attempts to find himself in poetry and writing were replaced by a 20th-century Babylon. The effect of John's time at Hamburg – the hardships and deprivations that he endured there – would filter through and provide justification for the later hurt he would visit on those around him.

CHAPTER NINE

1961–62

Great Charlotte Street

THE CHALLENGE TO aspire to the post-war American 'classless' culture was spearheaded by the novel controversial rock 'n' roll heroes of the teenage population. The appeal of rock 'n' roll for British teenagers was rooted in their belief that they didn't have to be clones of their parents, and the late '50s and early '60s saw the emergence of a teenage culture that would morph into what many would later see as a ground-breaking reflection of working-class representation in Britain. When Brian Epstein, the man who would manage The Beatles until his death in 1967, made his way through Liverpool city centre in the autumn of 1961, he was in part embracing this democratisation of working-class popular culture.

Liverpool's relatively full employment at this time and the advance of wartime baby boomers into teenagers meant a thriving business for stores like the Epstein's NEMS (North End Music Stores). The first NEMS store originally opened in the Walton area of the city. The success of this store saw the opening of city centre premises in Great Charlotte Street, with Brian as its manager. It was from this store that he took the short ten minute walk towards the river and the market district of the city in November 1961, accompanied by his assistant, Alistair Taylor.

As the 1960s unfolded and John and the band began to take tentative steps towards doing battle with the blandness of pop on both sides of the Atlantic, and British cinema was supporting the notion of bottom-up change in a growing awareness of society's working class. For the first time, ordinary people played leading roles, reflecting the drama of life in such films as *Saturday Night, Sunday Morning*, *This Sporting Life*, *The Loneliness of the Long Distance Runner* and *A Taste of Honey*, in which working people were no longer portrayed as chirpy cockney soldiers in war films, or criminals with gruff 'Burglar Bill' voices, but as characters in their own right set against their own familiar backdrop. The affluence of the '60s meant a growth in white goods such as washing machines, vacuum cleaners and TV sets – once the preserve of the middle class, such 'luxury' items were now widely available, and it was this more accessible pricing of electrical goods that benefited a number of local retail businesses, including the Epstein family.

Brian and Alistair headed for the 18 stone steps that led down to a warehouse converted into a club – The Cavern, located at 10 Mathew Street. The popular story behind Brian's visit apparently stems from the request from teenager Raymond Williams for a copy of 'My Bonnie' by The Beatles. The single was recorded in Germany with The Beatles (named as The Beat Boys on the label) as the backing band for Tony Sheridan, and hadn't been released in the UK. This apparently provoked Brian's interest in a band he hadn't heard of before. This version of events seems unlikely; Brian was savvy enough to know what the teenagers who visited his shop were into. After all, he was a column contributor to local music paper *Mersey Beat*, set up by John's old college pal Bill Harry to give information and keep track of dates on the hundreds of rock 'n' roll bands in the Merseyside area.

Brian's interest in The Beatles was a departure from his past experience. Previously, Brian's ambitions had been based in theatre, having attended the Royal Academy of Dramatic Art (RADA), which he left due to his dislike of the discipline applied by some of the staff on the course. Brian then returned to the family business in Liverpool, his previous aim to be an actor seeming like folly. But now the idea of managing a rock 'n' roll band in a music-mad city like Liverpool sparked a new sense of creativity.

A nervy Brian (in his two-piece hand-tailored suit, shirt and tie), head down, eased through The Cavern doorway with the body language of a man being looked for by the police. Once down the steps of The Cavern, he entered the three dark and poky connected barrel ceiling rooms, where Brian's senses would have been overwhelmed with the smell of sweat and disinfectant. The disinfectant was needed to keep away the smell of the drains that flowed into the Mersey's tide and then back up the waste pipes in the toilet. The smell of sweat emanated from the audience, seen through a dimly lit room as a sea of bobbing heads, teenagers clapping, stomping and singing along with the band, trying to dance as much as their packed in bodies would allow. Brian took in all the energy, the pure pleasure on the faces of the youngsters, with the uninhibited display of a satisfied need. This was *life*. And Brian decided he needed it to counter his own meanderings through the boredom of a family business and also to salve his sexually repressed and unhappy life.

What Brian witnessed on stage that day was John leading The Beatles, doing their best to look like they weren't bothered and were really, to all intents and purposes, just farting around in Paul's front room. The music bounced and careered around the acoustically unsympathetic warehouse brick walls, and the amplified vocals and instruments screamed disjointedly and distorted. The electrics of the club regularly shorted due to condensation on the walls finding its way into the fuse box. The Beatles ate on stage, smoked, changed broken guitar strings, larked about, talked to and joked with the audience – anything to prove to those watching that they weren't bothered. The Beatles, after all, had 'seen and done Hamburg'. The audience consisted mainly of office girls, shop assistant boys and girls bunking off from school, with a sprinkling of art and university students. Compared to Hamburg, this was the stabilisers on your bike version of rock 'n' roll. But it was here that The Beatles would form a communion with their fans over the course of 292 performances. The litmus test of appreciation came with the night time audience in the dockland and inner-city clubs. This audience included mill workers, female line workers at sugar refineries, stacker truck drivers at warehouses; these were the ones who could tell John what songs were on the latest Ray Charles LP, or the date that Buddy Holly died and the type of aircraft he flew in and even the pilot's name. These were the ones who kept John on his toes at the Tower Ballroom, Litherland Town Hall and Aintree Institute.

At The Cavern, The Beatles acted in 'self-defence' as they messed about, knowing that their lunchtime gig had been turned down by the local bands made up of workers who, during the hours of nine to five, had 'meaningful employment'. The Beatles didn't want word to get back to the likes of Derry and the Seniors that they were really that interested in proving themselves to such an easily pleased audience.

By now, The Beatles had taken to wearing their Exis-influenced leather trousers and jackets. At The Cavern the management rule was 'no jeans', so it was either slacks or leather trousers. While John, Paul, George and Pete were more than happy to dress up in their leathers for a night gig in a dance hall to an audience of 400–500 people, putting on a show in the same leathers for shop girls from Woolworths or clerks from a nearby insurance firm for the lunchtime Cavern sessions just didn't have the same appeal.

Brian's first impression of The Beatles' lunchtime Cavern sets must have seemed like a musical version of the Marx Brothers. But the ability to relate to the audience produced a genuine partnership between band and fans; young girls passing sandwiches up to Paul, Paul in turn passing them to the rest of the band, John cadging cigarettes from fans – everyone had a part to play. If The Beatles looked like they were laughing at the audience, then they were also doing the same to themselves. All this was playful, confident and adept, a watered down version of what they played and learnt in Hamburg. What Brian witnessed that afternoon on 9 November was a joyous, natural, raw, uninhibited jolt of adrenalin. He wanted in.

During this time, John led a double life, his time split between this new rock 'n' roll lifestyle and Mimi's attempts to turn him into one of the sharp-elbowed middle classes – these attempts had failed but, nevertheless, he still found himself anchored in the beliefs that were inculcated in Mendips. Just as Mimi was mortified at the courtship of her sister Julia by John's father – 'that ne'er do well Lennon' – so was her reaction on discovering John's hopes of becoming a musician. She was convinced that he'd make a show of himself and more importantly, of *her*. It wasn't just that she disliked John's chosen lifestyle, but that, at every turn, she did her utmost to stop him and turn him into something *she* wanted him to be.

Mrs Harrison, on one of her many visits to support George, bumped into Mimi after a lunchtime Cavern session. Mimi, according to Hunter Davies, was there 'to pull John out by his ear'. 'Aren't they great?' Mrs Harrison enthused to Mimi, whose reply was that 'she was glad someone thought so'. 'I met Mimi a few times after that', said Mrs Harrison. 'She always used to say, "We'd all have had lovely peaceful lives but for you encouraging them"'.[1] Further contrast to Mimi's attitude is provided by Paul's father:

> I had to go to The Cavern to give Paul the sausages or chops or whatever it was. I'd be in a terrible rush and I'd just have time to fight off the fans and give Paul the meat. 'Now don't forget, son,' I'd say, 'Put this on Regulo 450 on the electric oven when you get home'.[2]

The supportiveness of the other Beatles' parents was patently not evident in Mimi.

The quandary John found himself in was that he wanted to be a writer and/or a poet, but his inner turmoil made this option too passive a role to satisfy the whirring of what was going around his head. He needed something more 'outgoing' and being a rock musician suited the bill. Mimi's success in keeping John out of Liverpool city centre and away from Mimi's dreaded *Liverpudlians* gave him a somewhat misrepresented view of his hometown:

> On the streets in Liverpool, unless you were in the suburbs, you had to walk close to the wall... and to get to The Cavern, it was no easy matter, even at lunchtime sometimes. It's a tense place.[3]

To get to The Cavern was not a case of taking Raymond Chandler's 'mean streets'. Mathew Street lies on the border of Liverpool's central business district and 50 yards from the main shopping area of Lord Street. For anyone who has recently walked down Mathew Street it's no more a walk 'down these mean streets' than it was in 1961.

This seeming lack of ability to distinguish between perceived dangers and what were real dangers did at times see John come unstuck – he was in many ways ignorant of the common courtesies of life. Indeed, much of his behaviour and confidence was based on fear, ignorance and blind faith. This was shown at college when, after leaving Ye Cracke, John ballet danced around a couple of men walking along nearby Renshaw Street. Much to the amusement of John's college buddies, John pranced around, tip-toeing, limply waving his arms, flicking his hair back. This impromptu dance routine was not appreciated. Within seconds John found himself butted squarely in the face. This case of a 'misunderstanding of local culture' and what should and shouldn't be seen as acceptable behaviour became a running theme throughout John's life. John's cousin Stanley Parkes supports the impression of John's ignorance of his own city; on summer visits to Liverpool he, John and his cousin Leila went on bike rides around the area but, under Mimi's instructions, 'we were never allowed to cycle our bikes into Liverpool City proper'.[4] In 'Glass Onion', John alluded to 'standing on the Cast Iron Shore' – a strip of waste land used as a council tip on the banks of the Mersey, its name coming from a long-redundant iron works that stood on the site, which was a magnet for local kids who might salvage the odd unwanted toy or even an old bike. The reference in the song to the Cast Iron Shore suggests that he was there, but the sight of young John rummaging through tons of household waste for a discarded cricket bat would have given Mimi a cardiac arrest.

Mimi kept an obsessive and psychologically tight rein on John. She had lost her husband to alcohol, lost a sister and also her new love, Michael

Fishwick. Her family had moved away and her involvement with her neighbours and her community was negligible. All she had left was John. She had long held control over him through manipulation and the use of guilt with her regular references to the twin Houses of Sin and Correction. Now Mimi faced a crisis – how she could hope to keep John at home if his girlfriend stayed around and his musical ambition continued to bear fruit? No wonder she was so biting to Mrs Harrison – she was losing John. Mimi's extreme version of middle-class values, her obsession with property, discipline and respectability, led John into a moral vacuum of black and white judgements where self-centeredness and a disregard for others' feelings held sway.

John had left the comfort of his class and was acutely sensitive to the accusations of being, in his words, a 'toffee'. His reaction was to redouble his efforts towards 'respectability' in the Mersey Beat scene with a ruthless abandonment and harshness in dealing with others. The success of Hamburg plus the growth in the band's musical competence meant the stock of the band had sky-rocketed. But this also compounded John's psychological issues. Now would have been a time to consolidate and build bridges with other local musicians; instead, John often used his new-found credibility to antagonise and generally act like a thug.

Mersey Beat musician Ritchie Galvin recalls an incident concerning a 'floating beat night' which took place on the *Royal Iris*, in which the groups used the captain's cabin to get changed in before their performance. Girls were coming and going asking for autographs:

> … and you know what ship doors are like. One girl had her hand on the jamb and John just kicked the door on her hand and laughed. No-one else laughed and the girl's hand was dripping with blood. To be honest, I never liked him much.[5]

Even The Cavern's long-time doorman Paddy Delaney wasn't immune to John's mood swings: 'John could turn on you and he could be very short with anyone. He'd have a go at you if needs be'.[6] This was John's big weakness – when he had the choice to impress with his generosity of spirit and his humour, which he had in spades, he often chose the contrary. It wasn't so much a case of his being self-destructive, more a case of self-flagellation; it seemed like at times he *wanted* to be disliked, hated as much as he needed to be loved. The dual influences of Julia and Mimi were at times revealed in dramatic mood swings between light and darkness. John had decided early on that one way to avoid rejection was not to offer yourself up to it, act like an emotional hard-case, cold and insensitive.

After a few meetings with Brian, John identified in him an easy-going, somewhat passive attitude, which he could manipulate, giving him an opportunity to develop a form of control over The Beatles that would take on a more subtle and formal guise. George remembers Brian's first visit to The Cavern, in which Brian talked about 'My Bonnie' and how he came back to watch them a number of times:

> It seemed like there was something he wanted to say, but he wouldn't come out with it... He just kind of watched us and studied what we were doing. One day he took us to the store and introduced us. We thought he looked rather red and embarrassed by it all.[7]

That Brian had gone to see The Beatles on a number of occasions before bringing up the idea of being their manager challenges the opinion that he instantly fancied John, Pete, Paul or George. If this had been the case, that he was smitten by leather clad John or one of the others, then Brian would have made his 'move' there and then. The fact that he called into The Cavern a number of times suggests that he saw the management of The Beatles as a business interest and genuine hobby.

John and the band had gone as far as they could on their own. Musically they were beginning to compete with the best local bands. They had a strong fan base and as many bookings as they could fit in. What they needed now was a record contract. John, though, was wary. He knew Brian was gay and it was not too long ago that The Beatles had shrugged off the stigma of 'pretentious art band' tag. John's view was that he had to be careful to avoid getting stuck with another derogatory label from having a manager who was gay – Britain was still a country in which being a practising homosexual was a crime punishable by a jail sentence. John hadn't come all this way to be derailed by the promises of a gay businessman with no understanding of managing a band, let alone experience of show business.

At the meeting in Brian's office, Paul was delayed due to taking a bath, and in reply to Brian's exasperated 'but he'll be late!' came George's oh so cool reply of, 'yes, but very clean'. When Paul arrived, Brian proposed the idea of managing them:

Eventually he started talking about being our manager. Well we hadn't really had anyone volunteer in that sense... At the same time he was very honest about it, like saying he didn't really know anything about managing a group like us. He sort of hinted that he was keen if we'd go along with him.[8]

John listened to Brian's pitch, weighing up his options. He knew, as did the others, that ultimately it would be his choice. He had done as much as he could to lead the band towards success, but he needed time to think. The prospect of being managed by a novice manager or having no manager at all needed to be mulled over. A second meeting was arranged.

Whereas most managers of 'beat groups' at this level would be content to get as many bookings for the greatest fee, Brian wanted more. He wanted to manage, really manage. In many ways he needed The Beatles more than they needed him. They were a complete unit, operating independently; they'd paid their dues at the 'production line' hours of Hamburg and were nobody's fools. On the other hand, Brian was a 28-year-old, cosseted, lonely, guilt-ridden, Jewish, gay man with a social conscience. All these vulnerabilities John would later ruthlessly exploit. Clear evidence of this social conscience came after the Six Day War, when Brian revealed the reasons for his refusal to help fund the Israeli war effort:

> ... because I'm as sorry for a wounded Arab as I am for a wounded Israeli. People fundamentally are all the same and I can't discriminate. People should have no greater concern for the suffering of one race than they have for any other. I believe in, and want to help as far as I can, to understand mankind whatever colour, creed, religion or nationality.[9]

The idea of managing The Beatles removed Brian from his humdrum life outside of being the manager's son of the family owned store, and got him back in the swing of his RADA days. Almost immediately upon meeting them, he found himself totally immersed in their use of language, irreverence, self-deprecating sense of humour and general well-rounded sense of street savvy. Essentially, they felt good to be around. On 15 December, John, Paul, George and Pete signed their names over four of the five sixpenny stamps on the management contract Brian had drawn up. The fifth postage stamp was for Brian to sign, but he didn't. The reason he gave was that the contract was for him to deliver a recording contract, which up until then he hadn't achieved. Alistair Taylor signed as a witness to the absence of Brian's signature.

Although having the status of being a well-known manager of a large, city centre music store, Brian also knew his limitations in managing John and the band. Finding bookings was not a problem; what was difficult was the promise to secure them a recording contract. He also had to change their stage act to something more professional and saleable. This meant a strict set of rules while playing and a change of stage attire. Later, John would blame Brian and Paul for dragging him kicking and screaming into ditching his leathers and wearing a suit, but these claims largely came after the break-up of The Beatles. At this time, John's hunger to achieve fame saw him admit that he'd 'wear a balloon' if it meant success.

As The Beatles proceeded to undertake their round of local bookings, Brian's promise to secure a recording contract was matched by John and Paul's resolve to use only their own original songs in the studio. Their songwriting sessions had been in place since 1957 – during this four-year period, the pair had become adept at intuitively finding the weaknesses of each other's efforts and putting forward alternative choices. This ability of John and Paul to complement each other and learn from one another's flaws and strengths had begun long ago in Paul's front room at Forthlin Road. It moved between bed and breakfasts in Scotland onto spare space in Hamburg, be it Astrid's living room or the grubby excuse for a bedroom in the Bambi. John's discipline and total focus in these sessions, not to mention his earlier efforts in reading and writing, would provide him with a huge reservoir of wordplay images, rhymes and alliterations to draw on and adapt within his songwriting.

Clinical psychologist Kay Redfield Jamison's research on creative endeavour reveals that it:

> can act not only as a means of escape from pain, but also as a way of structuring chaotic emotions and thoughts, numbing pain through abstraction and the rigors of disciplined thought, and creating a distance from the source of despair.[10]

From this perspective, from the early age of five, John used his imagination as a barrier against the trauma that ran throughout his life. The security that this act of creativity gave him also led towards a second area of safety – that of the future. With his unconditional belief in his own success, the songs produced would be rewarded with the prospect of fame, fortune and, most importantly, peace of mind. That was the plan. Essentially, John's work was a means to an end, although not necessarily a happy end.

In the short time that Brian acted as manager, he moved fast. He pulled in favours and used the NEMS shop's buying power to persuade Decca's A&R assistant Mike Smith to make his way up from London to watch The Beatles play The Cavern. On the basis of the band's performance, an audition was secured at Decca's West Hampstead studios. Brian travelled down by train the night before. On the date of the audition, snow fell down all day. John, Paul, George and Pete travelled down to London huddled and freezing in the band's van. The number of bookings had grown so great that a roadie in the shape of an old school pal of Pete's, Neil Aspinall (who would later be joined by Mal Evans as driver-cum-roadie), had been hired and was behind the wheel as they ploughed their way down the M6 and M1 motorways. The burden of leadership, for John was not only for success for the band, but for some sort of validation for himself of the last five years. The swagger, the burning of bridges, the bluster of self-assured success was to come down to the next 24 hours – New Year's Day 1962.

After the audition, during which they gave an adequate account of themselves, running through such numbers as 'Like Dreamers Do', 'The Sheik of Araby' and 'Three Cool Cats', they travelled back up to Liverpool. The band was totally unaware that, on the same day at the West Hampstead studio, there was another group there hoping to secure a recording contract – Brian Poole and the Tremeloes. And there was only room for one band.

It helped that John and the band were so busy with bookings and had the steady and novel input from Brian's management – this all acted as a distraction to the impending decision from Decca. Nevertheless, when the rejection came it was crushing, especially for John – it was his band. He had steered it to where they were now. Even a readers' poll in Bill Harry's *Mersey Beat* proclaiming The Beatles as the best band in Merseyside couldn't soften the Decca decision. All that was left was to carry on playing. The Beatles resumed business as usual on the music circuit. Brian had copies of the Decca Tapes made and proceeded to unstintingly spend his time touting them to potential London record companies.

The Beatles fulfilled their weekly bookings in places such as Barnston Women's Institute, Thistle Café, West Kirby and the Pavilion, Liverpool. One ray of hope, in the shape of a TV recording of *Teenagers Turn (Here we Go)* at BBC Manchester, saw The Beatles performing in their new Beno Dorn worsted stage suits, their performance being broadcast the following night. While they busied themselves with their bookings, the Decca rejection transpired to be the first of more than half a dozen rejections which included major labels such as Pye and Philips. The pressure was on Brian to deliver, but, as much as his own well-mannered and softly spoken approach appealed to the record executives, the 'Decca Tapes' didn't.

On top of the strain of coming up with a record deal, Brian had the additional worry of being blackmailed. He had propositioned a man in a public toilet who proceeded to beat him up and steal his wallet. On discovering Brian's identity and contact details, the man demanded money in order to keep quiet over Brian's sexuality. Brian contacted Rex Makin, the family solicitor, who in turn informed the police. The case ended up in court and in the local newspaper. Brian was referred to as 'Mr X'. Although the man was convicted and Brian kept his anonymity, it is highly likely that, as the friendship between Brian and John developed, John would have been informed of this. It was this kind of incident that John would use against Brian in his own 'legitimate' distaste towards homosexuality.

Not long after the Decca snub, Peter Eckhorn contacted Brian via John. He wanted The Beatles for the Top Ten Club. Contract arrangements were made for a 12-week engagement starting in April. The success and improved finances of The Beatles now meant they could afford to fly from Liverpool to Hamburg.

During this period of progress for The Beatles, John kept in touch with Stu who was at art college in Hamburg. The letters they exchanged revealed a candid view of each other's lives and, as with his letters to Cyn, John revealed an ease of expression in the written word that in many times he failed to achieve verbally. What wasn't discussed in the letters was Stuart's degenerating health. Almost from the time of Stu leaving the band he began to develop headaches. As the pain began to become more persistent and severe, Stu's mother made arrangements for him to have a meeting with a consultant at the University of Liverpool. After the examination, nothing was concluded as to the source of the condition. So despite the blinding pains in Stuart's head, he had returned to Hamburg.

The day before John arrived in Hamburg, Stuart's condition became so grave that he was rushed to hospital in an ambulance. On the way to the hospital Stuart suffered severe convulsions and, despite the efforts by the ambulance crew, he died of a brain haemorrhage before they could reach the hospital. When John arrived at the airport, Astrid was there to meet him with the news. The one person in whom John could really confide was gone. The one person he wanted so much to be like, whose company he coveted more than any other, was dead. The one who, in his presence, John could comfortably revert to type as to who he really wanted to be – a poet-cum-writer, was no longer there for him.

The latest rejection by Decca followed a cycle of rejection by the other recording companies, the déjà vu element of the small town dance halls and inner-city social clubs, the constant doubts about whether the band was good enough – was it all a Lennon-motivated pipe dream? A manager who seemed all gloss and no substance, a manager that other band members watched and sniggered at, and now... Stuart. Maybe it's not surprising that, on being given the news, all John could manage to do was to cling on to Astrid and gaze numbly down over her shoulder at the arrival room's floor.

CHAPTER TEN

1962–63

The Grapes

STUART SUTCLIFFE WAS buried a week after The Beatles began to play their 12-week engagement at the Top Ten Club. The service took place in the parish of Saint Gabriel's Roman Catholic Church, where Stuart attended mass and where he had served as an altar boy. Strangely, although Liverpool has a large Irish Catholic population, none of the other members of The Beatles were Catholic. George was baptised as a Roman Catholic, but it was left at that – no Holy Communion, Confirmation or RC schooling. Paul's mother was Irish Catholic, but again nothing tied him into a formal sense of Catholicism. Only Stu, a church-going Scot, fulfilled the religious criteria that many would have expected The Beatles to possess, hailing from a city with such a strong Catholic influence.

Neither John nor any of the other members of the band attended Stuart's funeral service or internment at Bluebell Lane Cemetery in Huyton. The events of the last couple of months had left John almost emotionally tapped out. The news of Stuart's death drained him of anything left. Any fleeting thoughts of a nerve-searing funeral service were soon blanketed by the security of a return to exhausting sessions on stage at the Top Ten Club along with booze, pills and casual sex. With John's upbringing fostering a lack of compassion and sympathy towards others, he seemed better equipped than the rest of The Beatles to cope; but much of John's toughness was a sham and the fragile nature of his emotional makeup meant the loss of Stu hit him a lot harder than he was prepared to show.

The second trip to Hamburg followed the pattern of the previous one, only this time The Beatles' reputation meant much better pay and conditions, and headlining with artists such as Gene Vincent. A month after the death of Stu, Brian had forwarded the copy of the Decca Tapes to EMI and was invited to a meeting with producer George Martin, the head of EMI's Parlophone division. This resulted in a delighted Brian sending a telegram to The Beatles in Hamburg: 'Congratulations boys, EMI request recording session. Please rehearse new material'.[1] John at last had the validation he so desperately needed.

The Beatles flew from their engagement at the Top Ten Club to London for the Abbey Road audition. The studio session consisted of recording four songs: 'Besame Mucho', 'PS I Love You', 'Ask Me Why' and 'Love Me Do'. George Martin joined the session towards the end to discuss the songs. When George Martin said, 'If there's anything you don't like tell me,' George Harrison famously replied 'well we don't like your tie for a start'. This response stemmed not from the opportunity to be funny (hah hah), disregarding the importance of the situation, but also being *funny* (as in standing up for oneself being confrontational and sarcastic). The Beatles were no mugs and had seen more of the world than people twice their age – they'd been let down, disappointed and dumped on lots of times. Previous record company rejections had not left them humble or grateful for this new offer from Parlophone, but cautiously defensive. So George's 'tie comment' was born partly out of this, not of arrogance or resentment, but a mixture of being funny and being *funny*.

The first 'Abbey Road' recording session that Pete Best made was to be his last. There have been many reasons provided for the sacking of Pete. There has even been a book devoted entirely to his dismissal. None of the reasons put forward on their own seem to give an entirely satisfactory answer as to why, after two years in the band, he was sacked in such a shabby way. The issue of Pete's competency as a drummer seems to be the one that is most commonly given. But this is contradicted by George Martin:

> I never suggested that Pete Best must go. All I said was that for the purposes of The Beatles first record, I would rather use a session man. I never thought that Brian Epstein would let him go. He seemed to be the most saleable commodity as far as looks went. It was a surprise when I learned that they had dropped Pete. The drums were important to me for a record, but they didn't matter much otherwise. Fans don't pay particular attention to the quality of the drumming.[2]

Another view put forward for his dismissal was that the success of The Casbah meant Pete's mother, Mona, felt she could have an input into the management of the band, and repeatedly tried to interfere in the band's affairs. This made the decision to get rid of Pete easier. Pete being too quiet and too good looking are other factors put forward, but these could have been overlooked when considering the huge success that the 'handsome Pete' could bring to the band. One incident that many cite relating to the sacking occurred after The Beatles' first radio broadcast at Manchester Playhouse, when Pete was mobbed by female fans. Paul's father attended the show and witnessed this, and consequently told Pete off for being 'selfish' for 'hogging' all the girls. But Pete didn't have to flaunt himself, as Bob Wooler recalls:

> He was very handsome [with his] dark hair... [He was] probably the most handsome of The Beatles at the time, and the girls used to sleep in his garden at night. They used to go berserk over him.[3]

As for being too quiet and not having a Beatle haircut, there were worse things. Besides, when Astrid styled John, Paul and George's hair, she told Pete that she wasn't able to give him this style, as his hair was too curly; Pete was never asked to adopt this hairstyle. It could be argued that even at this stage, Pete was pencilled in to be sacked, so don't bother with a new hair style; this would only complicate things. Even when Decca rejected The Beatles, Pete was slighted: 'I was hurt I was last to know about it. The others knew a couple of weeks earlier. They let it slip out in a casual conversation one day'.

An insight into the manoeuvrings of Pete's sacking was revealed in a television documentary interview. Pete recalls travelling with Brian and John: 'One particular occasion when Brian propositioned me,' Pete informs the interviewer, 'and the answer was no, John was in the car.' Later on when they stopped for a drink, John approached Pete and asked him what Brian had said. Pete's response to John was 'The gaffer just propositioned me to spend the night with him.' John laughed and said, 'You're joking aren't you? What did you say?' Pete told the slightly amused John 'I said no, what'd bloody hell do you think I said?'.[4]

John's question to Pete is interesting: 'What did you say?' Most young men would have not asked a question but more likely make a statement along the lines of 'The cheeky sod!' But the uncertainty in 'What did you say?' suggests Pete's answer from John's point of view could have been 'yes' or 'no'.

At this time of Pete's sacking nothing happened in the band without John first giving it the green light. The *axe was about to fall* for Pete when

Paul, George and Brian met with Cavern DJ Bob Wooler in a city centre pub to talk about Pete being removed from the band. According to Wooler, 'We held a late meeting in a pub after hours and discussed it'.[5] Bob Wooler was informed of the intended sacking in an attempt to gauge the response of the fans to Pete being dumped out of the band. Wooler was shocked and informed the trio there would be uproar. But Paul, George and Brian had invited Wooler there not for his opinion, but to bear witness that John was not at the meeting. When the news of the meeting emerged and Wooler confirmed that John wasn't there, it would clear him of any involvement. But as the group leader, he always had the casting vote. Philip Norman's *Shout!* suggests that John's absence was due to him going to meet Cynthia, who was to inform him that she was pregnant. This seems unlikely. If John wanted to be at the meeting, he would have been there. That John supported this development was certainly demonstrated when he hurtfully described Pete as a 'stray drummer' The Beatles had picked up.

Later, during Beatlemania, a reporter questioned John as to what Pete was doing outside The Beatles. John replied: 'He was writing that he was glad about the way things worked out: he was glad he missed it all'.[6] Pete was actually working in a bakery for £22 per week, so John's comments are wide of the mark and totally indifferent to Pete's feelings. If Pete was glad for not being a Beatle at the height of Beatlemania, he must have been in an extremely small minority of males in that age group. In actual fact, after being dumped by the group, Pete Best went into a spiralling decline of depression, which climaxed when he attempted to take his own life. John's indifference to someone who was a member (and a major player in the early development) of The Beatles for two years is hard to understand. Perhaps John was trying to play down the importance of Pete Best in the 'apprenticeship' of the band, the logical conclusion being that Pete's dismissal was insignificant.

Bill Harry, then still a close friend of John's, provided the following view:

> I felt an injustice was being done, but not because Pete was getting kicked out on the brink of success. That's the luck of the game. I felt that there should have been some truth about why he'd been put out. They should have said, 'we've decided that we get on better with Ringo, and we want Ringo with us'. Instead, they suggested that Pete Best wasn't good enough.[7]

The reasons for sacking Pete were undoubtedly complex. For one thing, Pete's middle-class, suburban background would make The Beatles a group of four ex-college boys – that old 'art school band' chestnut they had been so keen to shed. While Paul and George had their working-class credentials in a period of the 1960s when being working-class was deemed sexy, Pete and John, with their background in comfortable suburbanite homes seemed too alike. But there were other reasons. Pete, although quiet, was not 'soft'. He boxed for his school and he could handle himself. While John definitely saw Paul and George as junior partners in the band, Pete, though considered a 'passive outsider', would still be prepared to stand up to John. This uncertainty for John, together with Pete's background, would ultimately lead to the decision that Pete was out and Ringo was in.

'We were cowards when we sacked him,' John later told Hunter Davies. 'We made Brian do it. But if we'd told Pete to his face, that would have been much nastier than getting Brian to do it. It probably would have ended in a fight if we'd told him.' John's conscience eventually got the better of him when he confided to Bill Harry that the way Pete was treated was 'despicable'.[8]

As The Beatles began to accept Brian's style of management, John's relationship with him developed into one of both tormentor and confidant. Indeed, long before Brian became manager, John was bigoted towards homosexuals. 'My God,' Bob Wooler recalls, 'how he ranted about "fucking queers" and "fucking fags!"'... He was very outspoken, indifferent to anyone's feelings. He didn't give a shite about anyone, really, but he was especially intolerant of gays'.[9]

Almost from the start, John had a fraught relationship with Brian. Minor jokes developed into stronger jibes and these continued into outright insults, which soon became accepted and then normalised. Being both Jewish and gay, Brian suffered doubly from John's prejudices. Not long after Brian took over The Beatles, he gave a press conference in the Blue Angel in Liverpool and while Paul was upstairs in the club, downstairs was a drunken John. Bob Wooler recalls that John was:

> shooting his mouth off, well away with drink or whatever. He said, 'Hitler should have finished the job', meaning that the gas ovens should have been more active than they were.[10]

Why Brian should allow incidents like this to slide is uncertain. Perhaps he was the first to realise the huge financial gains possible from the group's continued success. Perhaps he had already begun to develop a taste for the cut and thrust, the adrenalin rush of a show business lifestyle. For one (or all) of these reasons, Brian evidently felt that John's infantile insults were worth the price he had to pay to be with The Beatles. The pressure of managing what would become the biggest musical act in the world resulted in the development of temper tantrums by Brian to his staff; the stresses and strains of this position not being helped by the constant jibes by John. Yet whereas John viewed these bouts of temper as a laughable sign of weakness, his own uncontrollable rages against others were seen by him as an indication of masculine virility. It seems that John's homophobic attitude was slow to lose itself. Ten years later, in Jann Wenner's *Rolling Stone* interview, he declared, 'I think Mick [Jagger's] a joke, with all that fag dancing. I always did'.[11]

John was, without a shadow of doubt, the leader. In the group's first radio interview for a local hospital station, the Cleaver and Clatterbridge interviewer Monty Lister made a mistake in asking George, 'by playing lead guitar does that mean that you're the leader of the group?' George, seemingly embarrassed, blurts out, 'No, no. Just, well you see the other guitar is rhythm: ching, ching, ching you see.' Paul realised that the radio listening audience still didn't know who the leader is. What they did know was that the rhythm guitar player (John) was the one who had been given the task of making a ching, ching, ching sound on stage. Paul quickly steps in and empathically declares that 'John is in fact leader of the group.'[12]

Back in Abbey Road Studios, George Martin attempted to foist a song by producer and songwriter Mitch Murray on the band. The song, 'How Do You Do It', proved unpopular and the boys actively opposed it in favour of (mainly) Paul's 'Love Me Do', which Martin felt was too slow. John and Paul stood their ground and, after a tepid forced demo of Murray's song, George Martin challenged John to come up with something better. John and Paul quickly reworked 'Love Me Do' into a more upbeat and forceful delivery. Although 'How Do You Do It' was jettisoned by The Beatles, it served as a useful ploy for George Martin in encouraging John to improve the group's first single. This was to be a precursor of the cat and mouse game that George would have to play, particularly with John, throughout the band's time at Abbey Road. Unlike Paul, who immediately committed himself to whatever time was necessary for the needs of the recording, John was often deemed to be blasé and even downright lazy.

Pete's replacement, Ringo, had known John since their days at Hamburg and was considered a better drummer than Pete. Just as important, he shared the sense of humour and outgoing nature of The Beatles. The good news for Ringo was that he was now part of a band with a recording contract. The bad news was that Martin was uncertain as to whether his drumming was up to scratch to the point of being able to record at Abbey Road. Ultimately, Ringo was left to play maraca and tambourine on the B Side 'PS I Love You'. If George Martin's refusal to allow Ringo to drum on the records continued, this would have left John in a difficult position. It would be a safe guess to say that John would not have challenged George Martin, who was an established figure with his Guildhall School of Music and Drama credentials and status as producer. Martin was quiet but firm in his attitude, well spoken, tall and dignified in appearance and manner. He was qualified in his field, was everything John had been brought up to respect and could prove pivotal in getting John where he wanted to be, and so at this period, John went along with what George Martin had to say.

Ringo's less-than-perfect introduction to the studio must have made him pause for thought. After being replaced with session drummer Alan White for the single version of 'Love Me Do', Ringo told Hunter Davies: 'I thought, that's the end, they're doing a Pete Best on me'.[13] Though Ringo did play on the LP version, being replaced like that rankled for years to come.

It has been suggested that Ringo, brought up in a terraced house in the Dingle area of Liverpool, was the only truly working-class member of the band. The major difference between Paul, George and Ringo centred on schooling: Ringo never went to a grammar school, his early schooling having been disrupted by a series of illnesses which began with a ruptured appendix. Up until senior school, though, Ringo's education was the same as Paul and George's. His school would have contained the same type of classmates with the same kinds of families, either living on a council estate like Paul and George, or living in a landlord owned house like the drummer himself.

Ringo's main difference and strength was in his grounding in a life of manual work. Working jobs such as a barman on a ferry service, waiter, apprentice joiner and railway worker gave him a different kind of maturity than that gained in Hamburg. From this emerged a different outlook. He wasn't as fully committed to stardom as the others and so the intensity and hunger for success never took a firm hold. Ringo's view on finding himself part of the world's biggest music phenomenon was philosophical. In response to an interviewer's question about the future, he said, 'Who knows what tomorrow holds?'.[14] This must have stuck in John's conscience when it came to The Beatles' *Revolver* album, with the inclusion of his song, 'Tomorrow Never Knows'. From this life experience developed Ringo's deadpan, droll sense of humour.

Before Ringo joined The Beatles he was already a star (albeit a small one) with Rory Storm and the Hurricanes. They were talented, and at one time more famous than The Beatles. Ringo also owned his own car, which was impressive, and he was reluctant to accommodate John's moods as easily as Paul or George. He may have been seen as just the new boy, but Ringo's grounding in a practical world of work soon showed. When questioned about what he wanted out of life, his reply was to own a women's hairdresser's, no doubt influenced by his then girlfriend (and later his wife), Maureen, who herself was an hairdresser. This level-headedness was brought about by having a life outside a rock 'n' roll band. While promoting *A Hard Day's Night* in the US, Ringo quipped with the interviewer that, 'John can act the goat'. John replied: 'If I wasn't in America I'd punch him.' Quick as a flash, Ringo shot back: 'You're not big enough and when you are, you'll be too old!'.[15] Street-smart quips such at these helped John keep his feet on the ground.

A week after Ringo joined the group, John and Cynthia were married. There was nothing particularly notable about the ceremony, except that a pneumatic drill was repairing the road outside which all but drowned out the proceedings, that George jokingly stepping forward when the Register asked for the groom and the fact that it was the same registry office where Freddie and Julia were married. Interestingly, though, Brian was John's choice of best man. One would have expected this position to go to Paul; they'd known one another (and been on the road together) for five years, while Brian was a relative newcomer of less than a year. This may have had a lot to do with John's manipulation of Brian, rather than demonstrating a respect for the position of best man. This was later repeated when Brian was chosen as godfather to John's son, Julian.

To John, the definition of marriage didn't seem to contain any idea of commitment. Almost as soon as the wedding was over, it seemed to Cynthia as if it had never happened. John had 'done the right thing' and avoided a possible scandal. There was a fly in the ointment, though, in the shape of Mimi. Mimi never accepted that John should get married and flew into a rage when the intended nuptials were announced. The fact that Mimi had previously taken an instant dislike to Cynthia and that John *had* to get married didn't help her disposition – she refused to attend the wedding ceremony. Under these circumstances, John was no doubt more than happy to steer clear of Mendips and continue the hectic touring schedule that Brian had set out for The Beatles. Brian's plan was to *blitzkrieg* the local venues with The Beatles advertised as 'Parlophone Recording Artists', the intent being to build up sales of their forthcoming single.

When Brian took over, not many groups in the UK had the benefit of a personal full-time manager, especially one with such an educated background and impressive network in the recording industry. Brian brought the energy and enthusiasm of all his previous unfulfilled aspirations at RADA and ploughed his passion into making The Beatles the biggest act around. This meant a gruelling schedule of playing a variety of venues, sometimes two dozen every month; radio, regional television appearances and another trip to Hamburg, all mixed in with regular lunchtime Cavern visits, the release of the singles 'Love Me Do' and 'Please Please Me', their first number one and their first album, and a nationwide tour. This all emerged within the nine-month period following the sacking of Pete Best, and John's hectic rock 'n' roll lifestyle and its steady progression of success sat in stark contrast to Cynthia's position.

Married life for Cynthia consisted, in the main, of being pregnant and waiting for John. Initially, they lived in a flat borrowed from Brian. Although close to the city centre, a stone's throw from their old Liverpool Art College, the accommodation suffered from a certain lack of privacy. In order to walk from their living room to the bathroom, Cynthia and John had to cross the common hallway and as the flat was on the ground floor, it made the unlocked bedroom door open to strangers walking in from the street. More importantly, Cynthia was in the vulnerable position of being left on her own most of the time. As her pregnancy progressed, her lack of friends nearby or even access to a telephone made her worry that, when the time came, she might be unable to get to hospital. A scare came during the pregnancy when Cynthia started to lose blood. Fortunately this took place on the same day her brother Tony had called around for a visit and the potential danger and a trip to the hospital was averted. On John's return home from touring, he suggested that Cynthia stay at Mendips until she gave birth. Either that or John would have to stay home more, and for John, that wasn't an option.

A year prior to her pregnancy, John had talked her into staying with Mimi while he was in Hamburg. This stay made Cynthia fully aware of Mimi's character and, not surprisingly, she found life at Mendips difficult. At this time, Cynthia found she had a role to play in Mimi's cats' welfare:

> I was expected to feed them, which made me sick. Everyday fish scraps were collected by the parsimonious Mimi from the local fish-monger, boiled and then boned. The kitchen stank.[16]

Mimi's purpose for Cynthia's stay was a case of keeping John in her debt, by 'helping out' his girlfriend and also having the chance to see how she could use the situation to her own advantage with regards to keeping John at home. Cynthia was about to make a second stay at Mendips and this would prove to be even more of a challenge, with her being seven months pregnant.

While at Mendips, even though she had just given birth, Cynthia was treated like one of the lodgers. Mimi's cats having the run of the house meant newborn Julian's cot, along with the baby himself, was constantly covered in cat hairs. If this wasn't bad enough for a new mother, Cynthia found that she 'was still feeding [Mimi's] cats, gagging daily over the smell of boiling fish'. There were no allowances made for the young mother:

> Living with Mimi was harder than I'd imagined it might be. Even though I was paying rent I had to do any chores around the house and she expected me to drop everything and come running to her... There was no refusing Mimi and I was treated exactly as her other two lodgers. She always had a reason why she couldn't do a job herself or needed help.[17]

Due to the touring commitments of The Beatles, it was three days before John would arrive and see his newborn son. John was immediately over-joyed, picking up the baby and carrying him around the room declaring, 'Cynthia, he's bloody marvellous! He's fantastic'.[18] But after the initial elation, John announced he was going to Barcelona with Brian for 12 days. A disappointed Cynthia knew John would go, no matter what she said, and gave her blessing. 'Cynthia (had had) a baby and a holiday was planned,' John revealed, 'but I wasn't going to break the holiday for a baby. I just thought I was a bastard. I was and went'.[19] This comment was made many years later and is interesting in that his son, Julian, is not referred to by name or being spoken of as 'the baby' but by the anonymous title of 'a baby'.

The trip to Barcelona at this time provides an insightful view into John's attitude. Why would he go to Barcelona knowing that the gossip mill in Liverpool would be in overdrive? It could be argued, why not? He'd worked hard, it was his band and he deserved a break. Part of Brian's reason for the holiday could have been to impress John with his own experience of the culture and tradition of the capital of the Catalan region, the works of Gaudi, the Sagrada Familia, the Gothic Quarter and a walk down the famous La Ramblas. The challenge from Brian that, *It's just a holiday, what are you scared of?* was taken up by John. To him it wasn't just a case of thumbing a nose at gossips back in Liverpool – it was an opportunity, when the band was on the cusp of success, to fully stamp his authority, and not only with Brian.

John's insecurities made the notion of dominating Brian appealing. In many senses John was an outsider from a very early age, no more so in his frustrated aspirations to be a cultured poet. John despised the educated middle class – not for their class position, he wasn't that political – but for their education. John had no education, in the formal sense of certification. He was at the same time dismissive and envious of those who did. Brian had an education that fitted right in with John's somewhat dual attitude towards those with a cultivated outlook. To have Brian under his thumb was his way of trying to put right his own lost opportunity.

John confused the notion of having control over Brian with that of having control over how others in Liverpool would interpret it. John had overplayed his hand in his belief that he could laugh off going to Barcelona with a gay man or even be impervious to the consequent remarks. He believed that it wasn't such a big thing, but to 1960s homophobic Britain, and especially in a rough and ready seaport as Liverpool, it was. John was always trying to push people and see how far he could go. That there might be a danger of a rumour going around the city that John was gay would have killed all his previous credibility. This was to be an unintended consequence of John's trip to Barcelona and one that he would attempt to put right at a party in Dovecot.

Paul took the view that:

Brian was gay, and John saw his opportunity to impress on Mr Epstein who was boss of the group. He wanted Brian to know whom he should listen to.[20]

The subtext here is that John needed to have Brian on his side to be the leader of the group. If John wanted to show Brian who was boss, he didn't have to go to Barcelona. He was doing that with every cruel remark made to Brian in Liverpool and beyond. What John really wanted was to show *Paul* who was boss. Even at this early stage, John was fully aware of Paul's superior musical skills and ambitions. Paul let John believe he was the leader, but to Paul he believed that he was the most valued member of The Beatles. 'John used to say, "I'm the leader of this group!" and we used to say, "It's only because you fucking shout louder than anyone else."'.[21] Paul clearly suggests here that John was only leader by default of starting the band and being the pushiest.

Paul's confidence was born of his own indefatigable self-belief in himself as a musician and performer. It also stemmed from himself as a person. Paul's teacher Alan Durband recalls that:

Paul was always liked by the other lads. He had what people often refer to as a 'Liverpool wit'. Yet he was also rather withdrawn. He had a lot of natural charm, which endeared him to his teachers. In fact, he was consistently voted the head boy of his class.[22]

This 'profile' seems at odds with that of John's time at school. John's own creativity was more than a match for Paul, but his confidence was undermined by his conscious and unconscious sense of victimhood. This feeling was in many ways valid, but it revealed itself in unsavoury ways at times in his 'justified' appalling behaviour.

John had spent more than enough time with Paul in the control room and studio floor at the Abbey Road recording to see first-hand his gift for playing and understanding the concept of music. Paul's confidence and ability to understand the technicalities of the recording studio, including getting the band on acetate, was something John would be loath to do, because it would betray his ignorance (and thus weakness) to others. These very early issues, between John's *laissez-faire* attitude in the studio and Paul's craftsmanship and need to be in control, were what would later be at the heart of The Beatles' demise. With the trip to Barcelona, John was to reaffirm just whose band it really was.

When John had time to take a break from the tours and visited home, he didn't stop long – the mix of Mimi and a newborn baby who was suffering from colic never encouraged him to spend too many nights under the Mendips roof. In her autobiography, Cynthia recalls at this time feeling like 'a single parent'. The months spent in the company of Mimi at least gave Cynthia a comprehensive insight into what it must have been like for John to be brought up on Menlove Avenue. The chores continued, including the hated boiling of fish for Mimi's three cats, and were accompanied by snide remarks about the baby and herself from Mimi as well her 'subtle' early morning use of a vacuum cleaner outside Cynthia's bedroom door – a hint for her and the baby to get up. Eventually, Cynthia could not take it anymore, and moved out to stay with her mother.

When John returned from Barcelona, it was a case of the same old, same old with The Beatles, with a frantic round of clubs and dance halls, radio interviews and TV appearances. In between these came an incident which for too many people would define John as a roughhouse, fighter and tough guy. But, as in many instances, all was not what it seemed and the real 'truth' is much more interesting and insightful than the perceived party line of The Beatles Story.

The bare facts of the matter are that John attacked Cavern DJ Bob Wooler at a party at Paul's Auntie Gin's, after Wooler made a comment about John, Brian and Barcelona. That is correct, but the reasons behind this act of violence are far more complicated. John believed he could cope with the sniggers and the snide remarks on his return from Barcelona. Given a normal set of circumstances he possibly would have, but the beating of Bob Wooler resulted in an article by a national daily newspapers forcing John to send an awkward telegram apology (put together by Brian) and paying Wooler £200 compensation. But how did John find himself in a set of circumstances for this to happen at all? The location of the party was important: it took place in Dovecot in Liverpool. Dovecot is a council housing estate in the district of Huyton, to which 50,000 residents from the inner-city's worse slums were moved between the wars. They were provided, in the main, with town house accommodation with front and rear gardens, the back garden being accessed by a curved, open doorway used by the residents of the tied houses. This was a well-kept, working-class housing estate – a place that Mimi had warned John about, as it was full of 'those types' that shouldn't be let through the door unless they're there to mend something. The second issue that worked against John was that those invited were, in keeping with the nature of the party, local neighbours – Paul's large, extended family and their friends, all intent on making Paul feel 'King for the Day'.

It was to be a typical Liverpool party, where Liverpool people practised their verbal gymnastics, where irreverence to status was the order of the day, where jokes were made at anyone's expense and slights against oneself were only to be laughed at. In essence, it was a cut-throat affair of 'get your skit in first'. While John had a good sense of humour, was witty and quick with a rebuff, this was mainly on his own terms or patch; for John, this was his first real dealings, in a social situation, and with drink involved, with such a large group of those outside his normal 'audience'.

Liverpool-born author Linda Grant gives a good 'analysis' of what could be expected at these gatherings:

> Liverpudlians meeting for the first time always ask each other the same questions: the first is which school did you go to, so establishing whether you are Catholic or Protestant; and then, if you are Catholic, the next question is which parish you lived in. These are the means by which the tribes identify themselves.[23]

The older men at the party would be quick off the mark to pull John's leg, with comments about the 'Beatle hairstyle'. 'Who did that to your haircut lad? Did you tell the police about the ones who did it?'. 'Alright son, are you in our Paul's group? Which one are you, George or Bingo?'

The intention of the Barcelona trip had been to trump Paul, but John forgot to take into account the party and its content. Now he'd trumped himself. It was Paul's party and he would be the Birthday Boy, receiving presents, slaps on the back, having drinks thrust into his hand and all John could do was look on in stoic silence. The idea that, as the leader of The Beatles, John might gain some kudos held no water here. This was a Liverpool party, so leave your ego at the doorstep. This was the kind of audience who would take great pleasure in taking anyone down a peg or two. A Woolton grammar school boy quoting the works of Keats, Kerouac or Ginsberg would have gone down like a fart in a frogman's suit and the notion of a family singsong would have sent John screaming into the street. Mimi's code of conduct and manners were totally redundant here.

What could John do? If he didn't make an appearance his absence might add fuel to the fire of the rumours of Barcelona. A no-show would also leave him open to the mutterings of leaving his wife and three week old son behind and the mutterings of; *what kind of fella is he*? Not turning up would also have looked like bad form to Paul and George. So with Cynthia on his arm, he entered Mimi's worst nightmare: but first, get drunk, and that's where it went from bad to worse.

With no Brian for backup and given that John knew what he was walking into, getting drunk may have seemed a good option, but the tension of the situation was heightened by drink. With raucous and coarse laughter, impromptu half-drunken dancing, loud Scouse accents, Mimi's version of hell on earth, this in itself conspired against John in that the summer heat only accommodated the ease with which he could drink.

When a drunken John passed Bob Wooler, who fancied himself as a wit and made a comment concerning John's time in Spain with Brian, the results were explosive. Bill Harry recalls:

> He leapt on Bob and battered him to the ground giving him a black eye, bruised ribs and torn knuckles, which Bob sustained when he tried to protect his face from John's foot as he was being kicked.[24]

Bob Wooler was taken to hospital. But John wasn't finished. Soon after, he passed a good-looking girl who was sat on the knee of Billy J. Kramer: John fondled her breast. The girl, Rose Leach, slapped him in the face. John punched her and, as she fell to the floor, went to kick her before being stopped by Billy Hatton, bass player with The Fourmost, who were the resident band at the party. Soon after, John left with Cynthia. Too drunk to realise the full extent of his actions, only the next day, with the clarity which comes from a hangover, did the full impact began to filter through with a confessional declaration to Cynthia that, 'I battered his bloody ribs in'.[25] That John 'battered his bloody ribs in' was true, but what was also true was that this was against a small, slightly built man who couldn't punch his way out of a wet paper bag.

John's inability to understand himself would see a recurring pattern of this kind of action. Clinical Psychologist Alice Miller hypothesises that:

A person who can understand and integrate his anger as part of himself will not become violent. He has the need to strike out at others only if he is thoroughly unable to understand his rage, if he was not permitted to become familiar with this feeling as a small child, was never able to experience it as a part of himself because such a thing was totally unthinkable in his surroundings.[26]

The demons behind his unhappiness, depression and uncontrolled anger were supposed to be remedied by his art and music, but this was proving elusive.

CHAPTER ELEVEN

1963-64
Liverpool Town Hall

THE INTRODUCTION OF Brian Epstein as their manager transformed The Beatles from a Merseyside rock 'n' roll outfit gaining bookings at the behest of local promoters to a polished band. Bookings were no longer made by the band contacting the promoter, but by the promoter contacting Brian. Gone were the days when Brian had to blackball promoter Brian Kelly, after a booking at Aintree Institute, for paying out The Beatles' playing fee of £15 in loose change. Alistair Taylor, long-time personal assistant to Brian, had the view that 'John never liked to let you think he was taking anything seriously, but he took success seriously and he wanted a lot of it'.[1] The debacle at Auntie Gin's and John's public apology were soon forgotten as Brian's campaign for The Beatles' success took shape. Venues such as Newton Dancing School, Irby Institute and Heswall Jazz Club would soon be a thing of the past.

Things were changing fast and it was obvious to all that a move from Liverpool to a London base was necessary. But much as John was enjoying success, his complex sense of insecurity wouldn't let go of the need to maltreat and ridicule Brian. Success or not, Brian continued to suffer caustic and snide comments from John. With Brian present back stage at The Cavern, John remarked, 'I see that new Dirk Bogarde film is at the Odeon.' Those in the room knew it was a set-up. To the obligatory question of 'Which one is that?' John's response was 'Victim. It's all about those fucking queers'.[2] That John wasn't content with the success of the band without having to initiate incidents such as this goes deep into his consciousness: at times, John's notion of happiness was measured by the degree of control he had over others.

The issue of John's homophobia was tied to the particular values learnt at Mendips, values which lumped together groups such as 'common and vulgar', foreigners and those whose sexual practices didn't live up to the norms of Mimi's inter-war, traditional values. John's dislike of 'queers' also stemmed from the Myth of Masculinity, in which anything not deemed masculine was seen as not only as a weakness but a threat to his virility. The major difference with John was that he 'celebrated' his homophobia; he went out of his way to hurt. Once, in a lift with Neil Aspinall and Brian, Brian asked for suggestions for titles for his forthcoming autobiography. John's suggestion was 'Queer Jew'.[3] This role seems to have been given passive consent by the fact that Paul, George and Ringo were conspicuous in their apparent failure to challenge this abysmal way in which John treated Brian, who was, after all, *their* manager as well.

Yet for all John's unkindness towards Brian, there also seemed to be an unspoken bond between them. The view that only Brian knew John well was common to those who knew them both. It is likely that the bond that held them together was that of a shared recognition and awareness of outsiders. This understanding began to take shape in Barcelona when, more importantly than any notion of sex, which may or may not have taken place, they may have shared their innermost secrets and fears. Over the 12 days in Barcelona, John could have divulged bitter disclosures to Brian of Julia, Mimi, Stu and Cynthia, Brian responding with his own confessionals regarding the mismatch of his faith and sexuality, his loneliness and his broken dreams of the theatre.

On his return from Barcelona, John became more homophobic and anti-Semitic towards Brian. He worried that they would be disclosed, and even worse was the thought of who they could be disclosed to. The comment by Bob Wooler at Dovecot was a warning. So to prevent any perceived signs of affection, the best course of action was *to keep Brian in line*. This was to be achieved by a tirade of insults and threats. Yet, within this mix of self-doubt and self-hate, there was recognition by John of the commonality of background and sense of being an outsider. Brian was only eight years older than John, the gap was much wider in the sense of maturity. John could have been viewed by Brian as a well-meaning but naughty school boy. John's humour was, without doubt, at times oafishly puerile. John had spent most of his life being tied to what Mimi wanted. This narrow outlook towards life was fine when being single-minded towards musical success, but it left him wanting when it came to social relations and responsibilities. The emotional trauma that was visited on him in Mendips saw him seamlessly compartmentalise social relationships and actions whereby his hunger for success was matched by his indifference to being married. His relationship with Brian could switch from rants on 'homos', 'cripples' and Jews to, within minutes, discussing details of the next gig. This anomaly ran like a thread through John's life.

Brian's management of the band saw him pack The Beatles' diary with bookings. In July 1963 they were booked every day, from the Odeon Cinema, Glasgow to the Playhouse Theatre, London. Other bands would have suffered from fatigue and discontent, but other bands hadn't had the discipline of Hamburg or the supreme confidence of two songwriters whose whole adolescent life had been honed to bring them to where they were now. On the brink of stardom, a little bit of travelling wasn't going to get in their way.

John's relationship with Paul also began to change. In 1957 at Saint Peter's fête, it was not only their age difference that made John the leader, but also the sheer strength of personality which forced Paul to follow. Paul was happy to let John work out his frustrations of his personal life on stage and beyond, confident in his own understanding that John's over the top personality and burning desire for success would pay dividends. The privacy of the regular songwriting sessions provided the only arena where John would allow some sort of democracy within the partnership, but this was forced on John by the sheer necessity of Paul's superior musical ability. Not that John would admit this publicly. The problem that John faced with Paul was that if he gave an equal share of leadership then what would happen if the next level of success depended on the band performing original songs, and Paul taking the lion's share of credits?

John, like Paul, was aware that the partnership of songwriting 'eyeball to eyeball' would not last forever. John's particular problem was that he found it difficult to write songs without the safety net of sessions with Paul. This caused further conflict for John – he was now dealing with the twin pressures of fear of failure that creativity can bring, and the fear of competitive comparison with Paul. One of his strategies for dealing with this, in the public sphere of Abbey Road, was to be apparently nonchalant towards the recording process – the opposite of Paul's pedantic approach of questioning studio technicians, going through retake after retake and trying different sounds. John's creative genius was largely developed in private, for he wasn't emotionally equipped to be judged in the studio, hence his laid-back attitude and a tendency to *get in and get it done*. The real centre of his creativity had its roots as a self-defence mechanism in the isolation of Mendips as a child – it was within his reading and writing that his personal declaration of art was. The studio provided a platform for others to support this genius.

The initial period of recordings saw Paul steal a march on John with the first single 'Love Me Do' along with the B Side of 'PS I Love You'. John could no longer browbeat the other members of the band about the content of their stage set, nor could he demand which Lennon and McCartney songs should be recorded. George Martin's opinion was important, and John's influence over him at this time was negligible, so unless he was going to stand by and watch Paul run away with the prize of recorded songs, he would have to 'up his game'. This is what he did in the shape of The Beatles' first number one hit, 'Please Please Me', along with the B Side 'Ask Me Why?'

In many ways, John put himself under pressure with his aggression and his generally poor attitude, but to him this was justified by his 'majority' role in The Beatles' success, particularly in the shape of 'his' hit singles. Even under his own demanding expectations, in the period 1962–1965 John was happy, or at least contented. The unbelievable amount of work that The Beatles undertook during their Beatlemania days, together with the novelty of the situation and John's development and success as a song-writer, kept his fears and insecurities at bay. Nevertheless, he was still wired towards the cruel 'jokes'. This even happened on live, peak time TV at the Royal Variety Performance. The Beatles were filmed entering the theatre, and for the benefit of the camera, John twisted his head to his shoulder and stuck his tongue under his bottom lip in another repeat of his routine mocking of those with disabilities.

Within the history of The Beatles, until the demise of the band, no one was prepared to challenge John's unacceptable behaviour. John's vicious-ness was explained by the rest of The Beatles with, 'Oh, it's just John'. It wasn't so much that this trip to the dark side was consistent, indeed, such behaviour was worse because of its inconsistencies. John's time at Mendips found him in conflict with those whom, in the early days, he had needed most – the working class, those whom Mimi found so disgusting – John 'lowering' himself not only to be with them, but to act like them, added to an already fragile state of affairs mentally. 'I told him off about his accent,' Mimi reported to Ray Coleman, 'I said, "What's all this Scouse accent about, John? You weren't brought up as a little Scouser. You know how to speak properly"'.[4] John responded with, 'It's about money; the fans expect me to talk like that'.[5] Here John owns up to his fabricated self, implying Mimi would readily identify with the notion of deception in return for monetary gain.

The recording of the *Please Please Me* album in a marathon 12-hour session saw the unprecedented delivery of eight original songs. The division of songwriting credits between John and Paul were about equal, but the pack leader 'Please Please Me' removed any previous concerns regarding John's songwriting capabilities. The confidence of John and Paul as song- writers also meant this self-assurance spilled over to George Martin when it came to The Beatles having the 'right' to choose which cover versions to record.

John's choice of cover songs on the first two Beatles albums reflects a state of mind that can only be understood with future insights into John's frame of mind. 'Anna', 'You Really Got a Hold on Me' and 'Baby It's You' are soul-saddened confessionals of John's feelings, hidden behind boy meets girl, boy loses girl love songs. Beside his genius as a songwriter, his confidence at this early time of The Beatles saw him produce cover versions in the first two albums that in most cases are as good, if not better, than the originals. John and the band grabbed the original by the scruff of the neck and kicked it around until it morphed into what seemed to be one of their own songs. The confidence of John's vocal abilities challenge the listener to believe this is his song and nobody else's. And yet, tying in with his flip-flop- ping of egotism and insecurity, he hated the sound of his voice. He con- stantly asked George Martin and, later, Phil Spector to cloak it in echo.

The choice of cover versions on the first two Beatles albums was a precursor of future roads in music that John and Paul were to travel. The comparison is stark. Paul's choices, 'A Taste of Honey' and 'Till There was You', reveal an eagerness to impress, objective 'on the nose' lyrics and an emphasis on the professionalism of the delivery. John's choices and inter- pretation reveals an empathy for torch songs, tales of unrequited love and an honest nakedness of emotion that he found all too easy to identify with and respond to. 'Anna' in particular shows John *par excellence* as an artist totally immersing himself in the angst of lost love. Indeed, in 'Anna' John is ladling up all his past – what could have been the rebuffs from Julia, Stu and from Mimi to art college. 'Anna' was what John could have been. 'Anna' was a hymn to the sense of his inconsolable loss.

The frenzy of what was to be termed 'Beatlemania' was a perfect antidote to a Britain shocked by a Tory Government that had become embroiled in a scandal that the tabloid papers could only dream of – a Russian spy and Her Majesty's Defence Secretary sharing the services of the same prostitute. The *ancien regime* of power being located in the public schools of Eton and Harrow, with their provision of the ruling elite inside the Conservative Cabinet, and the landed gentry who for centuries had assumed a position of *noblesse oblige*, were suddenly under attack in a sleaze-fuelled scandal.

The Beatles presented an alternative to and a distraction from the constant newspaper coverage of a national embarrassment and a government in turmoil. Economically, the country was enjoying an unprecedented boom, income was rising and relatively full employment meant extensive con-sumerism in the shape of cars, motorbikes, cookers and washing machines, which were all made available through hire purchase and easier credit. Britain's economic situation was part of a wider, west-European post-war growth and this consumer boom put pressure on the BBC to entertain more and educate less. The need for the BBC to compete for an increasing share of audience figures with the commercial ITV meant accommodating the new teenage market. This made The Beatles 'hot property' to both the commercial and state-funded TV channels.

The whirlwind of demand and pressures on The Beatles' time and personal lives could have led to in-fighting, sulks and ego trips, but this did not happen. The extreme intensity of the living and playing arrange-ment in Hamburg had much to do with lancing any boils of discontent. That John and the rest of the band endured so much says a lot about the resilience of what Du Noyer calls a 'mutual sense of Scouse assurance'.[6] It's been estimated that The Beatles gave in excess of 1,400 performances. For John, this sense of group solidarity and sharing of triumphs and failures presented an antidote to the anger and resentment he still held for the loss of both Julia and Stu.

This sense of hurt was sadly matched with an equal willingness to hurt. During the same period in which he was standing naked and bleeding singing 'Anna', he acted in a manner that in other circles would have ended in a punch up. In April, The Beatles, along with Del Shannon, the Springfields and a host of other acts, played the Royal Albert Hall for a BBC Radio Special *Swinging Sound '63*. The band performed 'Please Please Me' and 'Misery' in the first act and 'Twist and Shout' and 'From Me to

You' in the second. At the Royal Albert Hall Paul met Jane Asher for the first time and made a play for her. The Beatles plus Jane went back to the flat of music journalist Chris Hutchins. Seventeen-year-old Jane came from an established and wealthy London family, living in Wimpole Street, Belgravia. Back at Hutchins' flat, John, who had had a drink, decided to see how far his new-found stardom could take him when it came to crass remarks and attitude:

JOHN: 'OK, there's no booze. Let's talk about sex. Jane, how do girls play with themselves?'

JANE: 'I'm not going to talk about that!'

JOHN: 'You're the only girl here and I want to know, how do you jerk off?'

CHRIS: 'There's only one jerk here.'

JOHN: 'Oh fab! No booze, no birds, insults from the host... What kind of rave is this? Bleedin' marvellous, I'm going in search of some crumpet. Call me a taxi.'

By this time Jane Asher was crying, and George Harrison was trying to comfort her.

JANE: 'You know, John, you can be very cruel sometimes.'

John made his way to the front door to find his own taxi and on his way responded with 'It's the beast in me'.[7]

Fame and power, in no matter what sphere they operate, can bring the worst out in people; but with John it was more a case of being deeply uncertain of himself, unsure of whether he really was happy and content or scared and hateful at the thought that it wouldn't last. The other members of The Beatles knew his moods better than anyone. 'I had been invited to see them play several times by Paul, but for some reason, I had never got round to it,' George recalls when first meeting John. 'I remember being very impressed by John's big, thick, sideboards and Teddy Boy clothes. He was a terribly sarcastic bugger from day one'.[8]

As with Ringo, George found the best way to deal with John was to give as good as you got. In ordinary life, this might work, but here was a young man who was the leader of the most extraordinary music act the world had ever seen. His face and those of *his* band were to be known to most teenagers in the western world. The world was his to have, and yet deep down inside there was always a part of him resisting and scared to show love and compassion. Sadly, it seemed he was happiest when he had his boot on the neck of his fellow man.

The image of John in Chris Hutchins' flat is a world away from the London Palladium Royal Variety Show and John's 'cheeky' comment aimed towards the Royal Family's Box at the start of The Beatles 'Twist and Shout' number: 'For our last number I'd like to ask your help: Will the people in the cheaper seats clap your hands? And the rest of you, if you'll just rattle your jewelry...'.[9] This show is generally viewed as a watershed. Eighteen million TV viewers were won over by The Beatles and, in particular, John's comment. The group came over as a combination of the musically novel, youthful rebelliousness, impudence and humour. Journalist and friend to The Beatles, Maureen Cleave, believed that, 'everyone loves them because they look so happy'.[10] And strangely for John, even with the moods and the slights to those around him, the period of 1963 to 1965 would be not only his most productive musically but, by his own standards, his most contented period during the life of The Beatles.

Prior to the success at the Royal Variety Performance, The Beatles had played in Sweden. As they flew into London, American talk show host Ed Sullivan was amazed to witness thousands of screaming young girls attempting to lay siege to their incoming plane. The result was a huge slice of luck for Brian and the band. Within weeks, Sullivan had contacted Brian and secured two TV appearances. Tied in with these appearances, Brian arranged with New York promoter Sidney Bernstein for further live appearances at the Coliseum, Washington, DC and two shows at Carnegie Hall. Before their trip to New York, the *London Evening Standard* put out a special supplement headed '1963... The Year of The Beatles'. Underneath a photograph of The Beatles it read: '1963 has been their year. An examination of the heart of the nation would reveal the word BEATLE engraved upon it'.[11] The Beatles were now on the front page of every national and local newspaper. Details of the shampoo they used, the food they liked and the clothes they wore formed the basis of articles from the broadsheet to the tabloids.

On their trip to New York, Phil Spector, who was in London at the time and who was terrified of flying, cancelled his flight to be on the same flight as The Beatles, because, according to George, 'he thought we were winners and he wouldn't crash'.[12] As they approached Kennedy Airport, local radio stations were announcing their impending arrival measured in temperature terms as '32 Beatle Degrees'. The press conference was attended by over 100 members of the American press corps, most with the intention of putting paid to this idea of Beatlemania and four little limey pipsqueaks. What happened, though, surprised everyone, including The Beatles.

From the start of the press conference at Kennedy Airport, The Beatles wouldn't go along with the series of usual mundane questions. They'd had enough interviews in the past 12 months to know that they wanted to play the game *their way*, that is, have a laugh. Asked about their hairstyles, George replied: 'We were coming out of a swimming bath in Liverpool and liked the way it looked'.[13] The Liverpool accent, moreover, threw the waiting journalists: it seemed to be a mix of English, Irish and Brooklyn/New York. Paul explained:

> Americans all spoke with accents that we like a lot and identified with. We felt we had a lot in common, phonetically. We say 'bath' and 'grass' with a short 'a' (we don't say 'bah-th'), and so do they... I think people from Liverpool do have an affinity with Americans, with the GIs and the war and that... It is almost as if Liverpool and New York are twin towns.[14]

It seemed to be a case of wise-cracking New Yorkers, meet your cousin, the wise-cracking Scouser.

For a year and more, The Beatles had to endure a seemingly endless and tedious series of interviews with the same banal questions, which gave an opportunity for them to exercise their right to respond to unoriginal or rude questions from interviewers with their own off-the-cuff put-ons. This was more a case of easing the boredom than trying to come across as smart arses. American based writer P. Willis-Pitts observed on their first press conference at Kennedy Airport: 'What the Americans didn't realise was that the wit and repartee are the substance of Liverpool life and that a group of Liverpool bus drivers would have proven just as charismatic'.[15] But from very early on, the US press were completely sold on the band. The Beatles' way of keeping their sanity on the treadmill of interviews was to turn most questions into a joke. 'Do you hope to take anything home with you?' 'The Rockefeller Centre.' 'Which is the bigger threat to your careers, the H-Bomb or dandruff?' Ringo: 'The H-Bomb, we've already got dandruff'.[16]

The American press corps taken aback by the way The Beatles looked with their identical suits and Beatle haircuts, and also by their sublime confidence and adeptness at not just answering their questions, but having the audacity to be genuinely funny with no hidden agenda towards hoping the press would give them 'good copy'. They were honest, frank and definitely unique. There was no stopping them.

On 9 February 1964, 73 million television viewers tuned in to watch The Beatles play six numbers on the Ed Sullivan Show. The performance was a resounding success. Even the seasoned host was awestruck:

> The Beatles first appeared on our show... and I have never seen any scenes to compare with the bedlam that was occasioned by their debut. Broadway was jammed with people for almost eight blocks. They screamed, yelled and stopped traffic. It was incredible.[17]

On the first day in New York, The Beatles received 37 sacks of fan mail. John and the band were totally taken aback by their effect. The promoter Sidney Bernstein exclaimed: 'Don't you realise this isn't showbiz? It's history!'.[18] The USA's coming out of mourning for the murder of John F. Kennedy, the highest teenage population in the history of the country and the large publicity campaign that The Beatles record company, Capitol, were prepared to undertake, all contributed to The Beatles' triumph in February 1964. Sir Alec Douglas Home, the then Prime Minister, even rescheduled his visit to the White House due to The Beatles appearance on the Ed Sullivan Show.

The Beatles now belonged to the world, not just Liverpool. Brian was to lament:

> In a way I'm sorry they've been so successful. John is a very unusual person... I got to know him well when we went on holiday in Spain last year... Now I'm closest to George; at least he's interested in the business side of work... It's just that I'm kept so busy managing their business affairs and I must share them with everybody.[19]

It seemed like everyone had a view of The Beatles: from cab drivers to *New York Times* music critic Theodore Strongin, who wrote, 'The Beatles are directly in the mainstream of Western tradition', and in answer to *The Times* music critic who argued that The Beatles' harmonies were pandiatonic, declared that:

Their harmony is unmistakable diatonic, a learned British colleague has described it as pandiatonic but I disagree, they have a tendency to build phrases around unresolved leading tones. This precipitates the ear into false modal frame that temporarily turns the fifth of the scale into a tonic, momentarily suggesting the mixolydian mode. But everything always ends as plain diatonic all the same.[20]

During Beatlemania, they were public property and everyone felt they had to have an opinion.

The strong interest in The Beatles didn't mean they were immune from rudeness and ignorance from certain sections of the press and other elements they came into contact with. One of the best books to be written on The Beatles is Michael Braun's *Love Me Do!: The Beatles' Progress*. Braun accompanied The Beatles for a six month period at the end of 1963 towards the start of 1964. A detailed insight is reported of the chaos and frenzy that followed the band everywhere they went. The US press seemed to have been won over by The Beatles, but Braun does cite incidents which would dog the band and generally piss them off, such as this in New York, when John sat down to eat his cheeseburger and a reporter from Associated Press put the question: 'Listen, I'm not too familiar with all this. What city are you from again?'.[21]

If John and the rest of The Beatles thought that lack of knowledge and understanding on the part of journalists applied only to Europe, it didn't. It was happy and thriving in America. A second example of this incompetence involved the renowned journalist Sheilah Graham of *Time* magazine: 'the door opens and George pops his head in. The Interviewer rises from her chair, "Now tell me quickly, which one are you?"'.[22]

Worse was to follow when The Beatles attended a charity function at the British Embassy in Washington in aid of the National Society for Prevention of Cruelty to Children. The debutantes and many of those present treated The Beatles as strange objects of interest to be pawed and pulled at. The ultimate insult came when one of these refined young women sneaked up and cut a lock of Ringo's hair. Soon after, The Beatles and Brian left, and John was particularly incensed.

For John, the triumph of America was bittersweet. He'd won. He'd succeeded. He'd showed them. Yet something deep inside gnawed at him. It was success, but not on his terms. In a short space of time, he'd gone from a tough, leather-clad rock n' roller turning in six-hour night shifts, going toe to toe with insults and obscenities with a flotsam and jetsam audience from the sex capital of Europe to inheriting the world, but there was a price. He desperately wanted to be an independently recognised, successful artist. Instead, now he performed a 'mechanised', 30-minute stage show, turned out in a Pierre Cardin 'bum freezer' suit as an 'international pop star' playing to an audience of thousands of screaming 14-year-olds, completing the set with a supplicant bow from the waist.

CHAPTER TWELVE

1964
Hansel and Gretel House

THE APPEARANCES AT Carnegie Hall, Washington and on the two Ed Sullivan shows, together with the steady output of successful singles, guaranteed an insatiable demand for anything Beatles: TV, radio, concerts and charity events. There was no stopping the juggernaut of Beatlemania. On 4 April, 1964 the *Billboard Hot 100* revealed that The Beatles had singles at 1, 2, 3, 4, 5, 31, 41, 46, 58, 65, 68 and 79. The band proved irresistible. But for John, insecurities would continue to haunt him.

The Beatles' relocation to a base in London at 13 Monmouth Street, Covent Garden, saw their first official office. It consisted of a single, first floor room which sat above a bookshop that sold sex magazines. Within months, Brian would move again to more palatial surroundings befitting his position as the manager of the world's greatest music act. One inevitability of The Beatles' fame was that it was only a matter of time before all four of them would move from Liverpool to London. The original intent was for John, Paul, George and Ringo to be living within a stone's throw of each other in the town of Weybridge in the Surrey stockbroker belt. It was John's idea to be such close neighbours. This notion of a Beatle idyll, each of them popping in and out of their mock Tudor mansions to borrow or return a cup of sugar, seemed to appeal to John in particular, and this idea of a Beatle commune would be rekindled with John's full support a few years later with an aborted attempt of all four Beatles and friends to live on a Greek Island.

John committed to the move to Weybridge by buying a mansion with the title of 'Kenwood', and was soon followed by Ringo. George instead chose a bungalow in nearby Esher and Paul rejected the notion of suburban living entirely and relocated to central London. This left just John and Ringo as neighbours. Although John had deliberately removed himself from the influence of Mendips, he'd now substituted one suburban home for another:

Weybridge won't do at all. I'm just stopping there, like a bus stop. Bankers and stockbrokers live there; they can add figures and Weybridge is what they live in and they think it's the end. I think of it every day, me in my Hansel and Gretel house. I'll take my time; I'll get my real house when I know what I want. You see there's something else I'm going to do, something I must do, only I don't know what it is. That's why I go round painting, taping, drawing and writing and that, because it may be one of them. All I know is this isn't it for me.[1]

Nevertheless, John was to live in his 'Hansel and Gretel' house for four years, moving out only when Yoko Ono came into his life.

The year 1964 would see The Beatles embark on a tour of Scandinavia, Holland, Hong Kong, Australia and back to the UK before then embarking of a 24-date tour of the United States. Everybody wanted them. The attraction of The Beatles to a worldwide audience was many-sided. One of these was their appearance. Paul recalled:

It helped that we were like a gang together… Mick [Jagger] called us the Four-Headed Monster because we went everywhere dressed similarly. We'd all have black polo-neck sweater and the same haircut, so we did look a bit like a four headed monster.[2]

With their unusual identical suits and hairstyles, they looked so alike that, in constant confusion, interviewers kept addressing them with interchangeable names.

A breakdown of the attractions of The Beatles during this period of Beatlemania was put forward by sociologist Dr Renée Short, who was cited by *The New York Times* in a series of three articles examining The Beatles: 'Publicitywise', 'Moneywise' and 'Peoplewise'. Dr Short addressed the last of these elements:

Most important answers to the Beatlemania question run much deeper than sex, status, and adolescent revolt… The Beatles constitute a treasure trove of such dualities. For example, they are male and yet have many female characteristics, especially their floppy hair-dos. They also play the dual roles of adults and children. They appear to be good boys who nevertheless dress and pose as bad ones… There is a Chaplinesque quality in their style. They convey the image of the absurd little man in an absurd, big world, bewildered but bemused by it at the same time. In America, as in England, the appeal of The Beatles is not confined to girls in their teens and younger, but spreads to boys and many adults of both sexes.[3]

Another selling point and novelty of the band was their sense of humour, wit and light-hearted attitude, which was supplemented by the unusual (even by British standards) Liverpool Scouse accent. As in the history of the city, The Beatles were from England, but not of it. Being interviewed about his accent, George stated: 'It's not English. It's Liverpudlian, yah see!'. The sense of commonality which their accent brought and the particular Liverpool humour helped support and hold the band together through the pressures of touring and the constant stream of inane interviews. This characteristic sense of solidarity and humour also had the benefit of masking John's negative comments and behaviour. For John, the Liverpool accent had become a badge of unique rebelliousness: he was fully aware of the negative aspects that his hometown accent had when outside Liverpool and revelled in the position of outsider. The accent suited John's notion of an outcast.

As Beatlemania showed no signs of abating, Brian felt that one way the inexhaustible demand for 'his boys' could be met was through the cinema. So in October 1963, negotiations started with United Artists to get work started on a feature film which was to become *A Hard Day's Night*. John and Paul delivered 13 songs in almost as many weeks for the soundtrack and album of the same name, this album being the first one to feature all Lennon and McCartney songs. But despite later film critics hailing *A Hard Day's Night* as one of the most influential films of the 1960s, John was generally critical of the film and his part in particular.

The task of providing a screenplay for The Beatles was given to dramatist Alun Owen. Although Welsh-born, he grew up in Liverpool and was well-versed in its culture; he wrote the TV drama *No Trams to Lime Street* and many TV plays in the shape of *The Wednesday Play* and *Armchair Theatre*. It was Paul who felt that Owen would be well suited to capture the group dynamic of The Beatles while on the road. Owen joined The Beatles' entourage for two performances in Dublin. The plan was for Owen to produce a screenplay based on an exaggerated day in the life of the group. Unlike *Help!*, *A Hard Day's Night* would have no real story, no first act, second act or denouement in the final third act. In actual fact, it could be argued that *A Hard Day's Night* was the precursor to the pop video.

The intention was to produce a (somewhat scripted) 'fly on the wall' documentary. It attempted to give some sort of insight into life on the road with The Beatles, playing set scenes and providing themselves with their own background music. John's initial view of himself and his role was that, 'we'll race through it all I'll probably lose all confidence by the time it's over'.[4] This view reflected a deep insecurity in John. As a young Quarryman, John had been well aware of his musical limits as a novice rock 'n' roller: to his audience, he was 'having a go', just like thousands of other teenagers in the UK at the time. In Hamburg, the audience judged him as an enthusiastic amateur – a case of guerrilla warfare with the audience, performing while fuelled on booze and pills. Back in Liverpool, John had the purpose of mind to believe that he was pushing at an open door for national success. And after all The Beatles' trepidation over American success, it turned out to be a walkover. After that, world domination was easy – the domino theory of South East Asia applied to rock 'n' roll. Now though, with *A Hard Day's Night*, John had no control over his accent, and his acting and guitar skills were available to all to be pored over and scrutinised up on the cinema screen. He didn't like what he saw. He was scathing of Owen's screenplay as being trivial and unreal; not at all capturing the 'real' Beatles. In conversation with the playwright, John once demanded: 'Why should I listen to you? You're nothing but an amateur Liverpudlian'.[5] Owen cut John to the bone with the response: 'Do you think that's better than being a professional Liverpudlian, John?'

When Ringo joined The Beatles, he had commented: 'Everyone loved Pete. Why get an ugly cat when you've already got a good looking one?'.[6] The disarming ease with which Ringo touched on his own perceived deficiencies was a polar opposite to John's response. Despite John's enormous talent as a musician and performer, his deep sense of anxiety stopped him fully enjoying this success. Instead of making any allowance for himself regarding his acting, he continued the pattern learned in his childhood of being his own biggest critic. Owen purposely scripted the band's lines short for this reason, to support the non-thespian Beatles, but John continued to torment himself over his acting abilities.

John's coping strategies against his own criticism operated on two levels, the easier one to understand being his throwaway remarks about his lack of acting ability in *A Hard Day's Night*. The second level was less direct and this was his criticism of Alun Owen's script. One way of deflecting negative comments was by being dismissive of the importance of the film. In the past, he'd witnessed and ridiculed many poor films starring 'rock 'n' roll stars' such as Tommy Steele and Cliff Richard, and even the later works of Elvis. He didn't want to offer himself up to the accusation of the film being an ego vehicle which turned out to be an embarrassing exposure of his acting efforts. So John got his own criticism in first; he treated his acting role as a laugh, not take it too seriously purely as a means of defence.

Nevertheless, John did enjoy large parts of the work on the film and his sense of fun and subterfuge can be found in the scene on the train (which probably stems from The Beatles' recent visit to New York) where he delivers a sharp in-joke concerning the use of cocaine – looking up at the camera, John smiles and proceeds to close one nostril with his finger as if to 'snort' a bottle of Coke. In many ways John's rebelliousness and attacks on phonies developed from the acute awareness of his own pretence of being working-class. Instead of discarding this notion of inter-loper and the anxiety which accompanied it, he ended up with a misguided sense of guilt and insecurity. The adulation for John and The Beatles centred on the new-found sexiness of the working class, the class that Mimi had done so well to school him into having contempt for, resulting in what he believed to be a practised charade. It festered into the confusion of wanting to identify with the backgrounds of the rest of The Beatles, which conflicted with his view of 'Why should I?'

The pull of the working class for John was firmly rooted in the back-grounds of his rock 'n' roll heroes such as Elvis and his dirt poor, shotgun shack background. If The Beatles were termed working-class in inter-views, John wasn't going to contradict anyone. The problem for John was that, for his art, he changed class codes, only to be forced out of his (working-class) rock 'n' roll leathers for (middle-class) silk and mohair, hand-cut suits reminiscent of Cliff Richard and The Shadows – the accept-able face of rock 'n' roll for middle England. Brian then coached The Beatles into a stage show as a planned, cohesive unit – the trademark shaking of the hair and cheeky smiles between themselves, along with the now famous synchronised group lowering of head to waist to inform the screaming audience, *your entertainment for the night is now over.*

At the end of 1963, sleazy, gangster-operated nightclubs had been replaced with televised variety shows. At times the compromise, or as

John put it, 'the sell-out', of mohair for leather, became too much. John thrived on the edginess of inner-city Liverpool and Hamburg. Early publicity photographs of The Beatles show them at locations in Liverpool with decaying Victorian warehouses in the background. Another location sees the group gathered on a 'bombed site', standing around a burnt-out car, wearing their leather coats and giving it their best hard-case looks for the benefit of photographer Les Chadwick. Looking, and better still being, working-class was chic. An insight into the early Beatles was that they 'unwittingly exploded this image of working-class youth', music writer Greil Marcus's point being that:

> Where authors had shown working-class youth as caged within a harsh physical world, resentful toward those they believed had made it that way, but resigned to their place in such a world, the Beatles presented working-class youth loose and free, glad to be out, unafraid to snub pretension.[7]

John wanted the raucousness and spontaneous humour that could be found in working-class life married to the cultured sensitivities found within parts of the middle class. Try as he might, he couldn't find a way to square the circle of these diverse elements. Instead of seeing the progress from Mendips to Liverpool Culture as a marriage and as part of his artistic development, he never acquired the confidence to do this and so for a large part of his life he was never happy in his own skin. It wasn't that Mendips/middle class was intrinsically 'wrong', it was his experience there.

The Beatles had become a global phenomenon. There was unprecedented demand for their albums and singles. They performed sell-out concerts all accompanied by the frenzied reaction of the fans. Their fame reached far beyond anything seen before. Their tinned breath sold on the streets of New York. Their unwashed hotel bed sheets were deposited in a bank vault, later to be sold off in pieces, each one inch square. People as eminent as Viscount Montgomery declared: 'I think I'll invite them down for the weekend just to see what kind of fellas they are'.[8]

Despite this, The Beatles were petrified when Brian arranged for them to attend a northern premiere of *A Hard Day's Night*, with a seven-mile 'parade' from Speke Airport through the streets of Liverpool to the Town Hall and finishing with a Lord Mayor's civic reception. 'The Beatles were nervous wrecks,' remembers the film's producer, Walter Shenson:

Even though they'd just come back from a world tour, they were scared about the appearance in Liverpool. 'Ah', they kept saying, 'you don't know what the people are like up there'.[9]

David Jacobs, who was to be the compère for the film premiere, travelled in the aircraft with The Beatles and was surprised to see how edgy they were: 'They were absolutely terrified'.[10] This was because, just like The Beatles, Liverpudlians love to prick the balloon of pomposity. The fear was that the deflated balloon could be represented by several miles of deserted Liverpool streets.

The comment by Owen of John being a 'plastic Scouser' hurt and worried John. The thought passed through John's mind – had he finally been found out? Had *A Hard Day's Night* revealed him for the phoney that he was, his middle-class accent overlaid with rock 'n' roll Scouse, smuggling himself in from Quarry Bank Grammar School to a world of bands made up of manual workers from Liverpool's factories, docks and building sites, horny handed, smoking Capstan Full Strength cigarettes, nicotine stained up to the elbows, dock workers living at home, a stone's throw away from the river, sharing a bedroom, no bathroom or inside toilet – these were the ones whose judgement John feared on the release of *A Hard Day's Night*. They were the ones. Not the film critics of the *New York Times* or the *Evening Standard*, but those 'back home'. That's why, when The Beatles returned to Liverpool for the northern premiere of *A Hard Day's Night*, while Paul, George and Ringo were concerned whether they would be judged negatively for leaving the city, for getting too big for their boots, for John it was a different ball game. It wasn't a case of *they*, but more a case of *him* being judged.

Neither John nor the other Beatles had anything to worry about. An estimated 250,000 people lined the streets of Liverpool, giving the group a heroes' homecoming.

At Princes Road it was mad. There were thousands of fans. They were everywhere. Most were in their late teens, but there were also kids with their mothers and dads. Some of the kids sat on their parents' shoulders. There were kids holding pictures of The Beatles cut out of magazines; some held the pictures high above their heads. Some waiting fans had plastic cowboy hats on, similar to those sold at seaside resorts with pictures of The Beatles pinned around them. Others had scarves with the names of the group knitted into them and some even wore Beatle wigs.[11]

Liverpool had fallen. The last ramparts had been breached. At the end of the route, as The Beatles stood on the balcony of the Town Hall surrounded by a selection of dignitaries, John's nerves and bravado got the better of him as he launched into an ill-timed Hitler salute for the tens of thousands of fans crowded below. Nothing was mentioned of this cackhanded attempt at humour – in many ways it just supported Pauline Sutcliffe's first impression of John, at art college: 'What is it about this guy? He seems to have no social skills'.[12]

John's unwillingness to accept himself for what he was had its roots in Mendips. Fifteen years spent there had left him with a residue of expectation towards being a grown-up extension of his middle-class childhood hero, *Just William*. Mimi projected her own idealised claims as his being one of the 'better half'. A point of constant friction between John and Mimi was his accent. As a developing 'tough guy Scouser' in a college full of middle-class students, John proceeded rapidly in this metamorphosis, laying it on thick with a broad Scouse accent. But to Mimi he was letting the side down, 'I brought him up properly, not to talk like a ruffian, ask anyone who knew him then... he didn't really talk like that'.[13] Mimi felt betrayed, that such an accent would be a measure of her not bringing him up right. By her own standard of refinement the thousands of inner-city Liverpudlians who spoke in their own accent were no more than 'ruffians'.

A telling example of Mimi's idealised expectations of John is revealed in a letter to a female fan. Mimi was usually dismissive of fans, but this one struck a chord with her own sensitivities. The fan, a 13-year-old from the affluent county of Surrey, had just started boarding school when her correspondence started with Mimi. In one letter, the young girl asked Mimi if John had gone to public school. 'No,' Mimi replied, 'he didn't go to boarding school; a big mistake on my part...'. Mimi's sad craving for recognition of her 'true' social status was shown by her claims for the missed opportunity of a private education for John. Instead of celebrating the fact that her nephew was more rich and famous than any other 24-year-old on the planet, she implied that if John had gone to public school he would have 'turned out alright'. Mimi's dislike of John's fame was largely based on the vehicle through which he achieved it; rock 'n' roll.

This, after all, was the domain of the 'rough types' and if it wasn't bad enough that John had associated himself with *those two from the council estates*, now he had *one* from the Dingle! God forbid if this one turned up to Mendips with John – she'd surely set the dog on him, if she hadn't already had Sally destroyed. John's modus operandi for achieving his phenomenal fame was disregarded by Mimi because now John spoke like a Scouser and played in a 'pop' group with real Scousers, generally making a show of himself and more importantly *her*.

George Orwell was born a few years before Mimi and, although he viewed himself as lower upper-middle-class, his perception of the attitude and views of the middle class, generally, towards the working class gives an insight into Mimi's own values. At an early age, Orwell was told by his parents that he was forbidden to play with:

> the plumber's children; they were common. This was snobbish if you like, but it was also necessary, for middle-class people cannot afford to let their children grow up with vulgar accents... So, very early the working class ceased to be a race of friendly and wonderful beings and became race of enemies. We realised that they hated us, but we could never know why and naturally we set it down to pure, vicious malignity. To me in my early boyhood, to nearly all children of families like mine 'common' people seemed almost sub-human.

Mimi's legacy to John was a similar inbred prejudice against 'common sorts', and was the cause of much of his anger. In essence John had to 'infiltrate' a section of the community that Mimi had indoctrinated him into believing was below his station. 'They had coarse faces, hideous accents and gross manners,' Orwell continues his description, 'they hated everyone who was not like themselves, and if they got half the chance they would insult you in brutal ways. That was our view of them and although it was false, it was understandable'.[14]

It was this sense of having to become someone he wasn't that angered John. A sense of being bogus with his adopted Scouse accent, a sheep in wolf's clothing.

The year that began with The Beatles' hugely successful appearances on the Ed Sullivan Show continued with a series of worldwide hit singles, the making of a feature film plus soundtrack, a tour of the Far East and Australia and a 24-date tour of the USA. In this context it is understandable that the energy and creativity would be at a low ebb at the end of the year. The Beatles would produce a weak album in the shape of *Beatles for Sale*. The previous vitality was missing. The Lennon and McCartney efforts were on the whole below par and the cover versions seemed passé. Compared to the previous cover versions, they seemed devoid of any resolve to impress the listener as to The Beatles' own good taste for their inclusion. The album's cover photograph of a world-weary Beatles reflected its tepid contents.

For all its frantic comings and goings, 1964 proved to be a fertile one for John in his music. He had been responsible for nine of the 13 tracks on the album *A Hard Day's Night*, with one more having been co-written with Paul. John could be well pleased with taking the lion's share of the writing credits. Only one small, black cloud could be detected on the horizon, and that was Paul's change in attitude towards who was the leader of the group. Yet John knew that any claim for leadership rested on the number of 'individual' song credits, and he had just proved beyond doubt that the crown was his. John was supremely confident as to who led The Beatles, and millions of fans knew as well. Many newspaper articles, after all, referred to him as 'John Lennon, leader of The Beatles'.

CHAPTER THIRTEEN

1965
Perugia Way

IN MARCH, The Beatles flew from London to Salzburg, where 4,000 fans awaited their arrival. The purpose of the visit was to begin to shoot their second feature film, *Help!*. The runaway success of *A Hard Day's Night* guaranteed the demand for another Beatles feature film. *Help!* would be a departure from their first effort. Not surprisingly, due to his fallout with John, Alun Owen was passed over in favour of Marc Behm and Charles Wood as screenwriters for the film. The budget had also changed, doubling that of *A Hard Day's Night*. This in turn allowed for the most notable change, moving from the black-and-white cinematography of *A Hard Day's Night* to the Technicolor of *Help!*.

Critical comparisons between *A Hard Day's Night* and *Help!* fell firmly in favour of the former, for the plot of *Help!* was a light comedy adventure and, as John recalled, 'we were extras in our own film'. The reasons were easy enough to find. For a start, The Beatles weren't that interested in making the film, and secondly, they were stoned most of the time. Gone were the previous comparisons of The Beatles in *A Hard Day's Night* to the Marx Brothers. Indeed, John's criticism of the director, Richard Lester, was, if off-beat, nonetheless true: 'He forgot about who and what we were, and that's why the film didn't work. It was like having clowns in a movie about frogs'.[1] Instead of *Help!* being a vehicle to display The Beatles' versatility, the outcome was that *real actors* such as Leo McKern, Victor Spinetti and Eleanor Bron became the focal point for the story.

The soundtrack to the film showed John on good form. His title song 'Help!' stands out as, once again, John bleeding in public. There are no allusions to childhood or love in the lyrics, just a raw pleading for help. No unrequited ballad of lost love, or sideways admission to an extra-marital affair, as in the later 'Norwegian Wood', just a deep cry to escape from the mental anguish that was depression. Another track, though not written by John, was also to be of significance to him inasmuch as it was a sign of things to come. This was Paul's 'Yesterday'. So much was it a

McCartney song, no other member of the group being involved in its writing or production, that an argument broke out between George Martin and Brian Epstein. Martin's contention was that the song should be put out under Paul's name alone. Brian was vehemently against it. He knew how much damage this would do to the cohesion and camaraderie between The Beatles. Whether John found out about this dispute between Brian and George is uncertain. If he did it would have done nothing for his already fragile self-confidence. What he was aware of was that 'Yesterday' was released by Capitol in America under The Beatles' name and reached number one in the charts, rapidly becoming a classic. This didn't bode well for John.

Like *A Hard Day's Night, Help!* was intended not just to reinforce the success of The Beatles but to satisfy the continually growing global market for anything *Beatle*. Some of this demand was stemmed by what became known as The British Invasion. By 1965, a swathe of British bands, led by The Rolling Stones, including The Animals, Manfred Mann, The Dave Clark Five, Wayne Fontana and the Mindbenders and Herman's Hermits, toured packed arenas – half-close your eyes, listen to the screams and use your imagination. The success of these substitutes was such that in 1965, one of those bands mentioned, Herman's Hermits actually sold more singles in America than The Beatles.

In fairness to the Stones, though, the flavour of their shows and their fans set them apart from the other groups that rode on the coat tails of The Beatles. The Stones' shows attracted what tended to be a more hard-edged audience. When writer, Tom Wolfe, quipped that 'The Beatles want to hold your hand, but The Rolling Stones want to burn your town down,' it must have raised a smile with John, especially when he considered he had travelled constantly for five years around the north west of England, playing gigs along the way in Scotland, experiencing long stretches of debauchery and violence in Hamburg's Red Light district, travelling and sometimes sleeping in scabby little vans, while Mick Jagger remained a homebird, living in Kent with his teacher father, Basil Fanshawe Jagger, and a mother who was an active member of the Conservative Party. As a student at London School of Economics, Mick (known as Mike to his friends), lived in a flat in Chelsea while studying a business degree; later, much to John's amusement, he was portrayed as a *bête noir* of teenage girls' parents. John could have been forgiven if he had muttered, 'Mick burn someone's town down, no chance. His mum wouldn't let him near the matches.'

The 1965 American tour was notable for The Beatles' appearance at the Shea Stadium and their meeting with Elvis. The whole tour replicated previous ones, only the venues were larger, as was the police presence. The Shea Stadium appearance was famous for its 55,600 audience paying record receipts of $304,000, which according to promoter Sid Bernstein became 'the greatest gross ever in the history of show business'.[2] The concert was shown coast to coast in American cinemas and on British TV. The security for The Beatles was straight out of James Bond movies – they were flown by helicopter to the top of the World's Fair Building then transported to the stadium in a Wells Fargo armoured van. 'If you look at the film footage you can see how we reacted to the place. It was very big and very strange,' Ringo remembers. 'I feel that on that show John cracked up. He went mad; not mentally ill, but he just got crazy. He was playing the piano with his elbows and it just got strange'.[3]

The visit to Elvis at Perugia Way, Bel Air, in between dates, proved not so historic. Elvis waited at his front door to welcome his guests, but once inside, The Beatles seemed to 'choke' upon being in the same room as their idol. The stifled atmosphere was only broken when Elvis announced, 'If you damn guys are gonna sit here and stare at me all night, I'm gonna go to bed'.[4] Later on, Elvis and The Beatles settled into an improvised jamming session. John in particular was disappointed, reflecting that 'it was like meeting Engelbert Humperdinck'.[5] During and after the meeting, John made a running joke of 'Where's Elvis?', this being a reference to both the regret and disillusionment of meeting his idol.

After The Beatles finished their tour of America, there was a small matter of receiving an MBE. This decision would in turn confer good publicity on the royal family and get them firmly on the Beatle bandwagon: John, Paul, George and Ringo were made Members of the British Empire. This was an opportunity not just for Brian to prove his worth in attracting worldwide publicity for The Beatles, but also for the royal courtiers to perform the same service for their employer – a global platform for the world's two biggest acts, The Beatles and the Queen.

A supposed incident, which garnered much publicity, concerning The Beatles smoking dope before receiving their MBE was later debunked by George: 'We never smoked marijuana at the investiture'.[6] It really was just

'Brian's Boys' acting the goat with the media. The 'admission' that the four of them smoked cannabis in the toilets of Buckingham Palace had given The Beatles another opportunity for the perception of being cheeky, cheerful, up-for-a-laugh Liverpudlians, a return to the 'rattle your jewelry' days. The 'confession' was seen by the public as a hoot, and newspaper cartoonists depicted The Beatles having a joint in the toilets at Buckingham Palace with supporting humorous comments or dialogue. In 1965, The Beatles still walked on water.

At the beginning of 1965, Ringo became the second member of the band to be married. His bride was his 19-year-old long-time girlfriend, Liverpool hairdresser Maureen Cox. Since Jane Asher was a permanent fixture with Paul and George had a steady girlfriend in former model Pattie Boyd, The Beatles had acquired a semi-domestic life in London and Surrey. Mimi and the parents of The Beatles also found themselves moving from their homes in Liverpool. The reason for these relocations was the constant stream of fans pestering them in their homes, which made their own move just as inevitable as The Beatles'.

George's mother, the group's biggest fan, and her husband chose to relocate to Appleton, some 15 miles outside Liverpool in the Cheshire countryside. Paul's father and his brother Michael moved 'over the water' to a bungalow in Heswall on the Wirral. At first, Ringo's parents were reluctant to move from their family and friends in the Dingle, despite the onslaught of fans knocking on their terraced house door and stealing mementos which ranged from the letter box to bottles of milk. Eventually Ringo persuaded his mother Elsie and husband George to move. They chose a small bungalow in the nearby south end suburb of Gateacre, five miles from their home in the Dingle, but near enough for neighbours and family to visit.

Mimi proved to be more selective. Her choice of new home was in Poole, Dorset, at a cost of £25,000 and 250 miles away from Liverpool on the south-east Coast – the most expensive by far or all the homes bought for The Beatles' parents, even more expensive than John's Kenwood home. Why she should choose such a faraway location had its roots in her desire to distance herself from the press and any questioning over how John came to be in 'her possession'. Mimi, like the parents of Paul, George and Ringo, suffered from the intrusiveness of the fans. Whereas the parents of the other Beatles chose to support their sons, Mimi's attitude was that

John's fame was an aggravation. As a natural extension of her negativity towards John's ambition to make it as a musician, Mimi proceeded to dismiss John's fame as pure luck, something that could have happened to anyone. Whereas the other parents of The Beatles celebrated their achievements, Mimi chose to treat John's success as a huge embarrassment. The other parents were quite democratic in their treatment of the fans, but generally, Mimi's was that of being dismissive and hostile to those who dared to show up at her front door looking for John or those who had the temerity to send letters. In contrast, George's mother answered the hundreds of fan letters a week herself, and even received an award for her efforts from a Beatles' Fan Club in Pomona California.

Mimi suffered as all the other parents did with regards to fans, maybe even more so, with John being regarded as leader of the group, and it was understandable that a move from Mendips was needed to avoid the siege of fans and the constant knocks to the front door. The final straw came when, according to her, she was burgled. She apparently left the back door open for the doctor as she wasn't feeling well and went to bed. Two female fans let themselves in. Mimi awoke to find the girls asleep downstairs surrounded by a blanket of toffee wrappers. After chasing the girls out, Mimi didn't call the police, but waited to be consoled by her bread delivery man.

The main reason for a move to the other end of the country, though, was more deep-rooted and less obvious. The fans were making life miserable for Mimi, yes, but the difference with Mimi when compared with the parents of Paul, George and Ringo was that their parents accepted the limelight and inconvenience that their own son's success brought. Mimi, though, had skeletons in the cupboard relating to how she came to 'acquire' John. In keeping with Mimi's lack of support for John and his music, she was also non-committal about his success and was extremely reluctant to commit herself to interviews.

Journalists digging into John's background would have found that his 'devoted' aunt had taken a child from his mother, a mother who spent the rest of her life being torn apart by this loss. If the reporters were to interview those in Mimi's neighbourhood, they would have been informed of a woman who didn't socialise or even make small talk, who never invited neighbours into Mendips and never accepted invites to others' houses. She didn't allow John to play with other children. If they interviewed the village tradesmen and one in particular, the fishmonger, they would have discovered how Mimi begged for hand-outs of fish scraps for her cats, despite her New Zealand windfall.

After John's death, Mimi became the fount of all knowledge regards her and John's life and she changed her opinion regards giving interviews, even 'admitting' to buying John his first guitar – that is the guitar Julia bought. Hunter Davies' book effectively whitewashed John's childhood but in a revised edition of *The Beatles*, the author revealed the pressure he was under from Mimi to rewrite large parts of the sections concerning John's childhood. As Cynthia Lennon points out:

> Most descriptions of Mimi that have appeared in print were based on interviews with her – she outlived John by eleven years. She loved to fuel the image of the stern but loving aunt who provided the secure backdrop to John's success. But that wasn't the Mimi I knew. She battered away at John's self-confidence and left him angry and hurt.[7]

John could have given an insight into his time at Mendips, but he never did. He would later describe Davies' book as 'really bullshit, you know… no home truths were written, my auntie knocked them all out, the true bits of my childhood'.[8] In many ways, one could understand John during his Beatles time and later for not criticising Mimi – how could he? How could he admit that at the age of nearly 17, he was taken on the bus to an interview to art college by his aunt, being kept in pocket money up until the age of 19, having to plead to go to Hamburg at the age of 20 when the other members of The Beatles were readily trusted to go? How could he tell of his time in his small boxroom while complete strangers, in the shape of students, came and went? Mimi's derogatory comments about Paul and George (which she herself recalls for the benefit of journalists), the abusive attitude to Cynthia, even after John and Cynthia were married – how could John admit his passive consent of this? John's 15 years at Mendips became an emotional nightmare. Anything John did that Mimi deemed as wrong was seen as an act of rebellion. Straying from Mimi's personal standards and values, or displaying signs of individuality were viewed as a personal attack on her.

Instead, his bitterness focused on Freddie, his seaman father, a 'song and dance man', a man who was never good enough for the Stanley family and one whom Mimi despised from day one. John told himself and others that Mimi was a fine, all-round good egg, but he knew better. He knew that many of Mimi's failings had been passed on to him, so an aunt who had had such a negative impact on him without any form of rebellion against her, could not be admitted. John had to block any idea of a less than happy time at 251 Menlove Avenue. He could never accept that after 15 years of Mendips how much he had succumbed to his aunt's way of thinking, the effect it had on him and the painful admission this would be. Psychologist Alice Miller points out that:

> Denial is both the most primitive and the most powerful of psychological defences. It employs a make-believe reality to minimize, or even negate, the impact of certain painful life experiences. It even makes some of us forget what our parents did to us, allowing us to keep them on their pedestals. The relief provided by denial is temporary and the price for this relief is high.[9]

Despite the adulation poured upon John by millions of fans and the sense of status he garnered, John's mental health veered from coping to desperate. Then suddenly it looked to him that he had found a safe haven in the shape of cannabis. In the Delmonico Hotel in New York, during the '64 tour of America, the band met up with Bob Dylan. The Beatles were huge fans and John was profoundly impressed with Dylan's adopted east-coast smart-arse, cryptic cat-and-mouse interview technique. Dylan's complete acceptance into the world of Allen Ginsberg and the rest of the East Coast/West Coast bohemian crowd, was something that John and Stu would have killed for in their student days. The relationship between The Beatles and Dylan was based on mutual respect and an understanding of each other's uniqueness. The Beatles' amazement at Dylan's repackaging and delivery of poetry and folk, of which the band up until then had never been great fans, was reciprocated in turn by Dylan's appreciation of The Beatles' killer humour and cool reinvention of his great teenage love of rock 'n' roll.

The meeting is largely remembered, though, for Dylan's supposed introduction of The Beatles to the appreciation of marijuana, but the fact is The Beatles were already familiar with dope, having been given a reefer by an older drummer in Liverpool. Their own drugs of choice were pills and booze. Over the next two years, Dylan's lyrics and the use of dope would have a telling influence on John. The impact of dope would begin almost immediately with the start of The Beatles' next feature film.

By the time it was to be shot, John and the rest of the band were heavy users. All it took was for them to get a reliable supply line in place and then John and the others got stoned to their hearts' content. John recalls, 'we were smoking marijuana for breakfast during that period'.[10] The novelty of the drug and its illegal status gave The Beatles another constituent of commonality along with their Liverpool background, accent, humour and shared band experiences.

For John, the drug's mellowing effect proved the antidote to the unstoppable and rattling thoughts which caused his bouts of despondency and depression. Unlike Paul, John found it difficult to switch off from the application of his artistic imagination when it came to dealing with everyday life, the consequence being the motor of creativity found in his music, poetry and painting stayed almost permanently switched on. The creative discipline needed for this intense train of thought resembled tramlines zipping along, carrying a myriad collection of tunes, words and phrases, each attempting to interconnect with the perfect companions. When John was in emotional distress or malaise, these tramlines of creative thoughts continued, but this time they were used to carry all his darkest fears and anxieties.

The importance of his art and the need for the success of this art was necessary for John to escape the unhappiness of his childhood. The loss of the mother at an early age is a well-established trigger for causing depression in adulthood. Writer William Styron, who lost his mother at 13, cites the prominence in depression literature of the 'irreparable emotional havoc' caused by the death of a parent, particularly the mother. Styron believes that:

> The danger is especially apparent if the young person is affected by what has been termed 'incomplete mourning' has, in effect, been unable to achieve the catharsis of grief, and so carries within himself through later years an insufferable burden of which rage and guilt, and not only dammed-up sorrow, are a part, and become the potential seeds of self-destruction.[11]

Taking this line of thought, the practice of wrapping himself in a protective blanket with his reading and writing at Mendips had a twofold effect. One was that he could immerse himself within his books and thus screen out the loss of his parents and the sterile environment he found himself in. But on the downside, his focus of attention could and did lead to a mulling over of negative events in his life. His capacity for creativity could be hijacked by thoughts of misery and despair. In a sense the defence mechanism John put in place to deal with his growing up became a 'wooden horse' for depression. 'I was never really wanted,' John lamented. 'The only reason I am a star is because of my repression. Nothing would have driven me through all that if I was normal'.[12] John was making a plea for understanding that for him stardom was an attempted route out of his poor emotional wellbeing and unhappiness.

The making of *Help!* proved to be a major turning point for John as a songwriter. Following on from taking the majority of credits on *A Hard Day's Night*, he continued to play a key part with the songwriting credits of *Help!*. But the same period saw him weighed down by severe depression. A combination of factors brought this on. The novelty and excesses of touring could no longer provide distraction from any embedded sense of depression. Another issue could have been the strain of being the focal point of The Beatles: the 'hard-faced one', 'the cheeky one', 'the witty one' or 'the rocker'. The other members of The Beatles could keep their heads down if they chose, but John couldn't, or wouldn't. Despite Paul's allusions to group democracy, John was the one who was seen as leader of the group. They were, after all, regularly introduced as John, Paul, George and...

Another reason for John's poor mental health at this time was his marriage. Unfortunately for Cynthia, John didn't make a good husband or father and it seemed to be a relationship where John's tolerance took the place of love. Maybe John felt he was forced into marriage due to Cynthia's pregnancy. It does seem evident that the role of fatherhood was not one that suited him. From John's viewpoint, part of his unhappiness was caused by married life, a life he wasn't suited to at the time. Finally, it may have been that the novelty and excesses of touring had run its course as a distraction from his depression.

John's state of mind was revealed by his weight gain during the filming of *Help!*:

> It was my fat Elvis period, you see the movie: he-I-is very fat, very insecure and he's completely lost himself. And I am singing about when I was so much younger and all the rest... Now I may be very positive, but I also go through deep depressions where I would like to jump out the window.[13]

There are some very revealing points about John's comment here. One is his switching between first and third person narrative. It's almost as if he's relating to someone else, such was the pain he suffered – he seems to be trying to distance himself from the memory. The other point is his almost casual comment about suicide. This would not be the only time John would refer to taking his life.

The effects of John's depression are on display for all to see in the song 'Help!', which opens with a lament to youthful naivety. 'Help!' was released the year after 'My Back Pages' and there is a detectable resonance in its lyrics with Bob Dylan's riddle-like recollection of his younger self. Their respective deliveries, however, could not be more different, Dylan's enigmatic, assertive bark a far cry from Lennon's pure on-the-nose misery. At the time this was missed by most. His macho image meant he was unwilling or unable to breach this tough nut exterior to demean himself by asking for support. During the time of his greatest need, John had isolated himself with the constant hurtful behaviour for which he had become renowned. It had become embedded in his nature. Paradoxically, his need for a hard-case stance to shed off his middle-class background and deal with his insecurities, were the very features that now left him adrift when it came to seeking support.

The lack of self-esteem that went with John's condition meant a sense of shame. Many people believe that depression is not actually a disease but a symptom of a personal or emotional weakness – they attach a stigma to it. For someone as 'in your face' and famous as John, seeking support for something for which the uninformed would suggest, 'pull yourself together', 'we all have bad days' and 'try to be positive' was unthinkable. The notion that cannabis alleviated his poor mental health was an illusion. The after effect of cannabis, besides bringing on fatigue, paranoia and anxiety, actually accentuated depression. 'Help!', 'I'm a Loser' and 'You've Got to Hide Your Love Away' were only the tip of the iceberg. Lack of self-esteem can be identified in many of his first person narrative song lyrics. Even his misogynistic lyrics, most notably of his unrequited love for his girlfriend which is readily replaced with a wish for her death in 'Run for your Life' (a line albeit taken from Presley's 'Let's Play House') can be seen as an attack turned on himself. The woman being attacked in the song is perhaps a substitute for John's distaste of himself. The woman being attacked in the song is perhaps a substitute for John's distaste of himself. The fact that John's songs are in the first person is not a matter of conceit. It was more a case of using his creative talent to try and salve his poor mental health.

The isolation of Weybridge impacted negatively on John. He had his games room, his music room and his art room – he had everything he wanted except the stimulation that was found in communication and interaction with others. All that was left for John was to watch TV, browse the daily papers and stare out of the window into the garden. If he was lucky and the gardener was about he could go outside and have a chat with him. Bob Dylan recalled his stay at John's 17-room, mock-Tudor mansion:

> The last time I went to London I stayed at John Lennon's house, you should see all the stuff that Lennon bought: big cars and a stuffed gorilla and thousands of things in every room in his house, cost a fortune. When I got back home I wondered what it would be like to have all those material things. I figured I had the money and I could do it, and I wondered if it would feel like anything real. So I bought all this stuff and filled my house with it and sat around in the middle of it all. And I felt nothing.[14]

Dylan's cutting comment gets to a core problem of John's, without any prompting – he'd used his wealth in the hope that this conspicuous consumption would give some small measure of satisfaction. Instead, all it provided was a constant reminder of the futility of equating money to peace of mind.

Dylan's own songwriting mastery came not only from his voracious appetite for books but also from his ability to soak up the experience and history of those around him like a sponge, the most notable and obvious being Woody Guthrie. John, on the other hand, included a large part of personal experience, conscience and unconscious, from art college to Hamburg and from Julia to Mimi. The searing expressiveness of many of his songs, both in content and delivery, left no doubt that this was anything but made up. No one could bare their soul in such a public way. Much as John recognised that Dylan's rhythmical gymnastics were a wonder to behold, his own lyrics would only reach such craftsmanship occasionally. The reason was simple – something was missing. Whereas Dylan was mostly the observer in his tales, John lived them, and that came out the moment the needle was dropped on the record.

While Dylan's sleight-of-hand lyrics were produced to dazzle and bewilder, John used his own personal history to deliver only so much and no more to give an insight into love, life and friendship. This was a vulnerability that John was willing to shoulder. Whereas Dylan delivered his lyric from a fount of sophistication and wit, John mined his lyrics from deep down inside.

The dexterity of Dylan's songwriting amazed John. Although in later years he ridiculed Dylan's lyrics with the pun of 'Stuck in the Thesaurus with the Memphis Blues Again', Dylan's ability to express himself in such an elusive and mainly dispassionate way gave rise to thoughts about what John might achieve with Dylan's lyrical sleight of hand to express his own wishes and sadness. What John failed to realise was that Dylan could achieve his role of the high priest of simile and metaphor juggle because he was something that John wasn't – Dylan was detached. He was brilliant because he had the confidence that what he was turning out was a work of high-class art.

John was equally brilliant, but because of the disapproval and criticism he received in Mendips, his self-esteem for a large part of his life bumped along on the bottom. It constantly forced him into his dark places in search of his creativity and, ultimately, his art. The openness in his lyrics is there for all to see. Dylan was a word illusionist, challenging you to guess the 'right interpretation'. John had no other choice but to be painfully direct, producing a sandwich board covered with heart-on-your-sleeve type lyrics that he paraded and onto which he constantly rewrote new lines, combing up further memories of his life for the benefit of The Beatles' next song.

CHAPTER FOURTEEN

1965–66
Candlestick Park

THE MID-'60S SAW the emergence of a more musically-mature Beatles, both in their songwriting and their studio technique: 'I think *Rubber Soul* is about when it started happening',[1] John said. *Rubber Soul* was the obvious precursor to *Revolver*, both major moves towards ever greater commitment to The Beatles being a studio band. 'With *Rubber Soul*, the clash between John and Paul was becoming obvious. Mind you, there's no doubt at all that Paul was the main musical force,' recalls Abbey Road engineer Norman Smith. 'He was also that in terms of production as well. He could tell an arranger how to do it just by singing a part. Most of the ideas came from Paul'.[2]

John and The Beatles were to a large extent forced to this position of a studio band due to growing issues concerning touring, but the problem for John was that, although touring was losing its attractiveness, he still needed the energy of live playing for the intense social contact it brought and the ego-lifting effect when on the stage. For John, the pumping adrenalin that came from performing or being chauffeured around at speed chased by thousands of fans, within a whisker of being caught, became his lifeline.

The Beatles welcomed the idea of taking more control over the recording process – artistically, all members of the band believed that the *Rubber Soul* sessions offered something new. It was the pivotal album in which the influences of rockabilly Carl Perkins, the falsetto gospel of Little Richard and the affected gurgling of Buddy Holly were left behind and replaced by The Byrds, Brian Wilson and Booker T and the MGs. The British Invasion bands had diluted some of The Beatles' cultural uniqueness. Without a change, musically there may have been some concern from The Beatles that eventually they could be viewed as another one of those British bands. Clear blue water was needed to be put between themselves and those who came after. John's whole idea of The Beatles was to be unique. Having to compete with clones of yourself just didn't make sense.

Rubber Soul's style and freshness of delivery was tailor-made for the

time – Carnaby Street centred London was up and running and the befud-
dling lyrics of Motown powered 'Baby You Can Drive My Car', counter-
balanced with the heart-wrenching photo album of 'In My Life', embraced
and reflected the modernity that epitomised the swinging '60s. The Beatles'
use of drugs didn't stop with *Help!*, and *Rubber Soul* was termed by John
as 'a pot album,' while he viewed *Revolver* as 'an acid album'. John pointed
out that they were not stoned while recording either album, but suggested
that drugs had become an important aspect of their life. The completion of
Revolver saw The Beatles 'officially' leave the simple world of girls who were
just 17 and move towards a more multidimensional and uncertain world.

Early that year, Brian flew to America to complete the final details of
what would turn out to be The Beatles' last tour of America, or anywhere
else. Even before the touring stopped, The Beatles' sense of independence
had grown. Unlike the relationship between Colonel Tom Parker and
Elvis, The Beatles had as much or as little influence upon their schedule
as they wanted. There were a few disagreements between Brian and The
Beatles over the direction which they should take. Brian had long since
learnt to stay out of the studio, let alone give advice with regards to music,
for fear of bringing out the wrath of John. There was the infamous
response of 'You count the percentages we'll do the songs', to Brian's
suggestion of an improvement to Paul's singing while recording an album
track. Brian's style was more a slight touch of the tiller rather than the
type of management seen in the early days of The Beatles, where he had
been meticulously concerned with controlling their public image.

But Brian lacked the business sense needed for an act as important as
The Beatles. During a meeting to negotiate with United Artists (UA) concerning the royalties of *A Hard Day's Night*, Brian immediately demanded
a seven and a half per cent cut of the profits. The UA executives cast glances
to each other as they had been convinced that they would have to start
negotiating at the figure of 20 per cent. This incident illustrates that
although Brian was well meaning and acted in good faith, he was also out
of his depth. Whether The Beatles, and in particular John, found out
about this financial naivety is unknown. Word of instances where Brian
fell short of adequately representing the band might well have filtered
back to them. Such disclosures of Brian's poor business acumen would
not have helped John's complex relationship with him. John's mood
swings meant that, when he moved towards his dark side, anyone and

everyone in his way was cut off at the knees. 'He was a Jekyll and Hyde. He could be one of the sweetest guys you ever met,' recalls Norman Smith, who had first-hand experience of John's moods, 'but he could also be one of the most terrible monsters, one of the most horrible. You'd better please John otherwise forget it'.[3]

John's friend and confidante Maureen Cleave, who knew him as well as anyone outside The Beatles' entourage, was one of the first to recognise the roots of his torments and inner conflicts. She states:

> I didn't think of John as someone who should be boxed in and get therapy. I thought that fame had relieved the pressure for him a little bit. But that Liverpool childhood was very scary for him.[4]

Fortunately, Brian had other acts to manage which diverted him to some extent from John's moods. One of those acts was Cilla Black. Brian took a particular interest in Cilla, with whom he formed a strong relationship. One of the features that Brian admired in Cilla was her lack of deference to The Beatles. The former Cavern Club coat check girl and guest singer at the Zodiac Club with local bands such as Rory Storm and the Hurricanes, The Big Three and Kingsize Taylor and the Dominoes, knew The Beatles when they were a 'bunch of scruffs' and preferred the sound of The Big Three to The Beatles.

Cilla was born in a flat above a hairdresser's shop in what many would argue was the toughest part of the city, Scotland Road. Her mother was a market stall trader and her father a dock worker. She knew exactly where Menlove Avenue was. In the neighbourhood where Cilla lived, a boy growing up there earned a reputation by how many fights he'd won, especially against older kids, unlike Woolton where status could be achieved by having the biggest conker collection. Cilla knew that John used what he believed to be a quick-fire sense of Liverpool humour as a cover for his cutting and derisive comments, believing it was acceptable because of his misconception that it was the norm that working-class people swore all the time and were predisposed to be sarcastic and bullying. Cilla was fully aware that through this image of hard case Scouser, John could smuggle in and 'legitimise' this attitude as a vehicle for his overbearing and misanthropic attitude. Cilla had John's number and from this insight in turn did her best for Brian by supporting him against John's perverted belief of what it was to be tough.

John was ashamed of Brian: being managed by a 'poof' further confused John's dual image of poet and tough nut; it brought shame on The Beatles, being managed by someone who was so open to be a victim to his sexuality, with the predators his position and wealth attracted. During a visit to Brian's home, John challenged a male caller with: 'Have you come to blackmail him? If not, you're the only bugger in London who hasn't'.[5] All the perceived weakness of Brian was from John's point of view immediately transferred to him. All of Brian's misdemeanours and the salacious gossip applied to John. It was another case of John not having the strength of character to see that Brian's life was Brian's, not his. It came down again to a lack of compassion towards Brian's life which reflected a weakness in his own humanity.

An example of John's professed 'hard edged attitude' that Cilla scorned took place at a party in the songwriter Lionel Bart's Knightsbridge home. John reduced a young German woman to tears by pointing out that her 'people killed six million of his [Brian's] relatives'.[6] Brian's friend and lawyer, Nat Weiss, believed that Brian's feelings towards John, despite the constant taunts and insults, 'were more than a sexual attraction. It was a sort of love which he felt'.[7] The love which Brian may have felt would have been brought on by an understanding that only someone in so much pain could lead his life looking to hurt others. Brian in turn believed this justified understanding, compassion and a large element of pity. In John, Brian recognised his own suffering. John's frustration and aggression came from not just Mendips, but also from wanting to be independent. He would have readily exchanged the role of world famous entertainer with an abundance of wealth, millions of adoring fans and a mansion in the country to be a self-determining recognised artist, someone who could follow his own path; someone like Stuart Sutcliffe.

Before the next tour of America, The Beatles had returned to Abbey Road studios for what would be their next album, *Revolver*. Their use of drugs continued. Although an overstatement, John was to claim to have taken a thousand trips on acid. This sense of hyperbole was intended to provide an insight into his dependency on drugs. His consumption was such that he claimed to be 'eating it'. Cynthia recalls many a time a stoned John returned to Weybridge in the early hours of the morning like a latter-day Pied Piper with a trail of acid heads, hangers on, fans and a generous contingent of the burgeoning hippy movement to continue their partying and later crash out at Kenwood while Julian lay sleeping upstairs. John's attitude on the surface was to be a free spirit, free of the confines and responsibility of both husband and father. The private and public John were miles apart.

An example of John's indifference to the distinction between his public and private views was shown in an interview with Maureen Cleave for the *London Evening Standard*. The interview, which resulted in great controversy, was initially intended to be a straightforward 'day in the life of a Beatle' piece. The content was essentially in two parts, the first a lengthy interview in which, as usual, John gave forthright views on a variety of subjects, followed by fly on the wall reportage in which Maureen Cleaves accompanied John on his day's events. The interview had taken place partly at Kenwood, which revealed a life of apathy that was not concealed by John; instead it was celebrated.

'Is this the laziest man in Britain?'[8] Maureen Cleave asks. John's claims to do nothing physical other than 'sex' may have been an attempt to be mischievous and provocative. The whole interview suggests that his inertia and lethargy were a result of his melancholia. In the published article for the *London Evening Standard*, Maureen Cleave reports John's total mistiming, by over two hours, of his appointment at his local GP and the revelation that when shooting *How I Won The War*, he confessed to losing 12 pairs of eyeglasses from the props department.

John's poor time management was well known. Maureen Cleave reports that when ringing John, his usual response was 'What day is it?' and then to ask about 'news from outside'. This poor recall supports the notion of John being lazy, a normal assumption given John's lifestyle, but this stupor can also be a reaction to depression, which affects memory. An impaired memory such as John's is quite common in those suffering from depression. There doesn't seem to be any evidence that John sought treatment for his depression before 1970, when he finally sought the help of Dr Janov and his scream therapy. Whether John's early reluctance was due to his fear of being 'outed' as a depressive or his stubbornness and sense of independence is difficult to say.

The 58 words of John's interview with Maureen Cleave which were to provoke a tidal wave of protests in the southern states of America, with many protests taking the shape of record burning and Beatles records being banned from radio stations, were as follows:

Christianity will go, it will vanish and shrink. I needn't argue about that; I'm right and I will be proved right. We're more popular than Jesus now; I don't know which will go first – rock 'n' roll or Christianity. Jesus was alright, but his disciples were thick and ordinary. It's them twisting it that ruins it for me.[9]

The argument that John puts forward was, in many ways, nothing new, inasmuch as there had been a steady march of secularism since the turn of the century, church attendances had plummeted and those that did attend were in the majority elderly. Confidence in churches to play a meaningful role in community was low or non-existent, and the role of faith-based organisations in the west was in question. What made John's words alarming was the arrogance and naivety with which he said them – the 'more popular than Jesus' incident became a worldwide controversy.

During the period the interview took place, The Beatles had an unprecedented three months off from recording and touring. This lack of structure in John's life wasn't really conducive to improving his state of mind. He needed to occupy himself with something meaningful. He could have spent this three-month period writing another book to follow up to *In His Own Write*, his previous book of poems, stories and drawings. The publication a few years earlier had won plaudits from around the world, and the *Times Literary Supplement* commenting: 'It is worth the attention of anyone who fears for the impoverishment of the English language and the British imagination'.[10] His talent for nonsensical stories and drawings, his sense of humour and surreal puns mixed with a bizarre collection of characters suited his sense of quick start to finish process which applied to *In His Own Write*. The second volume was called *A Spaniard in the Works*. The book sold well, but writing a book was not as satisfying to John as songwriting, nor was writing this follow-up book as easy. His second venture into authorship found him revealing that:

> I could only loosen up with a bottle of Johnnie Walker and I thought, 'if it takes a bottle every night to get me to write...' That's why I didn't write anymore.[11]

Part of the *In His Own Write* content had already been completed while he was at school and college, plus everything was happening so fast during that period that he never had time to think. But with his writing of *A Spaniard in the Works*, some of the frenzy surrounding The Beatles had dissipated and doubt had set in. The long hours and discipline needed to be a full-time writer didn't suit him. The previous ideals of poet/writer with its discipline of solitude paled in attractiveness when compared to the group dynamics of playing in the band and its instant gratification. He'd learnt to prefer short bursts of creativity and the 'chaos' of words that could be put together as lyrics in songs, rather than put together in the thousands and turned into a book. The isolation of being an author didn't sit well with him; the process of songwriting was more immediate than that of the long slog of deferred gratification of being an author. John was under pressure to write for the public in book form, but as he readily admitted, most of his writing was for himself. It was a form of therapy.

In a poem in a letter to Stu written while in Hamburg, John poignantly recalls his childhood as a time when everyone he loved returned that love with hate and he was dogged by the sense that he was a spectator on life, constantly aware of his own stupidity. The raw honesty of the poem is tempered both by a matter-of-fact directness and by an admixture of facetiousness, a 'trivialising' style which he sometimes deployed defensively, for example after returning his MBE, with the suggestion that one reason for doing so was 'Cold Turkey' slipping down the charts. The poem is a confession, a plea for understanding; it signposts a future of genius drenched in misery.

John's mental health condition seems to reveal symptoms of a form of bipolar cyclothymia, in which mood swings, although not as severe as full-blown bipolar disorder, reveal long periods of depression followed by a buoyant outlook. The copious amount of drugs John consumed temporarily dampened these symptoms, but later exacerbated them. His resistance to seeking help for his depression stemmed from not only the symptoms that come with the disease (in particular lethargy and lack of self-worth), but also his aggressive and abusive manner, which left him fully aware of perceived signs of 'weakness' on his part if seeking medical attention. This self-destructive approach exposes a misanthropic attitude, a repressed rage behind the misery.

Old school friend Peter Shotton, on a visit to Weybridge, gave an example of this uncontrolled hostility, when he found himself in the early hours of the morning with a drunken John in a London nightclub. The piano player in the club was Jewish, and before too long, John began with shouts of abuse in the shape of 'creepy Jewboy' accompanied by 'they should have stuck you in the ovens with the rest of them'.[13] Incidents like this in John's life abound – as though his self-worth was so low he wanted to be disliked and introduced a form of self-flagellation via the expected criticisms from those around him. It could be that he believed he was unworthy of love and kindness because he wasn't capable of returning this love and kindness, all he knew was how to withdraw into his patterns of aggression and resentment. At times his lack of self-worth spilled over into self-loathing, which in turn spilled over to 'acceptable' targets such as Jews, 'spastics' and 'queers'; his art acted as a buffer against such despondency and negative behaviour. Kay Redfield Jamison's view concerning artists with depressive episodes, cited earlier, is clearly relevant again here.[14] There is the question as to why didn't he recognise these episodes of unacceptable behaviour when outside his depression and seek to remedy them. It could well be that his bigotry was a fundamental part of his nature and he never actually believed there was anything untoward in it. This defence mechanism of denial took the shape of a list of those to who were to be held responsible for his pain.

John's mental health issues were largely misinterpreted, at times his belligerent and spiteful behaviour was put down to 'that's just John', but it would be unfair and misleading to see John as an ogre going around trampling on everyone's feelings. A large part of John's 'Beatle' life was lived just as the other members of the band. On his good days he could be extremely generous, good natured and good company, but when his black clouds of depression came around, the anger and mean-spiritedness came out and were remembered by others with particular clarity. John's own creativity was always going to be compared, by himself and by others, with Paul's. This was continually going to present problems. When his leadership slipped, so did his self-worth.

The radical development of The Beatles' music wasn't just driven by keeping ahead of the pack that was led by Mick and The Stones. More importantly, there was a complex brew of cut-throat competition and reciprocal support between John and Paul. On the surface it might have seemed that this was a friendly rivalry and it was portrayed as such, but it wasn't. It was a competition of adversity. Each needed the other in various ways and each tolerated the other's foibles because the semi-dependence on one another was based on an acceptance of the need to hold together the all-important production of The Beatles' lifeblood – songs. During the *Revolver* session, John admitted to Paul that, 'I probably like your songs better than mine'.[15] Later, he disclosed his acceptance of Paul's ability as a tunesmith:

> Paul has a special gift when it comes to making up tunes. I find myself using tunes which already exist and fitting my words to them... I realise I'm pinching an old American hit... With me, I have a theme which gets me started on the poetry side of the thing. Then I have to put a tune to it, but that's the part of the job I enjoy least.[16]

An early pointer of Paul's leaning towards tune had been in The Beatles' appearance in a 1963 edition of the TV music programme, *Juke Box Jury*, where invited guests where asked their opinion on the latest single releases. Steve and Eydie's 'I Can't Stop Talking About You' prompted Paul to judge that 'people will whistle to this one'.[17] The title of the long-running BBC 'progressive' music show *The Old Grey Whistle Test* came from the yardstick that the early professional songwriters in London's Tin Pan Alley used to determine whether a tune would be a hit or not – if one of the 'old greys' (that is, the elderly cleaners of the office block) was heard whistling it. That was it. John's strength was his lyrics, but nobody whistles lyrics.

It's likely that if John and Paul had worked without major criticisms of each other's work, then they never would have moved out of the *A Hard Day's Night* period. Though often brutal, this honesty was key to the development to their songwriting skills. Their critical observation of each other's work, built up over nearly ten years, generated an acute sense of one-upmanship which John in the end found impossible to deal with.

During the American tour, a reporter put the question: 'Do any of you have plans to record on your own?'

JOHN: We do at home... We might.

GEORGE: In fact we have done, I think. Well 'Eleanor Rigby' was Paul on his own.

JOHN: And we were just drinking tea.[18]

John was aware of Paul's ability to gain independent success outside The Beatles, in the shape of cover songs and as in 'Yesterday'. Neither John nor Paul was under any illusion as to the importance of writing credits. They were fully aware the reward for the writer who produced the most successful songs was the leadership of the band.

An interesting footnote to Paul's 'Yesterday' is his uncertainty of it actually being 'his' song – so uncertain was he that he hadn't pinched it from someone else, he carried it around for six months before recording it, constantly checking his own validity of ownership by asking others if they were familiar with its tune. Paul seemed to have a gift for subconsciously letting other musicians' tunes and production techniques 'stew' until he could reinvent and adapt them into his own original songs, whether these tunes came from rock 'n' roll as in Little Richard or soul in the shape of Marvin Gaye, or even Jazz – note Dave Brubeck's 'Kathy's Waltz' (1.01–1.06) whose seven notes give Paul the intro to 'All My Loving'.

The final Beatles tour started in disorder and headed quickly to disaster. In Germany, they played Munich, Essen and then Hamburg, their first visit since 1962. The two shows at Hamburg's Ernst Merck Halle saw frustrated fans hurl stones and tear gas canisters at the cordons of police who were barricading the surrounding streets. The next stop after Germany would be Tokyo, but, as if an omen for their whole tour, their flight was delayed due to Typhoon Kit moving towards Japan. In Tokyo they were met with protests over the venue for their concerts, the Budokan cultural centre being the imperial palace of sumo, which was considered too significant a place of national importance for pop groups. The Beatles had to have a police and a military escort for the two mile journey from their hotel and, once inside the Budokan, found the stage built up to eight feet high to ensure safety against any protesters.

If The Beatles were hoping for third time lucky with their next stop in the Philippines, they were in for a disappointment. The Philippines was run by authoritarian leader Ferdinand Marcos, who had a history of despotism, political repression and human rights violations. After playing two shows to audiences of 45,000 at the Rizla Stadium in Manila, there followed a misunderstanding by Brian. This concerned an invitation to The Beatles from President Marcos to attend a palace garden party. Here the first lady Imelda Marcos and 300 children of the Philippines ruling elite waited. The result of the misunderstanding resulted in a no-show at the garden party by The Beatles. The outcome of this perceived slight was a wave of hate by the Filipino officials and public, leaving The Beatles and their entourage in fear of their lives.

Threats that The Beatles may not be able to leave the Philippines from an official from the Department of Income Tax if a payment of $80,000 tax wasn't forthcoming led Vic Lewis, the promoter of the shows, (after consulting Brian) to reluctantly pay it. 'I have never been so terrified in my life,' recalled George. 'We will never go back there.' On their journey to the airport, The Beatles and their party had run a gauntlet of angry officials aiming feet and fists at them, with Brian having his face slapped, leaving him cut and bleeding. Mal Evans had his ribs kicked. When finally on the plane, they found it delayed for a very long forty-five minutes, and George recalled it felt like hours. Even with the loss of their fee, The Beatles and those with them felt this was a small price to pay. The soon-to-be profound believer in Eastern philosophy, its music and peaceful coexistence with the world, George, declared: 'If I go back. It will be with an H-bomb to drop on it'.[19]

The tour of America that immediately followed the Philippines proved a case of out of the frying pan and into the fire. The comments by John about Christianity had been picked up by TV and radio stations. Local churches and the Ku Klux Klan turned it into a crusade against them. In fairness to John, many of the protesters were using The Beatles as a form of proxy protest against what they viewed as the liberalisation of America resulting from Lyndon B. Johnson's Great Society, which aimed to eliminate poverty and racial injustice. The Beatles were lumped together with escalating protests against the Vietnam War, riots in cities and anyone connected with left-wing issues, and found themselves under attack from the moral majority.

Against this backdrop, it was no surprise that John looked like an easy target for right-wing Christian groups. With The Beatles' recording of 'black songs' along with their well-known admiration for Afro-American artists and their views against the war in Vietnam, it was also no surprise that the most vehement protests against them came from the Bible Belt, where extreme nationalism and racism were prevalent. Nevertheless, John was still shocked and bewildered at the news coverage and protests that his comments had caused. What he went through in facing the American media that summer was an emotional version of being placed in stocks or a public flogging. It was a painfully vulnerable John who faced the TV cameras for interviews. These showed him looking shaken and upset, making a genuine and emotional act of contrition. This was a totally new sight of John; one who was standing in the mud asking for forgiveness.

The comments concerning The Beatles being 'more popular than Christ' had a tremendous impact on John's state of mind. It was the delayed response. After such a comment, he may have had the chance to prepare himself for an adverse reaction, but in the UK it never created the controversy that it later did in the States. After The Beatles broke up, he bitterly revealed that 'one had to totally humiliate yourself to be a Beatle'.[20] The protests by insulted churchgoers and John's public acts of contrition are humiliations that would have readily come to mind.

Midway through the tour and after numerous explanations and apologies by John and The Beatles' press agents, the Memphis City Council decided to cancel both the planned afternoon and evening concerts. They stated their reason as being that they were opposed to having 'municipal facilities used as a forum to ridicule anyone's religion'. Outside the venue, the Ku Klux Klan nailed a Beatles album onto a wooden cross. In spite of the fact that the city council had previously cancelled the show, Brian, with poor judgment, agreed to fulfil the date. During the afternoon show, a member of the audience threw a firecracker onstage. The explosion that followed saw the heads of Paul, George and Ringo spin round towards John, expecting the worst.

The Shea Stadium concert, the venue of The Beatles' greatest triumph, where only 12 months previously they were paid a king's ransom to play, was short of being a sell-out by as many as 11,000 fans. Tickets had being given away at the last minute to mask the swathes of empty seats. From New York, The Beatles flew to the west coast to play Seattle, Los Angeles and what would be their last public performance (outside the Apple rooftop) at Candlestick Park, San Francisco.

Inside the dressing room after the Candlestick Park concert, George slumped into his seat and declared, 'That's it. I'm no longer a Beatle'.[21] Although John and Ringo felt the same, it was a unilateral decision by George to announce the end of live playing for The Beatles. George had come a long way in confidence terms since his 'ching a ching a ching' days at the hospital radio interview. This increased influence showed itself in his songwriting credits on *Revolver*. An interview at the time revealed George's views on The Beatles' music:

GEORGE: But whatever we do has got to be real and progressive. Everything we've done so far has been rubbish.

JOHN: George is being a bit blunt. You can always look back and say what you've done before is rubbish, especially in comparison with what you're doing today. It was all vital at the time, even if it looks daft when you see things differently later on.[22]

George is not referring to *Revolver* here, which included three tracks of his own and his 'discovery' of the sitar. But to offhandedly dismiss six previous albums and all the singles of Lennon and McCartney songs, including 'Help!', 'Michelle', 'Rain' and 'Yesterday' seems unfair to say the least. His own contribution in the previous six albums amounted to five songs. John's response puts the notion of 'progressive' into context. But the implication of George's view on *Revolver* demonstrates the radically changing group dynamics.

Although George was the chief advocate of stopping touring, this would prove to be a somewhat poisoned chalice. George's dilemma was that, while The Beatles toured, he had as much publicity and fame as the other members of the band. But when the band stopped playing live, he depended to a certain extent of his being a 'Beatle' through his input on new albums and this meant needing song credits to prove to himself and others as being a '*bona fide* member' of the band. Essentially, as the visual profile of 'Beatle George' diminished alongside the band's stage presence, he was subject to the unintended consequence of an increased pressure on him to gain status with his songwriting.

George's input on *Revolver* gave him the confidence that his songwriting was something he could build on in the studio, whereas time spent touring kept him anchored to being the sideman of John and Paul. It was no surprise that in less than 12 months' time, when accolades where being heaped on *Sergeant Pepper*, George's view on the album was that he preferred (his three song credit) *Revolver* to (his one song credit) *Sergeant Pepper*. But for all the disinclination towards touring, at least there was a vitality and sense of camaraderie about the problems they met on the road. They were shared problems, but in the studio it would be the steady journey into self-contained individualism with every man for himself.

Original site of the Flat Iron pub John Lennon's grandfather Jack used to perform song-and-dance routines regularly at this pub. In a strange coincidence, an illustration of this pub featured in the feature animation *Yellow Submarine* (1968). Map 2, location 11.
Courtesy of Liverpool Record Office, Liverpool Libraries.

Penny Lane Map 1, location 6.
Courtesy of Liverpool Record Office, Liverpool Libraries.

9 Newcastle Road John Lennon's first home. John lived here until he was five years old, when he was moved to stay with his Aunt Mimi at Mendips. Map 1, location 5.
Courtesy of Liverpool Record Office, Liverpool Libraries.

20 Forthlin Road Paul McCartney's childhood home. Map 1, location 13.
Courtesy of Lipinski, Wikimedia Commons).

12 Arnold Grove George Harrison's childhood home. Map 1, location 3.
Courtesy of Liverpool Record Office, Liverpool Libraries.

10 Admiral Grove Ringo Starr's childhood home. Map 2, location 13.
Courtesy of Liverpool Record Office, Liverpool Libraries.

Mendips 251 Menlove Avenue. John was sent to live at his Aunt Mimi's house in leafy suburbia when he was five years old. Map 1, location 11.
Courtesy of John Darch, Wikimedia Commons

Quarry Bank High School The grammar school for boys which John Lennon attended. His record here was one of shoddy work and delinquent behaviour. Map 1, location 9.
Courtesy of Liverpool Record Office, Liverpool Libraries.

St Peter's Church The very first meeting between John and Paul took place
at a fete held in the grounds of this church in 1957. Map 1, location 12.
Courtesy of Liverpool Record Office, Liverpool Libraries.

Rosebery Street One of The Quarrymen's first appearances was at a street party in Rosebery
Street in 1957, where they played on the back of a stationary coal lorry. Map 2, location 10.
Courtesy of Liverpool Record Office, Liverpool Libraries.

Ye Cracke Pub This pub was a regular haunt of John's when he was at Liverpool College of Art. John's tutor Arthur Ballard frequently held tutorials here. Map 2, location 5.
Courtesy of Liverpool Record Office, Liverpool Libraries.

Gambier Terrace John Lennon lived here as a student with original Beatles bassist Stuart Sutcliffe. Map 2, location 7.
Courtesy of Liverpool Record Office, Liverpool Libraries.

The Pavilion The Quarrymen took part in various 'skiffle contests' at this venue in the 1950s. The Beatles on performed once at The Pavilion on 2 April 1962. Map 2, location 9.
Courtesy of Liverpool Record Office, Liverpool Libraries.

NEMS The North End Music Stores offices where The Beatles signed a contract with Brian Epstein on 24 January 1962. Map 2, location 2.
Courtesy of Liverpool Record Office, Liverpool Libraries.

The Cavern 10 Mathew Street. The Beatles played this club frequently in the early years, first appearing as The Quarrymen in the late '50s. This photograph shows the original Cavern club in 1973, just before it was demolished. Map 2, location 1.
Courtesy of Liverpool Record Office, Liverpool Libraries.

The replacement statue of John Lennon that is currently outside The Cavern, referred to in the introduction. Map 1, location 1.
Courtesy of GHM.

This university building was renamed The John Lennon Art and Design Building in 2003. It features a self-portrait of John above the entrance. Map 2, location 1.
Courtesy of Rep0n1x, Wikimedia Commons.

CHAPTER FIFTEEN

1966–67
Cavendish Avenue

BY 1967, BRITAIN'S swinging sixties was in full tilt – flared trousers, beads and floppy hats were *de rigueur* in London's Kings Road and beyond. The mood of a new dawn breaking was driven by all things new and modern. Full employment brought a period of optimism and consumerism on a scale never seen before, a cultural revolution whose motor was the newly empowered youth scene. Tied into this emphasis on style was what became known as the 'permissive society'. Conventional moral codes were challenged at all levels of society in the shape of sexual freedom, movies, homosexuality and literature and the arts in general.

Historian Arthur Marwick's examination of the elements that gave birth to the swinging sixties believed that Britain's post-war elite exercised a 'measured judgement', which supported:

> traditional enlightened and rational outlook who responded flexibly and tolerantly to counter-cultural demands... striking changes in public and private morals and... a new frankness, openness and indeed honesty in personal relations and modes of expression.[1]

One of those modes of expression was to be found in the music of the *avant-garde* and what was to later become known as psychedelic rock. Paul summoned up the new challenge and attitude:

> We feel that only through recording do people listen to us, so that is our most important form of communication, we have always changed our style as we went along and we've never been frightened to develop and change... We take as much time as we want on a track, until we get it to our satisfaction.[2]

The feelings expressed by Paul in an interview given to a *New Musical Express* journalist concerning The Beatles' decision to stop touring made it clear that, like John, George and Ringo, he had recognised the futility of playing their latest material to a live audience. Normally a group would tour to tie in with the release of their new album, but on The Beatles' last tour and three months after the release of *Revolver*, they never performed a single track from the album while on stage. The gap between what was produced in Abbey Road and what could be, in some ways, replicated in the likes of Shea Stadium had become almost impossible because of the experimental recording and production techniques, and complex vocal harmonies. If The Beatles attempting to perform tracks from *Revolver* on stage was impracticable, to deliver a credible version of *Sergeant Pepper* tracks to a stadium full of fans was unthinkable.

The notion of an alter ego band in the shape of 'Sergeant Pepper and his Lonely Hearts Club Band' or a loose idea regarding childhood and Liverpool, had become a sketchy brief for a concept album, of which 'Strawberry Fields' and 'Penny Lane' were to be part of. 'Strawberry Fields' was conceived when John was filming in Almeria for *How I Won the War*. Even at this relatively early stage, John was considering his position and whether or not to be in The Beatles. The reasons he gave for taking part in that particular film was that he was asked by Richard Lester, who had directed *A Hard Day's Night* and *Help!*, and the film itself was anti-war (but only slightly), along with his concerns as to what to do with his life after The Beatles had stopped touring.

During a break in filming, John was interviewed and asked what the impact of his role as an actor on the set meant to being a member of The Beatles: 'For the last six years, I have been a Beatle. It's been a jolly life and we've had a good many laughs, but it can't go on forever'.[3] Even three years before the break-up, John was looking for alternatives. A month after the comments he was to announce: 'We've no intention of splitting up. We're always going to be recording'.[4] He was caught in a dilemma; he wanted to leave The Beatles because of the increasing pressure he felt constantly having to compete with Paul and longed to become his own man in the world of music and writing. But leaving The Beatles would lead to uncertainties with which he could not deal. *How I Won the War* gave him time to think of a possible for a way out:

> If I stopped and thought about it I was going to have a big bum trip for nine months so I tried to avoid the depression of the change of life by leaping into the movie.[5]

Being a Beatle was addictive; the money, the fame and the power meant membership was just as much a gilded cage as the wasted months spent in Kenwood. John needed time to think.

The idea for *Sergeant Pepper* came from Paul during a return flight to London. Previously Paul had flown to France for a motor tour, then onto Spain. He eventually flew to Kenya, where he stayed at the foot of Mount Kilimanjaro in the Treetops Hotel. Here the rooms where built into the ancient Kenyan trees. During this time, John languished in stockbroker Kenwood, steadily supplied with drugs and hangers on. Paul's globetrotting left him full of verve and with a yearning to self-educate; John's days were spent lying on the couch as he half-watched a muted TV while browsing the daily papers for the sixth time.

Paul's notion for the album was simple – a parody on American West Coast bands' penchant for convoluted names such as *The Quicksilver Messenger Service* and *Big Brother and the Holding Company*. It would be an alter ego type group that The Beatles could hide behind. The first title considered was named 'Dr Pepper', after the soft drink, but when this caused legal problems with the drinks company, 'Dr' was switched to 'Sergeant'. *Sergeant Pepper* was seen and talked about as The Beatles' concept album, but once 'Strawberry Fields' and 'Penny Lane' were released as a double-sided single due to pressure for a new Beatles release, the notion of a concept childhood album went out of the window.

The enthusiasm of The Beatles to nail their colours to the mast of experimentation and non-conformity, and a break with convention meant the good ship *Sergeant Pepper* would be one of the first to pull up anchor and set sail in uncharted waters to the isle of psychedelia where people 'skipped the light fandango' and the land was populated by 'white rabbits'. During the making of *Sergeant Pepper,* even though John produced what was probably the best track on the album in the shape of 'Lucy in the Sky with Diamonds', and the other song credits were almost evenly shared, it was essentially the overarching concept and experimental production techniques that made it Paul's album.

Touring had showcased John's best qualities: his ebullient leadership; his showmanship; his strength of personality; and his witty and unpredictable contributions in press conferences and TV interviews. Touring, however, was replaced by the studio, and Paul's superior knowledge of production techniques and greater share of writing credits brought about an irreversible power shift.

During this period, John's mental health problems and copious drug-taking seemed to be firmly entrenched. Even before the pressure to deliver songs, his deep unhappiness had resurfaced again. 'I was in a big depression in *Pepper* and I know that Paul wasn't at the time. I was going through murder,' he recalled.[6] As with many people suffering a self-defeating and distorted vision of themselves in a depressive condition, despite all his past triumphs John felt inadequate and belittled his talent. Paul would never have been so open. Barry Miles, a close friend of both John and Paul, was one of the few in their close circle of friends to recognise John's mental distress at this time, later commenting that, 'Lennon was going through a very neurotic phase'.[7]

What Barry Miles didn't realise was that the 'neurotic' image that John presented was also the combined result of high doses of acid, marijuana, lack of sleep and not eating, all having the effect of increasing John's mental frailty. Perversely, the acid and marijuana that John had put his faith in to hold back his depression gave a diminishing return of the required effects and eventually both drugs were used mostly through force of habit.

From John's perspective, if the pain and effort that had gone into creating his songs was outdone by Paul's superior songs, this in turn devalued his efforts and all the pain and emotional distress he had invested in the work. It wasn't just an issue of ego relating to having an 'A' side, it was much more important – his songs, and their success were a validation of him as a person. A gamble was made by John on his confessional songs. This took on an all-or-nothing importance, in the shape of achievement of public acclaim which meant his own self-validation, or a non-acceptance could result in staring into the abyss of depression again. John's fatalistic declaration that Paul's songs were 'better than mine' could have been a subconscious attempt to distance and disengage himself from the race for 'A' sides. Psychiatrist Anthony Storr points out the importance of artists using their art as the only *bona fide* means of communication: 'In fact, the work may be a much more valid piece of self-expression than what is revealed in action or conversation in "real life"'.[8]

Driving forward the theme of the times, *Sergeant Pepper* was instantly described as psychedelic. It came out at the beginning of what would be termed progressive rock. One of the first of these psychedelic bands were Pink Floyd. 'The Floyd' eventually found themselves recording their album *The Piper at the Gates of Dawn* in the Abbey Road studio next to The Beatles. Much has been made of John not visiting the studio in which Pink

Floyd were working, unlike Paul, George and Ringo. Some have read into this that John was fearful of The Beatles' crown being taken by these psychedelic upstarts. But this was not the case. John never visited Pink Floyd because it smacked of studio wizardry; what Paul was becoming so adept at. And what Paul had brought into Abbey Road was what made being in Studio Two so insufferable.

Paul's move into London's counter-culture set saw him mixing with the likes of William Burroughs, John Cage and Allen Ginsberg, and attending 'alternative' concerts which included the likes of Luciano Berio. This entree was in the main due to Paul's friend and 'mentor', Indica Bookshop owner and *bon viveur*, Barry Miles and his friend John Dunbar. Both were acquaintances of Peter Asher, brother of Jane. It was Miles and Dunbar whose arts and cultural grapevine kept Paul in touch with the great and good, the weird and the wacky, of the arts world's margins. The peculiar point about *Sergeant Pepper* is that for all the pronouncements of its psychedelic nature, with Paul at the cutting edge of all that was new and wonderful, it wasn't a really psychedelic, let alone an avant-garde album at all.

Even though Paul was seen as the one who steered *Sergeant Pepper* along the course to the new frontier with a combination of cutting-edge lyrics, musicianship and studio experimentation techniques, what he produced in the shape of tracks turned out to be largely 'pop' – 'Lovely Rita', 'Fixing a Hole', 'When I'm Sixty Four,' the ballad 'She's Leaving Home', and the rock song, 'Sergeant Pepper'. The only tracks that could lay claim to the avant-garde or psychedelic were John's 'Lucy in the Sky with Diamonds', 'Being for the Benefit of Mr Kite' and the joint effort of John and Paul with 'A Day in the Life'. Here Paul's middle eight was stitched to what was the body of John's song. This is not to say Paul's influence was absent in John's songs on the album, but outside these last three songs there was nothing cutting-edge or progressive about them other than (albeit important) production techniques, who some argue were overblown.

Sergeant Pepper was a classic album, but paradoxically what gave it impact was unique packaging, innovative production values and its unintended hidden messages from 'fixing a hole' to 'meeting a man in the motor trade'. The album's 'real meanings', alternative interpretations and reversed track made *Sergeant Pepper* the Rashomon of the music trade.

Paul's songs were excellent, but not avant-garde or psychedelic; the production gave a nod towards the forthcoming notion of 'progressive music' but *Sergeant Pepper* was no more than a tint of these strands. The Beatles would have to wait until the *White Album* to be fully immersed in the notion of avant-garde in the shape of 'Revolution 9', by which time, the concept would be seen by many as passé, having been overtaken by revolutionary and progressive rock.

George Martin rightly pointed out that, taking into account the overall aims of *Sergeant Pepper*, 'When I'm Sixty Four' and 'Within You and Without You' were 'alien' tracks. In the case of 'Within You and Without You', George made the mistake of displaying an undying passion for his love of Indian music with the belief that this commitment equated to a good album track. *Revolver*'s 'Love You To' worked because George made the effort to convey a crossover of Anglo-Indian music, which the listener appreciated, but George's delivery of 'Within You and Without You' goes totally native and comes across as a surly challenge to and denouncement of any listener who was too thick to get it, or, God forbid, didn't like it.

Previously, Paul's badgering 'school prefect' mentality had served well towards blending the talents of The Beatles in the studio. But it had now become a burden to John and later George and Ringo. But in redressing the balance somewhat, Paul was faced with the thankless and emotionally draining task of pulling the band together after the end of live concerts had reduced the amount of social time they spent together. Truth be known, the other Beatles were still demob happy from their 'tour of duty' mentality ending, enjoying their 'freedom' in swinging London, and had begun to view the studio in the same manner as being involved in the tiresome elements of being on the road, a case of having to clock in and out. An additional source of conflict that would also surface was Paul's non-acceptance of John as leader of The Beatles. To Paul, John was the leader because he was more up-front and vocal about being the leader, so for Paul, John was the band's self-appointed leader.

In *Many Years from Now*, written by Paul's friend Barry Miles, Paul gives his account of the *Sergeant Pepper* period:

> I had a rich avant-garde period which was such a buzz, making movies and stuff. Because I was living on my own in London and all the guys were married out in the suburbs... They were very square in my

mind… It was quite heady and very artistic. Like showing my movies to Antonioni, stuff like that, dead cool really and watching movies with Andy Warhol round at my house. My place was almost the centre of the social scene at one point because I was on my own. There was nobody to hang anyone up, this big house in St John's Wood. It was like a salon, almost. I used to go to avant-garde music concerts. That was me, all that Stockhausen shit in the Beatles.[9]

On giving consideration to Paul's comments, one would be hard pressed not to enquire, 'is there no end to this man's modesty?' Yes, Paul did all these things and more, and he introduced elements of Stockhausen into the album. But for all of the Stockhausen and the pastel suits and gate-fold lyric adorned album, it was Paul and John's genius as songwriters that made *Sergeant Pepper* the *tour de force* that it was. The additional elements on *Pepper* were individual and unusual supporting packages which helped lend a sense of novelty and charm.

This self-confidence of Paul's had an effect on John. Such was the weariness of the depression and drug taking that he'd lost confidence in his musicianship. He now wanted to distance himself from any painful comparisons to Paul's motivational and aspirational lifestyle. John found himself in a suburban angst *par excellence*; the gilded cage of Kenwood. This had become a mirror opposite of Paul's 'salon' in St John's Wood. It's easy to imagine John lounging on his couch in Kenwood, smoking dope, his poor mental health and fragile ego taking him to an interpretation of the *Sergeant Pepper* suits as a declared subconscious loyalty to Paul. Who was Sergeant Pepper? Who wrote the title album's song and sang it, who initiated the album cover and the psychedelic Salvation Army uniforms? Whose idea was it? Before John could roll another joint, John, Paul, George and Ringo had become, Paul, John, George and Ringo.

It should be borne in mind, though, that John's moods swings from extreme buoyancy to self-loathing were not an indication of John being a 'weak' or 'self-indulgent person' – these features are a recurrent theme in the history of creative people. Dr Marilyn J. Sorenson, believes that:

Those with low self-esteem have one thing in common. On some level they share a deep-seated fear that there is something wrong with them and wonder if they may be unlovable or unacceptable.[10]

Most of John's negative self-comparisons with Paul were illusions; and artists are beings of imagination. John's poor self-perception had its sources in his perceived lack of love in childhood. Eventually, it lead to a repressed rage behind the misery. Once there was a cheerleading side of John with his pre-fame rallying cry of, 'Where are we going fellas?', which prompted the response from the rest of the band, 'To the Toppermost of the Poppermost Johnnie!', and the imaginative fever he needed to sustain all the long midnight shifts in Hamburg and the hundreds of cold, boring hours in the back of a van. John could reverse this imagination of despair, but the help he needed in 1967 was to be found in professional medical health care, not that of acid and pot.

John's deep anxieties as a Beatle were neither new nor confined to the *Sergeant Pepper* period, but were displayed from the very beginning, starting with his distaste for his own voice in the recording studio. John's comments regards his voice are well documented, as is his view that he was unattractive and his self-proclaimed 'fat Elvis period' during the mid-'60s when his weight went up while his self-confidence went down, and his overall condition was that of isolation and loneliness. Even though he had achieved all he had set out to and more, he was still bitterly critical of himself. An earlier example of John's insecurities came during a break in the 1964 tour of America. The Beatles' early official photographer Dezo Hoffmann found himself sacked by John in Miami for the crime of taking a shot of him on a water ski with his wet hair swept back. John believed that this made him look as though he was receding, and Hoffmann was dismissed. All the attributes of Paul's which were an asset to John in 1957 in the shape of musical skills, ambition, organisation and determination had now turned against him. While touring, John could depend on his force of personality to be The Beatles' leader. The snatched songwriting sessions with Paul amidst the frantic schedule distracted him from his depression. After touring ended, however, Paul set up semi-formal songwriting sessions and these had a different effect on John. With his fragile ego, John felt he was being set up to be judged against Paul in these sessions, and he felt he was coming off second best. With his low self-confidence and negative thought patterns, he could well have seen these Paul-initiated sessions as a way for Paul to rub his nose in it and to challenge his position as the 'leader' of the Beatles.

In many ways, *Sergeant Pepper* was a con trick. This is not to say it wasn't a brilliant album containing typically high-quality songwriting and musicianship, as one would expect from The Beatles. Its innovative studio production techniques made it a classic album, but even the red noses for the orchestra in the finale of 'A Day in a Life' wasn't inventive, as 12 months previously, Brian Wilson had supplied his own studio orchestra with plastic fireman's hats for the track 'Fire' on the album *Smile*. As John bluntly put it after the band split up:

> *Sergeant Pepper* is called the first concept album, but it doesn't go anywhere. All my contribution to the album have nothing to do with this idea of Sergeant Pepper and his band; but it works 'cause we said it worked.[11]

John's (submerged but nevertheless) introvert character meant he found himself left out when it came to Paul's urbane lifestyle during the recording of *Sergeant Pepper*. John, meanwhile, found himself stuck in the heart of the English Home Counties. But this is unfair on Paul. It's more than likely that Paul would have been more than willing to buddy up with John on his jaunts around London. The reason John felt isolated during the recording of the album was due to his admission that he 'was in more at the start, later on I sort of succumbed to marriage and eating'.[12] John's decision was influenced by the increasing studio expertise, discipline and confidence that Paul was exercising at Abbey Road. After a couple of weeks John couldn't take it. Hence he was in 'in more at the start.' and then 'chose marriage and eating' as opposed to recording. Geoff Emerick recalls at this time that while Paul directed sound engineers around Studio Two, instructing them as to what should be done, where it should be done and when it should be done, John sat indifferently, unnoticed, a million miles away, warehouse eyes staring blankly at the wall.

George Martin's view of John and Paul was that they were polar opposites. He viewed Paul as:

> probably the best bass player there is, a first class drummer, brilliant and competent piano player... Paul needs an audience, but John doesn't. John is very lazy, unlike Paul. Without Paul he would often give up. John writes for his own amusement. He would be content to play his tunes to Cynthia, Paul likes a public.[13]

Paul was always going to be George Martin's type of studio musician. Paul's diligent, meticulous and dutiful commitment to his work contrasted with John's 'let's capture the moment' spirit. Eventually, John realised that the increased focus on the studio meant that Paul had become more an integral part of The Beatles than he was. Somewhat forlornly, he admitted that, 'George [Martin] was always more like a Paul McCartney producer than for my music'.[14]

Audio engineer Geoff Emerick's comments support George Martin's about John being lazy. This is not the full picture. John's 'laziness' is far more complicated. The 'laziness' on which George Martin sits in judgement is a reflection of John's inner conflicts. If John was as idle as George Martin claims, how does this explain his output of songs in the studio in previous years, when John and Paul would have an equal say in polishing and completing songs in the studio? In the case of A Hard Day's Night, almost all of the writing credits belonged to John, not to mention the tremendous amount of effort by John, along with Paul and George, during their live 'musical apprenticeship' just to get in the recording studio in the first place. The simple answer to the view of John being lazy is that this lethargy was a reflection of his main concern to protect himself from the loss of his self-esteem. Others' perception of John's indifference in the recording studio was encouraged by John as a safety net – as a message to Paul and George Martin that the artistic values being set 'don't apply to me', coupled with the hidden fear of going head to head with Paul's musical capabilities.

Another major element in understanding George Martin's misdiagnosis is the context of John and Paul's methods and background. John didn't like school and was a poor pupil. Paul, on the other hand, liked school and was a model pupil. John was autodidactic; he rebelled and was used to being disliked. Paul accepted a more prescribed type of learning – due to his background, he was largely a conformist and liked being liked. The movement towards The Beatles taking more control in the recording process seemed fine at first until John realised the amount of work in learning the vast swathe of technical details that were required for this transition, the same study skills required as if in a classroom. For John, Studio Two had transformed itself in to a Quarry Bank classroom. The recording studio had become a competition of who could master the intricacies of the recording equipment the best and the loser of the contest being deemed 'lazy' by the judge.

Cynthia Lennon provided some insight into John's need for an audience:

He wanted to stand out. He needed an audience, and he always got an audience because he shocked. John didn't let anyone off lightly. John's attitude was to fight insecurities, hence the aggression that came out in different ways. He would never allow people to see his insecurities. John had a lot more tragedies in his life than most. I think the fact is that he didn't want people to see his weaknesses.[15]

An indication of John's insecurities came during the recording of the song 'Good Morning, Good Morning'. John claims, 'I was never proud of it. I just knocked it off, to do a song'.[16] The reason for John's dismissive attitude was that, like many of his songs, he painfully reveals himself, this time as a nine-to-five, frustrated company-man character. John's intention with the song was to deliver a cynical commentary, a finger on the pulse of suburban angst, but he ended up giving an all too clear insight into his own lifestyle at this time. With the lyric 'somebody needs to know the time, glad that I'm here', John seems to be saying, with a huge dose of sarcasm – maybe in the studio you think I'm crap, but I can at least give someone the time of day, *I have some use*. Without any illusions or subtext to deflect from the true source of the comments, 'Good Morning, Good Morning' was a little too close to home, its lyrics reading like an entry into John's diary.

With the loss of 'Strawberry Fields' and 'Penny Lane' from the album, the notion of a theme was abandoned. It's interesting to speculate that if the demand for a single to be released had been resisted by Brian and the childhood theme had run through the album, what would this have meant to John? Would the idea have energised him or involved him more in the production process of the project? Would it have inflated his self-esteem; produced a cathartic effect and more 'Strawberry Fields' and 'In my Life' testimonials, eliminating once and for all the corrosive influences of Menlove Avenue, the heartbreak of Julia and Stu, the guilt of his treatment towards Brian? Would it salve the emotional distress that caused him to display such anger and destructiveness?

John had on many occasions attempted to use the richness of his imagination as a songwriter to reinvent his childhood. 'Strawberry Fields' is a song about a fictional childhood interlaced with the place he wanted to be *now*. It is also a song about denial. In 'Lucy in the Sky with Diamonds', so desperate was he for an untainted childhood that John 'invaded' his own son's early years by 'lifting' Julian's watercolour painting of his playschool friend Lucy, who was in the sky with… diamonds. John's emotional distress meant that he had to use his mind to take him anywhere but where he was then. Some children created imaginary friends; John created an imaginary childhood. It was a childhood that was safe and welcoming. A more robust John may have chosen to write about Gladstone House, the boys' remand home near to Mendips that he viewed from his bedroom window. But this 'big boys' borstal' and its realities and hardships of life were too painful to write about, too close to home, an opulent Merchant's mansion transformed into a young boys 'prison' while a 17-room mock Tudor manor transforms itself into… maybe much the same.

Storr makes the point that 'many people of this temperament [depressive state], during the course of childhood and adolescence, give up hope of being loved themselves, especially since they habitually conceal their real natures.' He continues:

> But the hope rises itself again when they start to create: so they become intensely sensitive about what they produce, more sensitive than about their own defended personalities in ordinary social life. To mind more about one's book or painting than one does about oneself will seem strange to those who are sure enough of themselves to *be* themselves in social relations. But if a book or painting contains more of the real person than is ever shown in ordinary life, it is not surprising that the producer of it is hypersensitive.[17]

The competition between John and Paul as to who was to get the 'A' of the next single or the largest number of credits on the next album was crucially more important to John than to Paul. For John, the rejection of his work was seen as a loss of self.

As *Sergeant Pepper* captured the air waves, it reflected the zeitgeist of the 1967 Summer of Love, West Coast 'be ins', 'happenings' and communes. The Beatles took it upon themselves to buy a collection of small Greek Islands. According to Marianne Faithfull, the idea was put forward by John. Seemingly it was a repeat of the communal living of Weybridge he had envisaged years before. During this time of the potential purchase, The Beatles had been introduced, via Barry Miles, to an amicable young Greek, whom the band christened Magic Alex. Alex's father, according to the version of events he gave at the time, was either a Colonel in the Greek Army or an officer in the Greek Army Intelligence. John in particular gave patronage to the young Greek, who was to all intents and purposes a bluffer extraordinaire in the realms of electronics, sound and light gizmos and high end recording equipment. Magic Alex was the inventor who professed to be capable of spinning crap into gold. He was in fact a TV repairman.

Magic Alex was brought in to act as the intermediary to the purchase of the islands from the Greek government. One sticking point of conscience might have occurred to The Beatles, especially given their growing interest in the teachings by the Maharishi Mahesh Yogi of the ideas of Peace, Love and Happiness. Six months previous to The Beatles' intended island purchase, the democratically elected government of Greece was toppled by a fascist military junta. The Greek press was censored and any opponents to the junta were tracked down, jailed and tortured. Particular targets for this treatment were students – long hair and rock 'n' roll were banned. Brian confided to his friend Nat Weiss that he thought it 'was a dotty idea' and consequently kept in the background. Magic Alex, always eager to please, negotiated the sale of the islands, pitching to the Greek officials the public relations coup that The Beatles residence could give to the regime. Also in the deal was the stipulation that The Beatles were to receive diplomatic immunity in that their luggage was not to be searched, the intent being for The Beatles' entourage to bring in as much dope and acid as they needed. In return for this, the band would pose for Ministry of Tourism publicity shots.

It seems perverse to think that a couple of months previously, The Beatles were in front of a worldwide TV audience of 400 million promoting their latest sing, 'All You Need is Love', while soon to be negotiating with a military dictatorship who imprisoned and exiled thousands of political opponents and detained thousands more in torture centres. It may have been a case of ignorance of the situation in Greece, but this seems doubtful. More than likely everybody knew the island was just a pipe dream. But once begun, the notion of a Greek idyll would have to be played out. The move encountered predicable glitches, the main one being the problematic need to exchange Sterling into Greek currency in order to buy the islands. This issue dragged, interest drifted into indifference and eventually, the idea became a minor embarrassment. The Greek commune was, unfortunately for John, his first venture into dealing with revolutionary politics, but it would be in the form of cuddling up to a military dictatorship.

It was only a matter of time before George's interest in all things Indian would move towards Transcendental Meditation (TM) and his eventual introduction to Indian guru Maharishi Yogi. This became a key aspect for the rest of his life. John's commitment towards TM was pragmatic – unlike George, who was looking for spiritual enlightenment, John was looking for peace of mind. Since Beatlemania, a large part of his life had been spent concentrating on writing songs alone or with Paul in the recording studio, or on the road performing. His free time was spent dossing around the sterile environment of Weybridge, mulling over what might have been. His social-ising consisted of being fawned over by sycophants and cup-bearers whilst in nightclubs getting high on drink or drugs. Unlike Paul, who could get along with anyone and had a large circle of friends who could educate and stimulate him, John never had this kind of confidence.

The semi-structured pattern of the Maharishi's teachings were welcomed by John, not just on the level of finding inner peace; just as important, and supporting this inner peace, was the interaction with people who weren't just hangers on. Being treated as an equal by others in the TM programme was exactly what John needed in terms of dealing with his torment and being overwhelmed by his own emotions without resorting to a life of self-medication.

Like John, Brian was trying to find himself. He was also having serious problems with depression. The band's decision to stop touring affected Brian in many of the same ways it affected John – lack of status, lack of a time structure and a lack of formal and informal socialising with The Beatles. Brian was never consulted on this crucial decision to stop playing live. At first he assumed 'his boys' were just a bit fed up and carried on making bookings, without their knowledge, but eventually, he accepted there would be no more touring. Brian was due to travel to North Wales to meet up with The Beatles and the Maharishi. Instead, after a weekend of disappointments, and of no-show guests at his weekend country home in Kingsley Hill, Brian returned to his Chapel Street home in London. He was found dead on 27 August, due to an accidental mixture of barbitu-rates and drink.

When the news arrived of Brian's death, The Beatles were crushed. The fact that they were away from their homes, surrounded by a frenzy of reporters and their inescapable popping of camera bulbs and glare of TV cameras, made it all the more painful. The sudden and overwhelming sorrow that was visited on them in North Wales had left them exposed and bereft of privacy for their grief. Brian, for all his business miscalculations, for all the conflict and pain his own sexuality brought, together with his temper tantrums was still the only one who in 1962 had believed in them. It was Brian who banged the drum for all to hear, who realised how good they were, who watched over them as though they were his blood. And now he was gone. 'I thought, we're fucked',[18] said John.

The massive blow to John was worsened by the fact that his relationship with Brian was so complex. What Brian and The Beatles had achieved and experienced together was immeasurable. Brian's sudden death threatened not a collapse of The Beatles' financial empire, but a collapse of the buffers and common areas of access. Brian had the negotiating skills essential to accommodate the dynamics within the core of the band: he was not as skilled at being a business manager as he was at being a counsellor and a friend. He provided 'neutral space' in the shape of his home, just as a mother would for her grown-up children to come together. His home, along with his office, eliminated the awkwardness and hierarchies that would have accompanied meeting at each other's homes. This provision of communal space was essential for The Beatles' flexibility and they would miss the spur of the moment 'letter drop' facility that Brian had offered: 'Let Paul know...', 'Tell Ringo I'll...'

Johnny Gustafson, whose band The Big Three were managed by Brian, recalls:

> Brian never seemed to have any close friends like we all did. I noticed that any men we saw him with, we would never see them again. Generally it was the wrong period for that man... he was too naïve. He learned about life in general later than the bands did. The musicians were very down to earth; we'd learned how to cope with the world partly through the Hamburg scene. But Brian had no grounding: he stepped right in at the deep end and was sucked into the whirlpool of drugs. And he had neither the experience to know how to escape from it nor the stamina to do anything about it. It was very sad and really upset me.[19]

CHAPTER SIXTEEN

1967–68
Foothills of the Himalayas

FOLLOWING THE DEATH of Brian and the global success of *Sergeant Pepper*, Paul's confidence in his ability to bring The Beatles together was such that he naturally assumed the role of unofficial leader. He looked towards building on the critical achievement of *Sergeant Pepper*. In the preceding 12 months, Paul had developed a keen interest in films and filmmaking. He had extended his interest from gifted amateur to conversing with the likes of Antonioni and Warhol. Paul's Cavendish Road home became a salon, around which the merits of the film genres of Italian Neorealism and German Expressionism could be discussed in great detail. Out of Paul's burgeoning interest in film came what was to become The Beatles' next venture. If John thought it was bad enough being outfitted in Pear-Drop-coloured suits for *Sergeant Pepper*, then Paul's next wheeze would see him involved with hand-held cameras, dressing up in more over-the-top costumes and sharing 100-mile coach journey with 50 actors and extras. The name painted on the side of the coach would inform the passengers of what they could expect: a Magical Mystery Tour.

The *Magical Mystery Tour* was meant to be a marriage of West Coast fun and weirdness tied to French New Wave cinéma verité technique using hand-held cameras in documentary style, but in the end, the reality was that The Beatles ended up with a good soundtrack, a charabanc and Paul pointing a camera and telling people where to stand. Part of Paul's notion, like the original idea for *Sergeant Pepper*, was rooted in his childhood – Paul would recall life as a youngster in Liverpool where neighbours would club together and hire a bus and driver to take them on a day out. The destination of the bus was a mystery, known only to the driver; but as Paul points out, it was usually Blackpool. The only mystery was why some of the neighbours on the coach didn't know this.

The notion that spawned the *Magical Mystery Tour* came from the American author Ken Kesey. While employed on the 'graveyard shift' as a member of care staff in a California veterans' psychiatric hospital, Kesey watched with interest as the medics administered LSD as a form of 'medication'. During his observations, 28-year-old Kesey not only offered himself as a paid recipient for the military-funded LSD testing at the hospital, but also began writing a novel based on the mind manipulation by corporate America played out in a hospital psychiatric wing. The novel was *One Flew over the Cuckoo's Nest*. The film rights were sold to Kirk Douglas for $28,000. Kesey then used this money to finance a trip with a collection of proto-hippies, crossing America to the 1964 World's Fair in New York where they handed out free, and legal, samples of LSD to all those who had the inclination of 'taking a trip'; soon after, in 1966, the drug was to be made illegal in the United States. The early exploits of Kesey and his entourage of 'Merry Pranksters' are chronicled by journalist Tom Wolfe in *The Electric Kool-Aid Acid Test*.

Using this and a very large leap of imagination, Paul decided to emulate the Merry Pranksters' journey. Instead of Kesey's DIY group-painted dayglow school bus, Paul's Mystery Tour took place in a bespoke hand-painted charabanc. While the Merry Pranksters zipped along Route 66 into Arizona and the New Mexico deserts, the Mystery Tour passengers waited at traffic lights on the A34 trying to make their way to Cornwall and Devon. The reason that *Magical Mystery Tour*, apart from its excellent soundtrack, was such a patent failure was not because The Beatles had overreached themselves; for the first time, they were unoriginal. Their attempt to use as a template the complicated combination of non-conformists, anarchists, seasoned drug users and a liberal dispensation of acid taken over a 5,000-mile coast-to-coast journey and to apply it to a sedate trip to south-west England was never going to happen.

The latter half of 1967 was taken up with producing *Magical Mystery Tour,* with a Christmas deadline for an airing on BBC TV. As the shooting of the film was taking place, so was the soundtrack recording. John was unhappy about the timescale he was given to complete new tracks for the proposed project. One of the reasons for his lukewarm attitude was that Paul had come to the table laden with completed songs, leaving him to play catch-up. John recalled after the break-up of The Beatles that, 'Paul had a tendency to come along and say, well he's written his ten songs, let's record now'.[1] In the end, John only contributed one song to the soundtrack of *Magical Mystery Tour* in the shape of 'I am the Walrus'.

In many ways, 'I am the Walrus' could be seen as John's first shot across the bow to Paul's steady takeover of The Beatles. Although John came to see the song as a particular favourite, nevertheless, the dirge-like tune with John spitting out a contemptuous and bitter vocal of nonsense lyrics worked out better than he initially expected. It is also worth noting that the 'yellow custard' references in 'I am the Walrus' are a (probably deliberate) 'mishearing' of a rhyme that had been popular in post-war Liverpool, where groups of children playing at 'making mud' in water-filled holes on bomb-sites would chant: '*Jolla molla* custard, green snot pie all mixed up with a dead dog's eye.'

John's accusation that Paul stockpiled songs until he was ready to begin a new album was in part true, but why shouldn't Paul continue to write on his own? John did. The days of an eyeball-to-eyeball partnership in their songwriting had long gone. The previous year, in an interview John gave to *Beatles Monthly*, he explained:

> It's too easy to put it off if we just meet without any plan and say, 'Shall we write something today?' If you do that you feel as though you're losing a free day. What we're going to do is make dates before-hand and sort of say, 'Right, Wednesday...'.[2]

In his own way, Paul did try to help John with his songs, indeed, more than the other way around. This is not to say Paul in this respect was more generous than John, more that he was better organised and more disciplined. Whereas John flags up as 'It's too easy to put it off...' Paul's attitude was far more pragmatic:

> We would normally be rung a couple of weeks before the recording session and they'd say, 'We're recording in a month's time and you've got a week off before the recordings to write some stuff.' You'd say, 'Oh, great, fabulous.' So I'd go out to John's every day for the week, and the rest of the time was just time off. We always wrote a song a day, whatever happened, we always wrote a song a day. And after that I'd pack up and drive back home and go out for the evening and that was it.[3]

Almost always, it was Paul who went to John's home in Kenwood. Only occasionally did John travel into London to work on songs. But if Paul were to travel out to Weybridge time after time with only *his* songs to work on, it would have looked like bad form.

John knew what Paul was like. Fortunately for The Beatles, Paul couldn't stop writing. The real reason for the complaint was that John's own inertia towards songwriting was making it easy for Paul to be seen as the leader of the band. Pete Shotton noted how, from the very moment John and Paul met at St Peter's Fête, from day one, in John's mind, he would have to look over his shoulder and wait for the time when Paul would be ready to push him aside as leader.

It could be argued, during this period of John's problems with lack of confidence, that Paul could have given him more support concerning his mental health, although this could have done more harm than good. Firstly, Paul wasn't totally privy to what John's particular issues were. To Paul it seemed a general malaise, brought on by too much drug taking. Secondly, approaching John on any personal level to do with his attitude and demeanour was problematic. Paul knew John and was aware that an offer to help on such a personal level could have been construed as patronising and ultimately would have ended in disaster. John's complicated emotional health issues and drug taking were too deeply ingrained for Paul to attempt a walk down memory lane, recalling the times at the art college, Hamburg and the *Ed Sullivan Show* in an effort to make a breach into John's prison of spiralling ill health. Notwithstanding the difficulties in the group at that particular time, if Paul could have helped John he would have, because he genuinely loved him.

Unfortunately, on *Sergeant Pepper* and *Magical Mystery Tour*, Paul took the reins of leading the group, but he did so in a cack-handed way that the rest of The Beatles were bound to chafe against. The obvious difference between *Sergeant Pepper* and *Magical Mystery Tour* (the film) was one of success. The achievement in album sales of *Sergeant Pepper* made it in some ways acceptable to the rest of The Beatles to go along with Paul's dominance in the studio. But when it came to the failure of *Magical Mystery Tour*, serious doubts were cast on Paul's ability to produce the goods. As *Magical Mystery Tour* progressed, it again became evident that Paul's well-meaning intentions of guidance left no room for equality. Eventually, Paul ended up coming across as a chivvying good friend, always there lecturing and informing about what was best. The one point of democracy that Paul conceded was in the script. This was probably due to Paul finding out that writing a script was not as easy as he first thought. He divvied out sections of loosely formulated scenes for the project that the other Beatles needed to contribute. In the end, scenes were written on scraps of paper, napkins and palms of hands. Eventually, it was agreed not to bother, but go with a loose idea based on a collection of scenes. The Beatles therefore decided that when it came to a screenplay they would be better off not being 'restrained'. In the film industry the belief is that you can make a bad film out of a good script but you can't make a good film out of a bad script. There was no mention about making a film without a script.

As *Magical Mystery Tour* was being put together, The Beatles found themselves pressed to come up with a new single. Paul had completed a song that would give the fans just what they wanted. In the theme of *Sergeant Pepper* and 'All You Need is Love', 'Hello Goodbye' seemed a seamless continuation of the multi-coloured 'Summer of Love', but 'Hello Goodbye' was a song which both John and George hated. In the promotional film for the song we see a glum, despondent George making no attempt to disguise his contempt for being made to dress up as another frock-coated *Sergeant Pepper* lookalike.

Notwithstanding both John and George's reservations, 'Hello Goodbye' was the second biggest selling Beatles single after 'She Loves You', spending seven weeks at number one. Paul had produced the goods again. How could John argue? John did argue, but he didn't have an answer to the question he had asked himself – how best to make an exit from The Beatles. He was in a bind. Leaving The Beatles was like being a guest at the Hotel California – you can check out anytime but you can never leave.

A year before, in November 1966, John had been invited to the opening of an avant-garde exhibition entitled 'Unfinished Paintings and Objects', promoted by his friend John Dunbar at the Indica Gallery in London. The gallery was part owned by Dunbar and Paul's friends Barry Miles and Peter Asher. The art exhibits that John saw that night consisted of items such as an apple on sale for £2,000, recordings of snow falling and, for the charge of five shillings, hammering an imaginary nail. To carry out the task, John reportedly offered payment of an imaginary five shillings. Dunbar introduced John to the artist responsible for the works, Yoko Ono. The pair chatted and struck up a rapport. The surreal and ridiculous elements struck a chord with John. Besides his music, he needed something else to fully complement his artistic temperament. The exhibition gave him an idea as to how to address this.

John, like many artists, was trying to communicate his inner-feelings through his art, but in his case these feelings produced a wealth of sorrow. Storr points out that 'the work may be a much more valid piece of self-expression than what is revealed in action or conversation in "real life"'.[4] John started to look at what he believed the limited sphere of 'normal' music held and began to contemplate more adventures in the form of art. In the months that followed the exhibition, Yoko contacted John by letter. According to Ray Coleman in *Lennon: The Definitive Biography*, John received a steady stream of letters from Yoko, some centring on avant-garde art, some asking for financial support towards her artistic ventures. Haiku poems and cards arrived at Kenwood, and this postal correspondence was followed by phone calls from Yoko repeating the request for John to provide financial backing for her exhibitions.

John's chauffeur, Les Anthony, who drove John into London on that night in 1966, gives an alternative view of John and Yoko's first meeting. He recalls John in the Indica meandering around, uninterested in the exhibition, and, after a short time, leaving. This was followed by Yoko chasing after John, totally contradicting the version provided by John and Yoko. The meeting at the Indica was given as the 'authorised' version, but this doesn't seem to have been the case. Paul had been approached previously by Yoko, who was making a request for original Beatles song manuscripts to be used as a gift for the 50th birthday of John Cage. Paul in turn suggested she contact John, who apparently gave her the original manuscript of 'The Word'. This manuscript is shown in John Cage's *Notations*, a collection of original musical manuscripts donated to the Foundation of Contemporary Performance, which displays a wide range of modern music. In *Notations*, the reader is informed that the manuscript was given to Cage by Yoko Ono. Yoko met Paul in 1965, almost a full 12 months before the apparent first meeting with John. Yoko was hungry for success and also to ingratiate herself with Cage, who could help with her career.

The problem with 'The Beatles Story' is that with the passage of time there becomes a continuous layer of different interpretations of the same events. And picking through the minefield of all those who knew The Beatles and getting an accurate description of events can be difficult, as in the case of the sacking of Pete Best. The Beatles story is riddled with inconsistencies, misdirection and 'credibility gaps'; John and Yoko's version of events that first night at the Indica may be accurate, or Les

Anthony's may be the truthful version, or it may be somewhere in between. What is certainly true is that events relating to The Beatles from 1968 until their ultimate break-up are as clear as mud.

Prior to their trip to India, The Beatles entered Abbey Road to record John's 'Across the Universe'. The recording turned out to be nowhere near to his liking. After The Beatles broke up, John believed Paul would 'sort of, subconsciously, try and destroy a great song.' It seems unlikely that Paul would 'destroy' 'Across the Universe', but whether he did or didn't is not as important as the point that *John believed it*. He called it a 'lousy track' and gave it to the World Wildlife Fund to raise funds. John's next effort during this time in the studio was 'Hey Bulldog'. This didn't fare much better than 'Across the Universe'. That being said, Abbey Road sound engineer Geoff Emerick recalls that 'Hey Bulldog' turned out so well that there was talk of putting it out as a single, relegating 'Lady Madonna' to the 'B' side. According to Emerick, George Martin ruled out this possibility by announcing that it was too late to make the change as the record sleeves had already been printed. It seems unlikely that this would be a valid reason; printing alternative record labels would never interfere with a Beatles single release. Secondly, George Martin was a hired hand – albeit an influential and important one, but nonetheless, his salary was paid for by The Beatles. He wouldn't be in a position to push John's song out of being an 'A' side. Whatever the real reason, John's hopes of bringing some sort of credibility back into the Beatles singles list sank.

John went from seeing 'Hey Bulldog' as being a contender for the next Beatles single to it being relegated to the 'half album' of *Yellow Submarine*. Here it rubbed shoulders with the title track, which was getting its third 'airing', and George's whimsical 'It's All Too Much' (which also deserved a better outlet). Two other tracks on the album were 'Only a Northern Song' and 'All Together Now', both throwaways – so bad it's only a shame they weren't thrown further. For the first time in ten Beatles singles, John had no part to play in either side of the release of 'Lady Madonna'. Instead, it was covered by 'Inner Light', George's tune attached to the words of a section of the Tao Te Ching. If John had hoped that his efforts in the studio would contribute in a positive way to supporting his fragile state of mind, then 'Hey Bulldog' was not going to be the one. As far as John was concerned, he was drowning and Paul was throwing rocks at him.

At the beginning of 1968, John received a visit from his father at Kenwood. Freddie had tried an ill-fated reunion some years before at the height of Beatlemania. But the visit foundered when he allowed himself to be used by the tabloid newspapers to gain personal information on John. The instant fame went to Freddie's head. Newspaper reporters went digging for controversial and personal quotes from 'John Lennon's long-lost dad'. Pint-sized Freddie may have been casting his mind back to his triumphant 'appearance' in wartime New York at Jack Dempsey's Bar. He declared to the gleeful reporters: 'I told him that he got his talent from me. I don't want to sound boastful, but I was doing what John was doing 25 years ago – and better'.[5] It was the first attempt at reconciliation between father and son, and it didn't go well.

Perhaps it had a lot to do with what was going on in John's life during Beatlemania and perhaps he categorised his dad as one of the hundreds of hangers-on that he was beating off with a stick. Freddie was criticised by John for being seen as a bum and being on the mooch for money. He wasn't, but in John's mind, his father was to blame for all his years of sadness. A second meeting took place at Kenwood where Freddie turned up unannounced. John slammed the door in his face. The third meeting turned out to be more amicable.

In 1967, Charlie Lennon (Freddie's younger brother) had recently found out that John believed his father was fully responsible for the break-up of his parents' marriage. 'It's about time you stopped listening to lies about your father and understand that it was not his fault,' Charlie wrote to John at Weybridge in an attempt to set the record straight, 'that his marriage broke up, any man coming home from sea to find his wife pregnant would have the right to ask for a divorce, but your father forgave your mother and took her back. Despite all that she ended up by walking out on him for someone else'.[6]

The contents of Charlie's letter shook John – never before had an alternative version of events surrounding the break-up of his parents' marriage been put to him. The letter from his uncle came a week before the death of Brian. This forced John to reconsider his view of his father, especially so when Freddie sent John a letter of condolence for Brian's death. The personal and emotional confusion of Brian's death and the introduction of Yoko Ono into John's life made reconciliation with his father a worthwhile consideration.

Following the letters from John's Uncle Charlie and Freddie, John wrote to his father. The letter that Freddie received from John gives some insight into the changes that were taking place in his life. The second half of the letter reads:

> I know it will be a bit awkward when we first meet and maybe for a few more meetings, but there's hope for us yet. I'm glad you didn't land yourself with a bloody big family; it's put me off seeing you a little. I've enough family to last me a few lifetimes. Write if you feel like. Love John PS Don't spread it (press I mean). I don't want Mimi cracking up.[7]

The nature of John's letter shows it being conciliatory and also to carry a sense of uncertainty: 'Write if you feel like.' The slightly confusing reference to the size of Freddie's family followed by, 'I've had enough of family to last me a few lifetimes,' is strange in that John's family, by any comparison, was small – there was some contact with Mimi's side, but this was sporadic and brief. His family from the age of five to fourteen was Mimi and George, and while George supported and cared for the young John, he played a small part in forming John's personality and had no significant impact on his discontented frame of mind. So why had John had enough of families to last him a few lifetimes? The clue to understanding this last point is in the 'PS'. At the time of the letter being written, John was in his late 20s and had abundant wealth and fame. He was fêted wherever he went and yet a possible reunion with his estranged father causes him concern and anxiety? The fear of the news of this meeting of father and son finding its way back to Mimi filled John with dread.

Around the time of Freddie's visit to Kenwood, John had further contact with Yoko who had organised another exhibition at the Lisson Gallery. John did not attend the exhibition, which bore the title 'Yoko and Me'. The undisclosed 'Me' was the patron of the exhibition, who was John. Yoko's overtures to John for funding had paid off. The attraction of Yoko to John was not initially sexual. For John it was a case of hoping to find someone – at long last – who could become a confidante and support his move to leave The Beatles.

In John's mind there was no one else out there to help him. Cynthia was seen as part of his guilt-ridden, domesticated lifestyle and thus part of the problem. The only people in whom he could have confided were dead. Initially, Yoko's presence within the Lennon household seemed innocent. Cynthia and John were apparently amused at a newspaper article reviewing Yoko's exhibition of close-up shots of people's bottoms. According to Cynthia, John's comment was: 'She can't be serious!'[8] It was not until later, when the letters began arriving from Yoko at Kenwood and Cynthia noticed John's keen interest in Yoko's book of haiku poetry, *Grapefruit*, that she began to question if there was more to John's interest than she first believed.

Cynthia's concern over Yoko's presence was the least of her problems. Her main and immediate worry was John's heavy drug use. Besides Cynthia's alarm over John's health, there was also a lack of comprehension as to why it had developed. Casting her mind back to Mimi, she questioned whether John's drug use was as a means of 'blotting out the pain of his childhood?' Cynthia observed:

> It seemed to me that, initially, success had done that. In the first couple of years, as The Beatles soared, John had been on a high and his confidence had blossomed. But eventually the fame and idolising had become too much, and I believe he had turned to drugs to escape. He soon became addicted to them.[9]

This was what was at the heart of what worried Cynthia – drugs John was using to try to come to terms with Mendips, and life since then. 'Once you're so depressed that you get into drugs, once you're on them, it's very, very hard to see the light or to have any kind of hope.' John himself was to declare: 'All you think about is the drug, and it's no good to us preaching at people and sayings don't take them, because that doesn't work'.[10]

Cynthia tried to make sense of John's mental state with reference to The Beatles' initial worldwide success and why this contentment didn't continue. But maintaining a healthy frame of mind doesn't depend on celebrity and adulation. Anthony Storr, in *The Dynamics of Creation*, points out that:

> Success does bring self-esteem reassurance and even elation to the depressive – but the improvement is generally short-lived. In the end, no amount of external success compensates for what has not been incorporated in early childhood.[11]

The beneficial effects of The Beatles' fame and fortune had petered out. Drugs weren't the answer and John's tolerance level was growing by the week. Philosopher and author Arthur Koestler's recollection of an experimental trip on LSD was not in sync with the much lauded 'mind blowing experience' of the '60s hippy generation: 'This is wonderful no doubt, but it is fake, ersatz, instant mysticism... I solved the secret of the universe last night, but this morning I forgot what it was'.[12]

John needed to look beyond the notion of fame and fortune, not to mention his lifestyle of drugs and cronies in Kenwood. Long before John met Yoko, his marriage to Cynthia was going through a rough period. The life he led in Kenwood, where he had far too much time to think, had now begun to be strongly associated with this bleak outlook. His indifference to Cynthia was matched by the apparent indifference to Julian, with whom he spent little personal time. On these occasions John would often bully and scream at the child for the least transgression. Julian found himself bearing the brunt of anger that was a spinoff of his parents' hollow marriage, and, more importantly, what had taken place in his father's own childhood. Miller contends:

> The fact that parents often abuse or neglect their children in the same manner that they themselves were abused or neglected by their own parents, even if (and especially if) they no longer have the slightest memory of those times, shows that they stored up their own traumas in their bodies. Otherwise they could not possibly reproduce them, which they do with amazing accuracy, an accuracy that comes to light as soon as they are prepared to feel their own helplessness instead of working it off on their own children and misusing their power.[13]

Even as John was at the height of his fame, he still found himself being held hostage to his childhood and repeating the patterns of his own 'parent', Mimi. His attitude towards Julian was in many ways one of indifference, not helped by the manner of John's divorce from Cynthia.

In an interview given in the late 1990s, Julian Lennon still felt the hurt over his father's conduct at this time:

> I have to say that, from my point of view, I felt he was a hypocrite. Dad could talk about peace and love out loud to the world but he could never show it to the people who supposedly meant the most to him: his wife and son. How can you talk about peace and love and have a family in bits and pieces.[14]

The issue of John's attitude towards Cynthia, Julian and close friends is complex. His aggressive and disdainful behaviour to a large extent can be traced to his own lack of emotional wellbeing and while it is reasonable to apply the adage of 'love the sinner, hate the sin', if one is on the receiving end of the 'sin', it is difficult to sympathise with their distress while they are causing you pain. Part of John's abusive attitude was due to the discontented state he found himself in, but he still had a responsibility to act with decent human kindness to others. Sadly, on many occasions, he failed to do this.

John was not totally unaware of the effects of his aggressive attitude and the opportunity which transcendental meditation presented became an attractive proposition. The Beatles, led by George, now made an even greater commitment to their mediation, with a two-month trip to the Maharishi's mediation retreat in Rishikesh, in the foothills of the Himalayas in northern India. John, Cynthia, George and Pattie arrived in mid-February, while Paul, Jane, Ringo and Maureen arrived four days later. The trip to Rishikesh showed a firm commitment by The Beatles to deal with the increasing pressure of their fame without recourse to drugs or drink. Ringo's early departure after a couple of weeks was a combination of Maureen's phobia of insects and his own childhood ailments. His stomach made the local foodstuffs a torture. He actually brought a suitcase full of Heinz beans in expectation of his dietary needs. Ringo's half-joking remarks about Rishikesh was that it was 'a bit too much like Butlins', the British holiday camp chain, may have rung true to Ringo with the ashram's regimental structure of set times for meals, lectures and meditation. This, though, is exactly what John needed. It was something to distract him from the recurring thought patterns of hopelessness and pessimism.

An added bonus at Rishikesh was the diversion and stimulation of the party of friends such as Donovan and new friends such as actress Mia Farrow and Beach Boy Mike Love and an assortment of authors and musicians also at the retreat. Previously, John's inability to allow himself to 'be himself' meant that he avoided social anxiety by never really being himself with others. The isolated nature of Rishikesh meant relative privacy. It's not surprising that during a period of eight hours' meditation per day and a disciplined order lifted John's spirit. It moved him to complete 15 new songs during his time at the ashram. Also revealing is that outside of John's eventual fallout with the Maharishi over allegations of the guru's conduct with women at the camp, John never came across as insulting or aggressive in the time he spent there.

Cynthia knew the marriage was in real trouble when John decided not to share a bedroom with her at Rishikesh. The reason John gave was that it would help with the meditation – this despite the fact that the other Beatles and their respective partners shared a bed while there. What Cynthia didn't know was that John and Yoko were exchanging letters and telegrams on a daily basis. Eventually, Cynthia began to be completely ignored by John.

The conventional wisdom is that Yoko Ono broke up The Beatles. This view is based largely on prejudice and ignorance. It is true that John's relationship with Yoko *contributed* to the break-up of The Beatles. Nothing Yoko did or said, with reference to the rest of The Beatles was done without John's blessing. This was to become obvious as the making of the *White Album* progressed. The simple reason for John's initial need for Yoko was that she was so utterly different from what he had been used to – how she looked, her sophistication, culture and background in art – so there was no history, no triggers that could set off the raw winds of despair with him. Yoko was a fresh start. Maybe the fresh start began earlier than we have been led to believe.

Following their initial meeting at the Indica Gallery in November 1966, and the approaches made by Yoko to John by letter and phone, in which she sought funds for her work, a second meeting took place when the Maharishi's assistant gave instructions concerning the trip to Rishikesh at a house in London. Here, Yoko was in attendance. She sat alone and silent, away from The Beatles and their partners. Afterwards, to the surprise of Cynthia and the apparent surprise of John, Yoko jumped uninvited into their car and requested to be dropped off at her home.

Considering the amount of interest from the press and public that The Beatles generated, it's fair to assume that this meeting was known only to The Beatles' close friends and associates. It was likely that Yoko attended the meeting through an invitation by John. It could be that the relationship of John and Yoko began earlier than they were later to claim.

A month before Yoko's 'carjacking', she had held another exhibition at the Lisson Gallery. Prior to this exhibition, Pete Shotton, who was employed by The Beatles at the Apple office, recalls a conversation with John concerning Yoko: 'Since she's an artist maybe I should try and help her out.' John told him, 'I haven't a clue what she wants, but I've told her to go and see you at Apple.' John continued, 'maybe there's something you can do for her.' Yoko came to the office. Pete Shotton recalls her entering the Apple office in a very tentative manner, seemingly uncertain of how to say what she wanted. What she wanted was £2,000 to fund her exhibition. Shotton was surprised by the figure requested (at today's value this would be £60,000). Before handing any money over he contacted John; John's response was 'give her what she wants'.[15]

The unusual aspect of this was that although John could be very generous when the mood took him, he wasn't a soft touch and he wasn't stupid with money. The question is why should he give away such a large amount to a person he had apparently only met a few times, and never alone? Why should he tell Pete Shotton he hadn't 'a clue what she wants' when for over six months Yoko had sent a steady stream of letters and made numerous phone calls requesting financial support for her projects? It could well be that Pete Shotton was used as a cover for the money leaving The Beatles' account.

Cynthia was encouraged by John to go on holiday to Greece with Magic Alex, Jennie Boyd and Gypsy Dave, a friend of Donovan's. Julian had been taken from Kenwood to be looked after by his nanny. It was during this time that John chose to invite Yoko to Kenwood. The same night Yoko arrived at Kenwood, John had invited Pete Shotton over to watch TV. Later on he commented to Pete Shotton that it would be 'nice to have a woman's company around'.[16] From there, John proceeded to telephone Yoko in London. John's casual, off the cuff, *oh, I just think I'll invite that Japanese artist over*, as reported by Pete Shotton, is at odds with John having paid Yoko's taxi fare from London. 'Usually he didn't handle money at all,' Pete Shotton recalls, 'so I was really impressed that he had the whole thing so carefully planned out'.[17]

Over the course of the next eight hours, John and Yoko produced the *Two Virgins* album in Kenwood's home studio. The album was in line with his previous venture into the avant-garde music scene – he describes it as 'far out stuff, some comedy stuff, and some electronic music'. *Two Virgins* was started at midnight and finished at dawn and then, John says, 'we made love... It was very beautiful'.[18] John and Yoko would later put the album out with the infamous photographs of them naked on the cover. The album is a good example of when artists confuse chaos with creativity.

The beginning of their relationship was complicated, but even taking into account Yoko being married with a child, the end of both marriages could have been achieved in a more honest and dignified manner than what transpired. Pete Shotton was invited there by John specifically to give witness to the whole one of those 'it just happened' events. In reality, what was being put into motion that night at Kenwood was a damage limitation exercise by John and Yoko, to mask the brutal, pre-planned event to come, which was Cynthia Lennon coming home to find her husband had moved in a 'new wife'. The likelihood is that John and Yoko had been having a relationship long before that night at Kenwood.

Within hours of the completion of the *Two Virgins* album, the *coup de grâce* to John and Cynthia's marriage was delivered upon her return home from Greece. She was confronted in Kenwood by John and Yoko sitting causally cross-legged on the floor, Yoko wearing one of Cynthia's towelled robes. 'Oh hi,' said John. Yoko ignored her. In shock, all Cynthia could think to do was to ask them if they wanted to come for dinner. 'The stupidity of that question,' she recalls, 'has haunted me ever since'.[19]

It's undeniable that John and Yoko were in love, but there was also a practical aspect to the relationship. Yoko had gained access to John's wealth, status and connections. For John, this was a way to get himself out of The Beatles through the predictable irritation he knew Yoko would cause in the studio. John wanted two things. He wanted to keep his wealth and his fame. And he didn't want to find himself in the throes of another depression. By freeing himself from The Beatles and moving into radical politics and the peace movement, coupled with Yoko's avant-garde alternative lifestyle and ambition, he could achieve these goals.

A week after John and Yoko had made their *Two Virgins* album, The Beatles prepared to go back into Abbey Road to record *The Beatles*, which would become known, almost instantly, as the *White Album*. John's mental health had begun to improve. This was due to a combination of reducing his drug intake, Rishikesh and his relationship with Yoko. John had not been in the studio since the middle of February and didn't return there for recording purposes until the end of May, a period of three and a half months. This was three and a half months without feeling helpless and inadequate under the gaze of Paul and George Martin. Abbey Road in the previous year had become the House of Horrors where many a time he would have to be stoned just to set foot through the door.

But now, with John and Yoko's relationship public knowledge, this was going to be his declaration of independence. Things were going to change. There would be no more being pushed aside when it came to the recording of his songs. This time John had Yoko in his corner, and when he and Yoko walked into Studio Two hand-in-hand, it was obvious to all those in the room that the brown stuff was about to hit the fan.

CHAPTER SEVENTEEN

1968
Abbey Road

WHEN THE BEATLES returned to the studios in May, John's life had undergone a radical change, and his marriage to Cynthia had moved closer to its end. After she found John and Yoko together, Cynthia fled Kenwood in shock, only to return a few days later to be reassured by John that the 'incident' with Yoko was of no importance. John informed her that he was returning to Abbey Road and would be committed to long hours in the studio. He suggested a holiday to Italy for Cynthia, along with Julian and their nanny. While Cynthia was in Italy, she received a letter from John's solicitor. He had filed for divorce. Regardless of what others thought of his treatment of Cynthia, John was committed to Yoko. It was in Yoko that he had put his faith to help challenge his low self-esteem and despondency.

Given his previous 18 months of lethargy, his marriage being in the doldrums and a new partner, whom the other Beatles and many others found 'strange', the recording of the *White Album* was always going to be stressful and tense. The fact that Yoko played an active part in the recording increased this tension enormously. John and Yoko were a team that went everywhere together. The *White Album* was to be a template of this unity. John felt that the album was his favourite and personal best with The Beatles. Due to the particular issues of drugs and his mental health, the creative aspect of John's character had been subdued from the start of *Sergeant Pepper* until now.

This time, John was determined not to be outshone or undermined by Paul's superior studio skills. The dissatisfaction John felt turned itself into a powerful tool for creativity. But his return to the studio with Yoko joined to his hip immediately had an unsettling effect on the other members of the band. The long-standing, many times unspoken, mutual understanding of John, Paul, George and Ringo was coming to an end.

John had always had a myopic tendency and a 'talent' to leap on the weakness of others. The weakness he identified now was that, as the

White Album developed, it became apparent that the other members of the band didn't want The Beatles to end, at least not at this particular time, but John conducted himself as if actively wanting the group to cease. John could now ignore their feelings. The John who returned to the studio had no intention of submitting to the needs of Paul. No more caring if Paul was George Martin's type of musician, no more acquiescing to The Beatles' musical needs; if it meant that he had to be arrogant, disrespectful or bombastic, then so be it. He had started The Beatles, it was *his* band and he wasn't going to work for or be told what to do by a junior partner in the firm that he founded.

From John's view point, he entered Abbey Road as leader, *John and The Beatles*; a different and dispassionate John was back, and with a new lover and partner for his art, this was John at his Hamburg, hard-faced, couldn't give a shit 'best'. Except this time it wasn't a drunken Kaiserkeller crowd that was confronted and mocked, it was the rest of The Beatles.

The *White Album* was The Beatles' first and only double album. The collection of songs that John, Paul, George and Ringo wrote while at Rishikesh would result in 30 new tracks being recorded. During the four and a half months it took to complete the album, longer even than the making of *Sergeant Pepper*, it turned into a form of emotional guerrilla warfare. The binding commitment of John and Yoko to each other resulted in Yoko accompanying him almost everywhere; this included almost all the *White Album* recording sessions. John's output of songs along with Paul, George and Ringo meant that the new album was going to have to be a double.

Such were the convoluted personal undercurrents within The Beatles, any consideration of culling the number of the songs they brought back from India would more than likely have resulted in the band's dissolution there and then. Criticisms of the content of the *White Album* centre on the sheer range of the songs themselves. Bringing together the likes of 'Rocky Raccoon', 'Revolution 9', 'Yer Blues' and 'Martha My Dear' was always going to present a challenge of 'theme'. In some ways, recording 30 songs, many demanding in their arrangement and delivery, over a period of four and a half months, within a maelstrom of personal and emotional discontent, was a great achievement – it is a credit to The Beatles that they even completed the album.

Having compromised in the early days and changed his tough guy

Hamburg 'leather uniform' image, now John had changed again... to a pastel coloured, braided and frock-coated suit. In his early days, John was of the opinion that 'avant-garde is French for shite'. But it was avant-garde that was going to play an important part in his ambition to leave The Beatles.

After The Beatles broke up, John was questioned as to when he had felt the band would end. The answer John gave was the *Sergeant Pepper* period. When pushed to be more specific by the interviewer, John replied, 'I don't remember. I was in my own pain'.[1] Kay Redfield Jamison has carried out detailed studies on those with depression who are also artists of one form or another. She believes there is a strong relationship between the creativity of these people and the swings within their mental health:

> Their associations are genuinely unusual. And having extremes of emotion is a gift – the capacity to be passionately involved in life, to care deeply about things, to feel hurt: a lot of people don't have that. And it is the transition in and out of the highs and lows, the constant contrast that can foster creativity.[2]

During the time recording the *White Album*, John's sense of hurt was kept under wraps. But he still sought some kind of collective responsibility from the rest of The Beatles who had, as he believed, in some way contributed to his sense of dejection. Paul couldn't comprehend why John had brought Yoko to the studio. He didn't get it. But it was obvious to John that Paul wanted to take over, and to rub salt into the wound the only person in the world who didn't recognised John as the leader of The Beatles was Paul himself. *Sergeant Pepper* was all about Paul, as was *Magical Mystery Tour*, yet Paul couldn't see how this displacement of John as the group's leader would affect him.

After five years in a succession of different line-ups in groups, John had been the driver behind The Beatles achieving their breakthrough success. Since Beatlemania, millions identified John as the focal point of The Beatles, yet it didn't seem to occur to Paul that taking John's crown would not be accepted by John. A combined effort of support by Paul, George and Ringo may have helped with John's illness, but it wasn't identified by them and thus no such support was made available. In addition, perhaps some consideration could have been shown towards the allocation of 'A' side singles, with reference to the inclusion of John's work, because with hindsight, what was good for the record sales wasn't necessarily good for the *whole* of the band. But being with Yoko meant John was back in control.

The introduction of Yoko as the new partner to John caught the rest of The Beatles by surprise. At first they found her presence strange, then awkward, then downright annoying. The reason Yoko at first wasn't taken too seriously as a threat to the group by Paul, George and Ringo was because they weren't privy to the troubles John had faced in the previous 18 months, and just how important Yoko was to him in dealing with his bleak mental disorder. But it wasn't long before Yoko had found her stride, making her opinions known to the rest of The Beatles and studio staff, at times coming across as subtle as a lead cosh. The view of the other Beatles was that her presence wouldn't last for long: it couldn't. But it did.

Yoko's background – her high-status upbringing and knowledge of the art world – had helped John regain some of his confidence in trying to come to terms with his diminishing influence in the group, and this is what he had been lacking in the two previous visits to Abbey Road. His drug abuse and depression revealed John to be in a very fragile and vulnerable state when he met Yoko. Yoko had been educated in the exclusive private school of Gakushuin, near the Imperial Palace, where she shared the same class with Akihito, the future Emperor of Japan. Her father was a one-time professional classical pianist. She was part of the eminent and powerful Yasuda banking family and a descendant of the Emperor. As with a many couples of the upper classes during that era in Japan, Yoko's parents had an arranged marriage, but the marriage would have been of Yoko's mother's choosing because 'my mother could have married anyone at all, being from one of the richest families in Japan'.[3]

After hostilities ceased between America and Japan in 1946, Yoko's father's position in banking took him to Scarsdale, New York. Yoko accompanied him and received an American education in Sarah Lawrence College, where she gained an insight into the bohemian side of New York. From her late teens, Yoko immersed herself in bohemian life as an avant-garde artist in the 1950s New York alternative arts community. In 1956, she married and later divorced Japanese composer Tochi Ichiyanagi. By the time she meet John, she had been married for a second time to American jazz musician, sometime film producer and art exhibition promoter, Anthony Cox. Their daughter Kyoko was born a year after Julian Lennon in 1963. When Yoko arrived in London in late 1965, despite her family's wealth, she was low on cash but hungry for success.

Six years after the 'sink or swim' experience of Hamburg, John had found himself firmly entrenched in rock star malaise. Yoko, despite her privileged background, had ducked and dived around the world for the past six years, mixing with a wide range of artists from the sincere to the glad-handers, back-stair crawlers and those with more faces than Big Ben. All these artists were all after the same thing – commissions for their work – Yoko was among them, ambitious and hungry for patronage of her art; while at the exact same time, John lay stoned at home, languidly awaiting a new muse.

John couldn't make a clean break with The Beatles. It didn't make sense. He had issued divorce papers to Cynthia while she was on holiday with their son. He had been having an affair with a married woman. The woman in question was tiny. She dressed in 'weird' clothes, had an 'odd' hairstyle, took photographs of people's bums, spoke like Betty Boop and came from the Far East. As a Beatle, there was some chance of John gaining a degree of acceptance of his relationship by the general public, but without his position as a Beatle, there wouldn't have been a snow-ball's chance in hell of his being accepted in any way or form by all but a small group of supporters and friends. For a time, he needed to be a Beatle in order to make the transition towards his own artistic and personal progression complete.

As John's relationship with Yoko progressed, he could now achieve what he had wished for since his time as a student. At Liverpool Art College with Stu, John craved to be a liberated, bohemian hipster, writing for the smart set. Instead, he found himself with a job, working as a 'Beatle' and rather than being with the smart set, he had to make do with an audience of hysterical, screaming 14-year-old girls. Now all this could be put behind him. His art now was going to be firmly influenced by Yoko. There was going to be change in his music. This change had already started before the *White Album* and it had its roots with Stuart Sutcliffe.

Everything about Stu had been different. His outlook, lifestyle, dress sense, talent, background; and John liked the notion of *different*. John's conversion to an alternative perspective of art had been made easier by Stu, who had already carried out the spade work back in Liverpool. John coveted everything about Stu – his educated and cultured family, his good looks, sense of cool, *everything*. John's manufactured, working-class virility clashed with his complex search for himself as a poet-artist. When Yoko was selling John the idea of avant-garde, she was pushing at an open door.

If John had decided he didn't need The Beatles, and it was no longer *his* band, then why should he be bothered about being seen as insensitive or concerned about their needs? To him they were passé. He required The Beatles in name only. He needed them as a status umbrella for his and Yoko's own projects. The Beatles served a purpose up until such time as he decided they didn't, at which point he could make a convenient exit.

The gradual introduction of Yoko would cause friction among the other Beatles to the extent that they would be happy to disband. John was not going to leave The Beatles to remain intact without him, certainly not a McCartney-led band which could well go on to bigger and better things without him: 'I started the band, I disbanded it. It's as simple as that,' was John's outlook.[4] By remaining a Beatle, John could use this time along with his fame and the finances of the band to support an alternative life as an artist with Yoko. But to fully complete his life with Yoko, The Beatles must end. 'In the case of people with a predominately depressive psychopathology, it is likely that the destruction precedes, rather than follows, the development of the new approach'.[5]

But the The Beatles' break-up was not down purely to one particular factor, the presence of Yoko. The break-up was more to do with the fact that the band members had developed in divergent musical directions, artistic changes that had overtaken The Beatles during the previous year.

It was obvious, well before the recording of the *White Album*, that John's lyrics were far more personal than those of Paul. The raft of songs brought back from Rishikesh by John and Paul heightened this contrast with John's introspective subject matter starkly at odds with Paul's eclectic use of pop. The most significant song reflecting on John's psyche was 'Julia', a joint homage to his mother and Yoko. John's whole outlook in life was shaped by his childhood, tied to the apron strings of misery:

> When this is so, the work, rather than the person, becomes the focus of self-esteem. Many people of this temperament during the course of childhood and adolescence give up hope of being loved for themselves especially since they habitually conceal their real natures.[6]

Anthony Storr's argument that art can offer comfort and understanding to depression, cited earlier, is clearly relevant again here. Storr's view gives a valuable insight into John's extreme defensiveness and feelings of being slighted when it came to his name being eased off The Beatles' singles roster, coupled with George Martin's and Paul's studio interpretation of *his* songs. The quickly deduced difference between John's first-person narrative and Paul's third-person within their songs held more importance than 'John's songs are a more personal statement'. John's songs were about his own existence. The lack of validation given to his songs was a lack of validation to his sense of self. This was going to change.

One venture which could have extended the life of The Beatles was their newly-formed company, Apple, in giving them the opportunity individually and as a team to develop new artistic talent. Instead, the reverse became the case. Apple contributed to a speeding up of the deterioration of relationships within the group. The formation of Apple was initially conceived as a means of paying less tax; Brian Epstein had been constantly on the lookout for ways in which The Beatles and himself could avoid the punitive British taxes ever since the group first made it into the high earnings tax band. Brian made arrangements for one such tax avoidance scheme by having The Beatles shoot scenes for *Help!* in the tax haven of Bermuda. After Brian's death, they were faced with a financial choice of £2 million which they had earned going to Her Majesty's Income and Revenue, or, alternatively, they could form a company to offset tax payable: 'we decided to play businessmen for a bit because we've got to run our own affairs now,' John recalled. 'So we've got this thing called "Apple" which is going to be records films, electronics – which all tie up'.[7]

Unfortunately for The Beatles, things didn't 'tie up'. To a large extent, the arms of Apple (film, electronics, studio, publishing, retail) were not a success, but the records division, unsurprisingly, was. The problem for The Beatles was that because of the nature of who they were as public figures, any failure of Apple was writ large. This was the case when TV cameras reported the chaotic scenes at the free for all in Apple's Baker Street boutique when it closed down. The closure was due to a combination of shoplifting, financial failure of the store, and The Beatles not really being that interested in being retailers. The entire stock was given away.

'Basically it was chaos,' George recalls:

We just gave away huge quantities of money. It was a lesson to anybody not to have a partnership, because when you're in a partnership with other people you can't do anything about it (or it's very difficult to), and at that point we were naïve. Basically, I think John and Paul got carried away with the idea and blew millions, Ringo and I just had to go along with it.[8]

The 'savings' of the £2 million that would have gone to the tax man in the long run proved to be a doubled-edged sword. There were successes – in the record division they signed the likes of James Taylor, Mary Hopkins and Badfinger. Whereas Paul involved himself with Apple artists such as the Black Dyke Mills Band, George with his old Liverpool friend and ex-Undertakers band member Jackie Lomax and Ringo with John Tavener, a classical musician and composer, John and Yoko never involved themselves in any other projects.

One of the first projects John and Yoko undertook was to distribute their *Two Virgins* album on the newly formed Apple label. John characterised themselves as 'two innocents in a world gone bad'.[9] The album consisted of tape loops and sound effects of musical instruments. The content in itself would have been difficult enough to sell. The contents of *Two Virgins* was never a floor-filler at the local clubs, but the sleeve packaging of a black and white photograph of John and Yoko standing full-length naked before the camera (shot at Ringo's Montagu Square flat) was going to be a tough call for the advertising people.

On the release of *Two Virgins*, Bryce Hanmer Ltd, The Beatles' financial advisor, resigned in protest over the nudity and John's use of drugs. Although put out on the Apple label, EMI refused to distribute it and in the end Track Records, run by The Who's managers Kit Lambert and Chris Stamp, acted as distributors. On John's part, The *Two Virgins* cover may be seen as an endorsement of Yoko's artistic tenets, her unorthodox confrontation of established norms and values, or it may have been a casting off of the 'old John' and a move towards bringing a quicker end to The Beatles.

John later commented that he had expected the rest of The Beatles to accept Yoko as 'one of them' while recording the *White Album*, but her presence raised the level of tension, as John no doubt knew it would. The previous atmosphere of cooperation was gone, fostering an 'I'm alright Jack' attitude, which was the polar opposite of what brought about The

Beatles' success. The 'family' stance that The Beatles had taken to protect each other was now lost to the insularity of the individual, and the introduction of emotional damage limitation. The four and a half months in the studio making the *White Album* would later be seen as a portrait of group dynamics in free-fall.

When The Beatles recorded *Sergeant Pepper*, John could not in any way or form have succeeded in introducing Yoko as he did with the *White Album*. There are a number of reasons for this, but the main and most elementary one was the essential need for the various degrees of musical collaboration between The Beatles in the studio. By contrast, many of the songs that came out of Rishikesh to be included on the *White Album* would lend themselves to a personal or independent production. Recording components which would have been thought up to include the entire band were now about limiting the other Beatles to side-men, or total exclusion. John's work in the studio, wrapped up with Yoko's constant presence, led to reluctance by the rest of the band to wait until invited to be involved.

This 'do your own thing' attitude carried itself over to such an extent that John, Paul and George could be found working on their own songs in separate studios at the same time. The result was a less than tolerant attitude when it did come to working on one another's songs. This isolationist approach was facilitated by the growing technical recording proficiency of The Beatles within Abbey Road. The result was a lack of reliance on each other's input, or that of George Martin. The early years of cooperation were replaced by increasing self-sufficiency.

The political unrest of the late 1960s, coinciding with the making of the *White Album*, saw John taking an interest in New Left politics. This meant a convenient amnesia about The Beatles' last venture into politics. It was only a short nine months previously that they were seeking to secure a life in Greece, where the military junta was in the process of torturing dissidents by jumping on their stomach or pulling out their toenails and fingernails. Miles remembers John's views on this subject: '"I'm not worried about the political situation in Greece, as long as it doesn't affect us," Lennon declared. "I don't care if the government is all fascist or communist."' Barry Miles recalls, 'I was horrified, I remember it. Paul was faintly embarrassed by it all, but John wasn't concerned'.[10]

The sad aspect of The Beatles' moral blindness on this issue is that the mentality of the Greek generals was not too far removed from those in the southern states of America in 1966. Those who saw John as the antichrist not only burned Beatles records but also burned crosses on people's lawns. It's difficult to know if John's road to Damascus conversion in his political views came about through genuine conviction or whether it was seen as a badge of honour – a move towards revolutionary chic and a further step away from the notion of 'loveable Beatles'.

'The year of Revolution', as 1968 was later termed, dovetailed with John and Yoko's own radical agenda in their music and their art. On the first of July, John ventured into his new art form by holding his own art exhibition, *You Are Here*, at friend Robert Fraser's Duke Street gallery in London. The show consisted, amongst other exhibits, of a rusty bicycle (donated by a local art college) and a collection of charity boxes. The previous year had witnessed a series of riots in many Afro-America areas of US cities. Anti-war demonstrations were increasing by the month. One in particular numbered a quarter of a million in New York. 1967 was a precursor for 1968, when an even greater number of anti-Vietnam war demonstrations and sit-ins took place.

Violent clashes between demonstrators and police on the streets of major cities around the world became commonplace. The invasion of Czechoslovakia by the USSR in 1968 and the gunning down of over 300 Mexican students and civilian protesters by the paramilitary before the Olympics were cases in point. Parisian students formed an alliance with 11 million French workers, which led to a national strike lasting two weeks in protest against the government and six weeks of street battles and confusion in Paris. It was against this backdrop that John chose the development of 'Revolution 1'. While the song's intention was to support the revolutionary zeal of the time, it came under attack by the New Left and, perversely, attracted support from the Right. The single version – the B-side to 'Hey Jude' – talks of the revolutionary destruction he wants no part of, but the lyric was changed in the album version, alternating 'out' with 'in', introducing an ambiguity that drew flak from both Left and Right on the political spectrum. The John Birch Society magazine gave this analysis:

> The Beatles are simply telling the Maoists that Fabian gradualism is working, and that the Maoists might blow it all by getting the public excited before things are ready for 'revolution' – 'it's gonna be all

right'. In short, 'Revolution' takes the Moscow line against Trotsky-ites and the Progressive Labor Party.[11]

In many aspects, far more radical than 'Revolution 1' was John and Yoko's 'Revolution 9'. 'Revolution 9', while it was never going to be a Beatles fan favourite, was at least an honest effort by John and Yoko at presenting a radical form of music to the general public. If avant-garde was about anything, it was about challenging preconceived assumptions and society's norms and values. It could be argued that 'Revolution 9' was a lot more interesting and challenging than the pedestrian and tepid 'greeting card' platitudes of 'All You Need is Love'. There just might have been a hidden agenda for the inclusion of 'Revolution 9' on the *White Album* as a test to see how far John and Yoko could bend the other Beatles to their will with its acceptance on the album.

Studio engineer Emerick recalls how, after the completion of 'Revolution 9', John asked Paul his opinion. Tactfully, Paul responded with 'not bad'. John snapped back:

> You have no idea what you're talking about. In fact, this should be our next bloody single! This is the direction the Beatles should be going in from now on.[12]

Paul was, not surprisingly, hurt by John's indifference to him inside the studio and out. Only recently, Paul had gone out of his way to support John by offering him and Yoko a safe haven from the press, after John's break-up with Cynthia. John and Yoko had accepted, only to move out a few weeks later.

This is another example of John's ability to freeze people out and compartmentalise situations, an attitude which Paul was at a loss to understand. But for John to be *himself*, subconsciously and consciously, he had to fight his upbringing. And it was these very values (Paul's strengths) which he had come to strongly associate with the punitive regime of Mendips. Paul's simple belief was that, in order to gain the recognition he desperately wanted, he needed to socialise with anyone and everyone on the road to stardom; John viewed this as 'phoniness', which ran counter to what he needed. What John needed was to save his *self* and in order to achieve this, he needed to kick against conformity and acknowledge and validate the injustice and pain in his life. So when John was to witness Paul at his 'best', charming all and sundry, buckling down to the needs of the studio, essentially bending to the needs of success (and the needs of The Beatles), this reminded him too much of the template that was laid out for him in Mendips as to what was needed to get on in life; to be someone just like Paul.

At the time of John and Cynthia's divorce, Paul also had his own cross to bear. In the middle of July, his long-term relationship with Jane Asher came to an end in a most public manner. Jane announced to presenter Simon Dee on the BBC1 chat show *Dee Time*: 'My engagement to Paul is off!'.[13] Paul was absolutely devastated: 'I hadn't broken it off!' Apple aide Alistair Taylor recalls: 'Jane's departure shattered him. It was the only time I ever saw him totally distraught and lost for words'.[14] This blow to Paul's ego further served to deplete what little goodwill existed within Abbey Road. While the Spartan conditions of Studio Two had served The Beatles well in the past, now the working environment began to match the feelings of Paul, George and Ringo. Emerick recalls the setting of harsh fluorescent tube lighting and 'bare brick walls adorned with huge mattresses stuffed with seaweed' in an effort to add some sparkle:

> EMI gave us exactly three fluorescent tubes with coloured gels wrapped around them, clumsily done. Needless to say, they gave out almost no colour whatsoever, but they remained, nonetheless, a mute symbol of the incompetence we had to put up with every day.[15]

It was easy for The Beatles to see the workman-like conditions of the studio as a prison. The condition and sour atmosphere claimed its first casualty in mid July. Emerick, who had worked with The Beatles for five years, quit, worn down by the miserable, unpleasant atmosphere and the group's relentless quarrels. A couple of weeks later, a criticism by Paul over Ringo's drumming on 'Back in the USSR' resulted in Ringo walking out, only returning after a two-week holiday abroad.

> I felt I was playing like shit. And those three were really getting on. I had this feeling that nobody loved me. I felt horrible. So I said to myself, 'What am I doing here? Those three are getting along so well and I'm not even playing well.' That was madness, so I went away on holiday to sort things out. I don't know, maybe I was just paranoid. To play in a band you have to trust each other.[16]

What could have been some kind of return to normality in the shape of their new single only widened the divide between John and the rest of the band. 'Hey Jude', which was never intended for the *White Album*, was performed on a September edition of the TV *Frost Programme* in front of a 300-strong participating audience. It looked like a return to the 'All You Need is Love' TV session. This time it was Paul who took centre stage, playing a grand piano and 'lording it up' on another 'Paul song' while John sat glumly on the floor with his guitar and contributed nothing to the opening bars. For all John's determination to do it alone on the *White Album*, he still couldn't produce a single that the others would support. By now most Beatle fans were fully aware of which singles were Paul's and which were John's, and they could see that more were coming from Paul. 'Hey Jude' went on to sell a massive five million copies in the first six months. It stayed at the number one position of the American charts for nine consecutive weeks. As much as John was regaining more control in the studio, the outside audience belonged to Paul.

Rishikesh helped detoxify John in body and mind, but he still found it hard to shake off his depression. John recalls, 'In "Yer Blues", when I wrote I'm so lonely I want to die, I wasn't kidding. That's how I felt... up there, to reach God and feeling suicidal'.[17] William Styron, who fought for many years with this crippling illness, wrote:

> Never let it be doubted that depression, in its extreme form, is madness. The madness results from an aberrant biochemical process. With all this upheaval in the brain tissues, the alternate drenching and deprivation, it is no wonder that the mind begins to feel aggrieved, stricken, and the muddied thought processes register the distress of an organ in convulsion.[18]

The fact that John's illness was mixed with his drug use made it far harder to identify and support. Only with hindsight does the weight of the crosses he bore become evident. While recording the *White Album*, to promote *The John Lennon Play: In His Own Write*, John gave an interview to the BBC2 arts programme *Release* concerning the roles of the American, Russian and Chinese governments:

> I think our society is run by insane people for insane objectives and I sussed that when I was 16 and 12, way down the line... I think they're all insane. But I'm liable to be put away for being insane for

expressing that, you know, that's what's insane about it. That's what's insane about it... It's not just a bit strange it's insane... Half the people watching this are going to be saying, 'Oh what's he saying? What's he saying?' You are being run by people who are insane, and you don't know it.[19]

Even though John hadn't yet found his political footing to articulate his views, nevertheless his previous press conferences with The Beatles had given him enough experience of interviews to deliver a much more eloquent view of political manipulation. The reasons why this turned out to be a jumbled rant may have had its roots in the stress and anxiety around the risk of him and Yoko becoming figures of public ridicule. It could also be attributed to the beginnings of John's use of heroin.

John's fragile state of mind made it easy for him to seek out and identify hard drugs as the answer. When William Burroughs was asked why he had become an addict, Burroughs replied flatly that a person didn't need a reason to become an addict; he needed a reason not to become one. John also identified Yoko as someone who could unconsciously protect and support him. Yoko became his safe house. In psychoanalytical terms, 'transference' indicates the 'inappropriate repetition in the present of a relationship that was important in a person's childhood'. It may seem a cliché when the term 'mother figure' is used to express a person's outlook and feelings towards a dominant female. Nevertheless, it seems that such a relationship existed between John and Yoko.

In his youth, John sought the protective cloak of masculinity to cover up his insecurities. Now he looked to Yoko for the same protection via an alternative form of creativity. The combination of strength and affection are what John transferred onto Yoko, but not in equal measures. The main influence of the transference is to be found in his 15 years spent with Mimi. John found himself facing 'the redirection of feelings and desires and especially of those unconsciously retained from childhood toward a new object',[20] together with 'a reproduction of emotions relating to repressed experiences, especially of childhood, and the substitution of another person... for the original object of the repressed impulses.'

The increasing amount of 'partnership responsibilities' that John gave to Yoko in the studio correlated to the increasing amount of tension in the band. Paul tried to counter-attack by bringing his new girlfriend to the studio, but this didn't last long. George made a better go of it with the introduction of a guest musician in the shape of Eric Clapton to play on 'While My Guitar Gently Weeps', regardless of what the others thought. But no matter who was brought in and no matter how many lips were curled and asides made against Yoko, Yoko didn't 'bite'. She had mastered not being affected by insults to a fine art; she just didn't *do* being offended. Trying to insult Yoko was like trying to herd cats. And strangely, the less offended she became, the more her confidence grew and she in turn offended everyone and anyone. 'She was soon treating us like a servant to order about,' recalls Pete Shotton. 'That's when it got hard. She rubbed lots of people up the wrong way.' George Martin declared that 'everyone was irritated by her'.[21]

Yoko's affluent background and her corresponding lack of under-standing of the customs and culture of working-class life may have con-tributed towards some of the tensions she caused. The residue of the Japanese caste system may well have been at play in the treatment of studio staff and The Beatles' entourage. For Yoko – with her private tutoring in etiquette, her ballet lessons, her social and educational needs catered for by a team of tutors and servants – dealing with those, to coin a Mimi term 'lower-class types' could be problematic. Not long after The Beatles broke up, John and Yoko gave an interview in which they discussed poverty:

JOHN: I'm not sure. I don't think I've ever been poverty stricken, so I don't know what it is. It's probably a pretty tough scene. It depends on the people though I suppose.

YOKO: There must be a line where it becomes masochism. I'm sure there are ways of getting out of poverty and there's a point whether you either decide to get out or not.

INTERVIEWER: A lot of people don't control their own destiny.

JOHN: We're hardly allowed to, the way things are set up.

YOKO: I find this in many people who are poor; it's a state of mind. They have a certain kind of pride that's almost incomprehensible.[22]

John shows sympathy and identifies the structural problems of society (such as employment) in the shape of a 'set up', whereas Yoko classifies poverty as a personal defect, a kind of bio-determinism. This apparent lack of compassion and understanding may have been at play in her treatment of those around her in the Abbey Road studios. Maybe residual ripples of the old Japanese system influenced Yoko in her assessment of the other Beatles – one whose father was a bus driver, another a minor office clerk and yet another a painter and decorator for the local council. They were obviously not merchant banking material, so why take their sons seriously?

The taxing recording sessions were followed in John and Yoko's case by even more anxiety and uncertainty as they were arrested on a drugs charge. While still living at Montagu Square, police raided the flat and found 219 grams of cannabis resin. John and Yoko were charged at Paddington Green Police Station with possession and obstructing the execution of the search warrant. At the time of the arrest, Yoko was pregnant. Due to this and to avoid the complications of possible deportation, John admitted to possession and was eventually fined £150 with 20 guineas of costs.

Two weeks after their arrest, *Two Virgins* was released in America. The notoriety of its cover meant that brown paper wrapping obscured the 'offending' parts of the photograph and the 30,000 copies that arrived in New Jersey were confiscated by the police. The album was roundly criticised as a pretentious collage of sound passing as art. Almost all the time during his fame, John's name had been inevitably followed by Paul, George and Ringo; now it was Yoko. The public categorically *didn't like it*. Initially, John believed he could deal with the criticism and pressure, but he'd totally underestimated the rapidly changing perception of him in the eyes of the British – and American – public.

John believed all those years as a mop top Beatle mattered for something. He was convinced that he'd be spared most of the general public's prejudices, but he misjudged. The public didn't like John's relationship with Yoko because it was all wrong. But what was it that they saw as wrong? That Yoko was Japanese, that Yoko was a radical conceptual artist, that Yoko was small and dressed in unusual arty clothes? Or maybe it was because Yoko wasn't Cynthia. The British, American and world public had invested a huge amount of interest, affection and love in John and, from their point of view, all this emotional deposit had been stolen by *this Japanese woman*. Worse still John had *let her*. This being the case, the public demanded justice, justice in the sense of pillorying them both in every conceivable medium and in every conceivable aspect of their lives.

A week after *Two Virgins* was released in America, Yoko was admitted to the Queen Charlotte's Hospital in London over concerns about the pregnancy. John stayed and slept in a bed next to her, and when the bed was needed for another patient he slept on the floor, thus forming the basis for the track 'No Bed for John' on their album *Life with the Lions*. On 21 November, Yoko miscarried. Whether the reason for Yoko and John's loss was the stress of the drugs arrest and the following trial, or the continuing pressure of being ridiculed by every tabloid newspaper and third-rate comic, or – according to Barry Miles – Yoko's previous abortions while with Tony Cox, or the element of drugs in their lives, or a combination of all (or none), no one could tell. The unborn child was named John Ono Lennon II and was interred at an undisclosed location.

The year ended for John and Yoko with a combination of tragedy, notoriety and farce. A few days before Christmas 1968, author Ken Kesey arrived at the Apple Office on Savile Row. He was invited to London for *Paperback Records*, a spoken-word project initiated by Apple. With Kesey came an entourage of flotsam and jetsam of the West Coast's counter-culture, which included a couple of Hells Angels (Old Bert and Smooth Sam Smathers) who brought with them their Harley Davidsons. Kesey's group were invited to Apple's Christmas drinks and dinner party, at which a fight ensued (or to be more accurate, Old Bert punched another guest over the accusation of him being a freeloader). Kesey recalls that, when it looked like an all-out melee might ensue between 'Yanks and Limeys', into the room stepped John, resplendent in Father Christmas robes, false white beard and red gown. Behind him stood Yoko dressed as Mother Christmas. At the sight of John those in the room froze, as John spoke, 'Awright then'. Kesey recalls: 'the thin white hands coming out of the white fur cuffs to hold back the two sides of the room like Moses holding back the waters,'. 'That's enough,' John declared.[23] The tension left the room and later John and Yoko in their role as Father and Mother Christmas dished out presents to the staff and their children complete with a series of festive 'Ho, Ho, Hos'.

Kesey saw John a few times after the near 'gunfight at the Savile Row Corral' and attended John and Yoko's Alchemical Wedding at The Royal Albert Hall. The performance consisted of the couple entering a large white bag on stage for 30 minutes while a flute played. During the perfor-mance a member of the audience rushed onto the stage, waving a banner condemning the British Government's role in the war of the African state of Biafra. He shouted at the bag, 'Do you care, John Lennon? Do you care?' A saddened and disappointed Kesey described this event as 'public humping' inside a bag. Despite this disillusionment, Kesey's lasting memory of John remained that of his appearance a few days earlier:

> I never saw anything as bright and clear and courageous as when he stepped between the two sides at the Christmas party. He was something. When he said 'Peace' even the warring angels listened.[24]

The proposed spoken word project with Apple's Paperback Records was never completed. The initiative, just like The Beatles themselves, fell apart. That day of the office party at Savile Row would be the last Christmas that The Beatles would gather together under one roof. The huge amount of mutual goodwill they had accumulated for each other over the past ten years and more, the thousand and more gigs, the travelling and the triumphs in the studio would finally bleed out. When the New Year of 1969 was rung in, it would see the convulsions and demise of quite easily the most influential set of musicians and songwriters the world has seen in modern times.

CHAPTER EIGHTEEN

1969
Savile Row

THE BIGGEST STUMBLING block to any kind of amicable working relationship during the making of the *White Album* and *Let it Be* was ignorance. Paul was still almost totally ignorant of the strong feelings of dislike that John held for him. If he had been privy to John's feelings, he could have had a choice of leaving the band there and then, or keeping out of John's way, or copying John's exit strategy of managed release from The Beatles. Paul's attitude to John was not much different to when they were boarding an old Commer van in the early 1960s and heading down the East Lancashire Road for a gig in Newton-Le-Willows or Manchester: Paul may well have felt that: *John's an awkward bugger with a big mouth, but he means well.* What Paul didn't grasp was that in John's eyes, Paul's increasing influence in the group meant the previous joking notion of '*awkward bugger*', had taken on a new and different dimension.

John's belief was that, in the studio, Paul was George Martin's 'blue-eyed boy', prompting him to get his retaliation in first. He told Martin with reference to the next album, *Let it Be* (initially entitled *Get Back*), that he didn't want any of his 'production shit' on this album, that 'we want this to be an honest album'.[1] By extension, some of the other albums weren't 'honest'. John's message to George Martin was that Paul got too much of his own way in the studio. In the end, Abbey Road engineer Glyn Johns was brought in alongside George Martin. John's lack of trust in George didn't stop there:

> He [Paul] subconsciously tried to destroy songs, meaning that we'd play experimental games with my great pieces, like 'Strawberry Fields', which I always felt was badly recorded... That song got away with it and it worked. But usually we'd spend hours doing little detailed cleaning-ups of Paul's songs. When it came to mine, especially if it was a great song like 'Strawberry Fields' or 'Across the Universe', somehow this atmosphere of looseness and casualness and experimentation would creep in.[2]

Due to John's conviction that Paul was out to make himself leader in the studio, he wanted production techniques to be brought down to a minimum, thereby levelling the playing field between himself and Paul. But Paul also supported John to get 'back to the basics', and in addition was keen to play live, with *Let it Be,* and as previous live shows of the band cemented John's public position as leader so Paul's proposal for the band to play a large live benefitted John's status immensely. Considering Paul's absolute conviction that The Beatles were the best band on the planet, it seems farfetched to believe he would risk this mantle for some spiteful sabotage of John's work. John, for most of the time in the studio, was unprepared for the recording process which left it to Paul and George Martin to direct proceedings, which was interpreted by John as their attempt to 'destroy' his songs.

On John's minimal production diktat to George Martin, it was Paul who wanted to bring the band together by the idea of a live concert to be recorded – and Paul supported the 'no production bullshit'. The lack of live interaction also put paid to the sense of solidarity and shared experiences, now there was less and less common ground between them. After his songwriting being re-energised due to Rishikesh and the support to his confidence provided by Yoko, why then, if John felt Paul was trying to destroy his work, didn't he do something about it? The answer can be found in the same interview, when John again brings up 'Across the Universe':

> The guitars are out of tune and I'm singing out of tune 'cause I'm psychologically destroyed and nobody's supporting me or helping me with it and the song was never done properly.[3]

It's now easy to see why, when recording the track pencilled in for the *White Album,* John admits that he was 'psychologically destroyed'. The depression he suffered had such deep roots that respite had been only temporary. The recording of the song was largely unimportant. What was important was that in his hour of need, no one was there for him. In John's eyes, as he was mired in depression, Paul was flaunting his unannounced though obvious new position as leader of The Beatles.

That he wouldn't allow anyone (until Yoko) into his life to support him is to a certain extent immaterial. The main point is John's perception that he was alone. It was in this frame of mind that John went into the *Let it Be* sessions and why the sessions even outdid the *White Album* in their levels of dissatisfaction. 'We couldn't get into it. It was dreadful, dreadful feeling at Twickenham Studio,' remembers John. 'You couldn't make music at eight in the morning in a strange place with people filming you and coloured lights... I was stoned all the time and I just didn't give a shit'.[4]

What seems surprising about the *Let it Be* project is that, given the major personal changes that had taken place during the past six months and the general lack of goodwill during the previous four and a half months spent in Abbey Road studios, that the Beatles would want to put themselves in the spotlight in such a way as to be filmed five to six hours a day as they worked on new songs in harsh studio conditions. It is certainly difficult to fully comprehend. The intended result for The Beatles in Twickenham was an album of new songs and a TV spectacular based on a live concert, and that a recording of how the album was made would follow. The idea came from The Rolling Stones' recent TV show *Rock 'n' roll Circus,* where John performed 'Yer Blues' with the Dirty Mac band comprising Eric Clapton, Keith Richards and Mitch Mitchell while Yoko knelt on stage near the band covered completely in a black sheet.

One of the issues which John had no influence over, but would support his goals in achieving the demise of The Beatles, was the breakup of Paul's relationship with Jane Asher. The five-year courtship had been, despite Jane being three years younger, one of equals. The initial courtship saw Paul living in the Asher household at Wimpole Street in London's fashionable Marylebone district, before they moved into a shared home. From here he gained entry into London's upper-middle-class society via Jane's parents, who were well established in the network of London's professional 'set'. Paul entered the London art scene through Jane's brother, Peter. The break-up came about as a result of Paul's womanising. When found with another woman in the home they shared in Cavendish Avenue, not even Paul's 'come to heaven eyes' could rescue him from his fiancée's wrath. Within days, Jane's mother had arrived to collect all of her belongings.

It couldn't have come at a worse time for Paul. The John and Yoko self-absorbed road show was getting ever closer to driving him over the edge. He needed Jane's companionship and council more than ever. With Jane gone, and in such a public manner, for the first time as a Beatle, Paul felt vulnerable. Without Jane there was no confidante, no equal, no real partner. Trying to talk to John was like hammering nails into his leg. He needed someone to confide in concerning the problems that John and Yoko were bringing to his door. Paul was looking for support from a partner of his own. He needed someone of more substance than the usual women he came across, someone with a pedigree, a sense of independence someone who knew her way around, someone like Linda Eastman.

Paul had met Linda a number of times before the couple began 'going steady'. Linda was a professional freelance photographer, commissioned to photograph rock stars on and off stage. She became a well-known face on the music circuit and this is where Paul first met her. Their first real contact came when they were at a Georgie Fame concert in 1967, while Linda was carrying out a commission to shoot 'Swinging London'. They met again a few days later at the promotional party for *Sergeant Pepper*. A year later, they met again in New York, where John and Paul were giving a press conference to announce the formation of Apple.

Four months after their meeting in New York, Paul phoned her and asked to take a flight to London. Six months later, they married. It seems unusual that, given Paul's reputation as something of a serial 'woman chaser', he would 'allow' Linda to do in six months what Jane Asher couldn't in five years – make him commit to marriage. Both women were from similar backgrounds. Linda was from a wealthy sophisticated East Coast family, her father a well-known lawyer specialising in representing show business clients. Before too long, Linda, along with her young daughter Heather from her previous marriage, had moved into Paul's Cavendish Avenue home.

In the six-month period between Jane Asher calling off their engagement and Linda moving in, the whole power structure between John and Paul had shifted, again from Paul to John, The division in The Beatles, the rumours, the jockeying for position and the role of Yoko within the Apple office forced Apple press officer Derek Taylor to make this observation:

> Yeah, sure I know John thinks we hate her and that we're all a bunch of two-faced fuckers running around behind his back snivelling and bad mouthing her, sticking pins in our homemade Yoko Ono voodoo dolls, but you know and I know what's happening and that's not happening at all. No one in this building hates her. Hate; that's a very strong accusation and an extreme assumption. I can't say as I blame him for thinking that sometimes, but the reasons he feels that way is because we don't love her.[5]

On the first week of January, The Beatles met at Twickenham Studios to begin rehearsing and recording of new songs. Twickenham Studios was coincidentally the same soundstage The Beatles had used for *A Hard Day's Night* in 1964. An agreed two-week period for rehearsals was pencilled in for the project, plus the live show whose venue was as yet unspecified. The view towards playing and building up new songs while being filmed was Paul's idea. One can understand his reasoning – The Beatles as they recorded a new album with film director in the shape of Michael Lindsay-Hogg would generate a large amount of novelty and interest for its intended audience. Lindsey-Hogg had directed previous Beatles promo films for the singles 'Rain', 'Lady Madonna', 'Revolution 1' and 'Hey Jude'. He had now been given the responsibility of a professional film crew who knew exactly what they were doing. Unlike *Magical Mystery Tour*, when it seemed to be a case of 'amateur hour gone mad' and of 'What happens when I press this button, Paul?' the idea of *Let it Be* was good in itself, but The Beatles' normal time for working was to start in the studio between 8pm and 10pm, not 10am. It was a shock to the system for them to be woken by an alarm clock on a dark January winter morning.

As the chauffeur-driven luxury cars ferried each Beatle to Twickenham, there was no disguising what they would come to expect inside the factory-sized cavernous film lot. This was to be *work*; work as in doing something you don't want to do, work in the shape of what a young John warned Paul about as an apprentice wire winder with Massey & Coggins back in Liverpool. The soundstage of the Twickenham lot gateway being slammed shut would give the same reminder as that of any other factory door: *Work*.

What is immediately noticeable in the filmed rehearsals is the lethargy and general disinterest of John, George and Ringo. This response by the other three Beatles to Paul's ideal was reflected in procrastination and indifference. The getting down to the business of working on their new material turned into meandering jamming sessions of their favourite artists songs. This jamming served the purpose of a protective bubble where anything goes and no one had ownership of what should be played. This was by far more attractive than the effort needed towards working out arrangements for each other's songs.

The playing of old songs became a sort of demilitarised zone, where safety was found in the music of old rock 'n' roll heroes. These jamming sessions were an attempt to ignore the elephant in the room. What comes out at Twickenham is how much Yoko's confidence had grown. As with the *White Album,* Yoko was continually at John's side. This was a far cry from when she arrived at the Apple office less than a year before, almost incoherently and timidly requesting funds from Pete Shotton from the 'wrong side' of the desk for her projects – now she was constantly answering questions directed to John. It seemed in this interaction with other members of the band that Yoko had convinced herself she was as important as any of the other Beatles. This went as far as her forcefully putting her ideas forward on where The Beatles should hold their concerts.

With the recording of the *White Album* and Yoko's continuous presence again, the rest of The Beatles were left confused and hurt. They had to share John and their recording studio with her. Eventually, this hurt subsided into a grudging acceptance of her presence. Now it was apparent to Paul, George and Ringo that they were expected to treat her as a musical equal. Far from the light footprint that was expected of Yoko at Twickenham, the reverse was the case.

The first thing that would strike any audience member watching the finished cinema version of *Let it Be* is of the sombreness and irritability that pervades the rehearsals. George was totally dissatisfied with being given the job of just laying down chord frameworks for Paul and John's songs. It is patently obvious that he wanted to be more creative in the overall construction and not be treated as a jobbing or session musician. At the same time, Paul seemingly felt unsupported in the decisions made by himself, while his own contribution to decisions from the others was negligible. During the rehearsals, Paul inadvertently rubbed George up the wrong way by recalling the recording of 'Hey Jude'.

Paul's previous directions to George to omit his guitar solo on 'Hey Jude' instantly exposed a sore point for George and provide insight into the storage of painful memories that surround the sessions. Throughout the relatively short set of rehearsals, over the course of ten days or so, was revealed a reservoir of gripes, slights and grudges that had been building up over the previous five years. These were brought up on Twickenham's sound stage. The hurt within the group built up in the recent past found a voice on the recording of *Let it Be.* Outside of the touching boogie piano duet between Paul and Ringo, for the most part the Twickenham section of the documentary meanders along, searching for some kind of spark or even a couple of the sort of wisecracks The Beatles had come up with at a hundred or more press conferences. Considering the amount of footage shot, apart from the performance on the rooftop, there wasn't a lot to cheer about. This poses the question – why bother? A week after beginning the project, George didn't.

Critics of Paul point out that he is placed firmly at the centre of the film, but the reason for this is simple – nobody else wanted to be. Nobody wanted to be involved, full stop. So although Paul was aware of the dangers of coming across as a 'pestering good friend', he wasn't left with much option. The other Beatles showed no willingness, which reduced Paul to always trying to fill pregnant pauses in discussions, which made him appear to be constantly leading. The soulless atmosphere of Twickenham's sound stage, together with the outside temperature hovering below zero, frost covering the ground, didn't help. It was only just getting light as they set off from their homes and became dark at four o'clock in the afternoon – even Paul's persuasive and upbeat attitude couldn't lift the interest inside the rehearsal studio above half-hearted. The following conversation from the Twickenham sessions sums up the attitude and response to the project:

PAUL: I'm only trying to help you and I always hear myself trying to annoy you.

GEORGE: [sarcastically] You're not annoying me anymore.

PAUL: We've only got 12 more days so we've got to do this methodically. I hear myself saying it. I never get any support. [silence] What do you think?

JOHN: What about?

GEORGE: [aimed at John] Hear no evil, speak no evil, see no evil.

RINGO: I'm not interested.

PAUL: I don't see why any of you, if you're not interested, got yourselves into this. What's it for? It can't be for the money. Why are you here? I'm here because I want to do a show, but I really don't feel a lot of support. [silence]

PAUL: I feel terrible [to John]. Imagine if you were the only one interested. [silence] You don't say anything.

JOHN: I've said what I've been thinking.

PAUL: There's only two choices. We're going to do it or we're not gonna do it. And I want a decision. Because I'm not interested in spending my fucking days farting about here while everyone makes up their minds whether they want to do it or not, I'll do it. If everyone else wants to do it, great but I don't have to be here. [silence] We should just have it out if this one turns out to be like [the *White Album*] it should definitely be the last – for all of us. There's no point in hanging on.

GEORGE: The Beatles have been in the doldrums for at least a year... Maybe we should get a divorce.

PAUL: Well I said that at the last meeting. It's getting near.[6]

It's obvious that Paul is making a heartfelt appeal to some kind of solidarity. This falls on deaf ears. Importantly, when Paul has had enough and ready to call it a day, there's no response. This was the time for John or George to tell Paul categorically that they wanted out, but they didn't. When Paul the mediator gives up and makes an open suggestion regarding the break-up The Beatles, there are no takers. Why?

Considering the dismal content of the conversation, it is a small miracle that the *Let it Be* sessions went further than this. It didn't help that John refused to communicate with anyone other than Yoko. John's attitude was one of being forced to be where he didn't want to be and he made no attempt to hide his disinterest or obtuseness. John had miscalculated; his aim was to leave The Beatles under his own steam. With this in mind, he now found himself totally disregarding his role in the band. This self-induced listlessness combined with his use of heroin made him, at times, almost useless. Yoko covered up some of the cracks resulting from John's inertia and became his lightning conductor for most of the criticism, which in reality should have been aimed at him. At the time of the Twickenham rehearsals, the relationship between The Beatles had reached an all-time low. The rehearsals had become a feeding frenzy of old wounds being opened, perceived slights, unrecognised credits and basic downright dislikes.

Twickenham had fast become a vehicle to deliver an act of contrition and penance, where John, George and Ringo exacted penance from Paul for the sins of vanity, pride and, worst of all, of coveting the leadership of The Beatles. John demanded penance from Paul for wrenching away what John had created and the validation he needed most as leader. George demanded penance from Paul for all the times he had been treated as a kid brother. Ringo resented Paul for bringing all this unwarranted trouble to his door.

Fighting a rearguard battle to try to add some structure to the sessions Paul suggested that they all bring their own arrangements for their own songs and show the others how to play what they wanted; this is where John miscalculated, for he baulked at this suggestion. The simple reason is that this would have meant work for him, which he didn't want. John's contributions, songs-wise, apart from 'Don't Let Me Down', were poor. At this rebuff, Paul stated that they had to improve things or cancel the whole project. George agreed. John was indifferent and again almost refused to communicate with anyone beyond Yoko. George added a further area of contention by declaring he didn't want to contribute any of his songs to the proposed album, due to his belief that they wouldn't turn out as well as they would in a studio environment.

John's strategy at Twickenham had been to be there in body but not in spirit; to keep his head down and hide behind the larger than life persona of Yoko and let the others do the recording. This wasn't working out, as the notion of any recording was drifting further away. Later on in the sessions, Paul brings up the issue of ground rules regarding showing up with a positive rather than a negative attitude; if there isn't a big change in their attitude, Paul declares, then he refuses to carry on with the project. Incredibly, at this time, George was in conversation with George Martin and hadn't listened to a word Paul had said. George wasn't as interested in being a Beatle as much as Paul. It wasn't him that was fighting for the crown. What John and Paul had underestimated was how little George wanted the band to stay together. John wrongly assumed that Paul, George and Ringo possessed the same eagerness for the band to continue. In the case of George and Ringo, they had reached a point where they could take it or leave it: 'it's no fun anymore', accepted Ringo.[7]

Rather than recording, The Beatles found themselves procrastinating by engaging in long, torturous meetings at Twickenham concerning anything other than how to solve the dominant problem underlying their discontent. Huge amounts of time and energy was given over to discussing and bickering over the venue for the live concert; Paul being in favour of a live concert, Ringo unwilling to travel abroad, John not bothered, and George uninterested in any live concert. The arguments over the location and type of venue were bitter attempts to disguise the steady disintegration of The

Beatles. At the end of each day at Twickenham, Paul could have been forgiven for thinking that it couldn't get any worse. But it did.

Things came to a head just over a week into rehearsals. A row between John and George, which involved John saying he would bring in Eric Clapton to replace George, resulted in George announcing he had quit. As he departed, George suggested that the Apple press office could deal with the news of his departure in a press release and that The Beatles might want to place an advertisement in the *New Musical Express* for a replacement. After George left, the remaining Beatles began an impromptu jam session at which Yoko immediately jumped up and stood in front of the mike to take part, continuously screaming John's name.

It's not certain what caused the row between John and George. Some reports talk of fists being thrown in the studio canteen. Whatever the cause, John's off the cuff suggestion about Eric Clapton was at best insensitive and at worst crass. George's walkout left John in a dilemma – it would seem that he wanted to coast along and do minimum work until such time as he chose to leave but to do this, he needed The Beatles. He had to compromise with the other members, which he didn't want to do, and in this particular case, settle his differences with George.

After leaving the sessions, George went to visit his parents for a few days. Later he returned to London, where a meeting was held at Ringo's house with the rest of The Beatles and Yoko. Any attempts to avert the break-up of the band foundered when George again walked out, as John stubbornly offered no meaningful contribution towards discussions. George believed that only The Beatles should have been in attendance. Paul, fearful that this would result in John leaving, didn't support George, even though he agreed with his view.

The following day at rehearsals, Paul and Ringo were in attendance. George didn't show at all and John made an appearance mid-afternoon. Paul's constant appeasement of John to accommodate Yoko in the rehearsal didn't yield any positive results. John was still detached from the proceedings. He only dipped in and out of the events when the mood took him, disregarding most of what was going on around him. John's heavy use of heroin saw him turn up to many sessions sleepy-eyed and incoherent, which meant he was unable to control the situation as he wished. In many ways, this was only a logical extension of their life outside the studio.

An incident on the set revealed the level of John and Yoko's drug use.

It came when Peter Sellars visited Ringo to talk over the film *The Magic Christian*, in which they were both starring. As Sellars was leaving, John confronted him with jokes about drugs, declaring that taking drugs was better than doing exercise. In an attempt to get in on the fun, Yoko contributed with her opinion that shooting up heroin *is* exercise. Sellars, duly embarrassed, quickly made his exit. Many bonds are forged through adversity and this seemed to be the case with John and Yoko, which added to their inseparability. Eventually both John and Yoko came to see themselves as artists tortured and purged by suffering. They hoped to be redeemed by faith and fortune.

A second meeting was arranged, which resulted in a pact by all of The Beatles to finish the project, but on the proviso that they relocate the rehearsals to Apple's new recording studio in the basement of the building at Savile Row, London. The idea of a show abroad had been jettisoned in favour of a live performance in front of the camera. A week's hiatus was given for The Beatles to get the attitude right for their visit to Savile Row. In between Twickenham and the Apple basement studios, John gave an interview to *Disc & Music Echo* editor Ray Coleman. Topics ranged from macrobiotic food, raising chickens and hens, looking to buy a farm, appearing in the nude and Apple.

John made an off-the-record remark in which he revealed that Apple was losing money and that 'if it carries on like this, all of us will be broke in the next six months'.[8] This view of John's turned up in the article itself. Whether or not John fully believed the financial situation to be so dire is uncertain. The fact was that Apple was having 'inefficiency' problems at the office, but generally its financial state was nowhere near as bad as John was suggesting it was. Paul was furious, primarily because it wasn't true, but also because, as everyone knew, Apple was his 'baby'. If Apple was to get into difficulties, then John could point to Paul and claim it wasn't his concern. What was his concern though, was the complete loss of his and Paul's songwriting catalogue and this had its roots in John and Yoko being photographed naked on the cover of their album. This comment of John's on Apple's finances had the effect of not only making Paul furious, but of shocking Apple financers and Apple staff. Paul was the most protective of The Beatles when it came to their image and John's mention of possible bankruptcy made them look like incompetent, wannabe businessmen.

The second, and far more important, consequence of John's comment was to bring the alleged financial uncertainties of The Beatles to the attention of Allen Klein, a New Jersey accountant who had moved into representation of musicians and managerial involvement with Sam Cooke, The Rolling Stones and others. He had a reputation for clawing back royalties from record companies for his artists. Klein was viewed as a tenacious 'street fighter' of a businessman, short and heavy in stature and known for his toughness in negotiations. He looked like the kind of man who'd been hit by lightning and liked it. Klein had had his eye on managing The Beatles for a long time. John's remarks about the band's insolvency set wheels in motion: Klein planned to be The Beatles' next manager.

Back in rehearsals, a few days after John's 'being broke' interview, it seemed nothing had changed. The initial rehearsals at Apple carried on as they left off at Twickenham – *dire*. Then there was the appearance of keyboard player Billy Preston. He was invited to the sessions by George. Billy Preston was a friend of The Beatles from their Hamburg days, when he played with Little Richard's band. The introduction of Billy Preston transformed The Beatles. Before, they had been behaving like surly fifth formers on detention. Finally they got themselves back on track to being The Beatles. From here on in they began to respond to their own collective energy. The introduction of Billy Preston, for whom The Beatles had respect as a musician and affection as a person, had a number of significant effects of the recording of *Let it Be*. The first was the fear of someone outside their entourage bearing witness to their behaviour. More positively, the additional scope of a gifted keyboard player like Preston encouraged The Beatles to freshen up their musical ideas and interact with each other through his being an 'intermediary'. Finally, Billy Preston's growing and welcome contribution to the sessions meant a decreased role for Yoko.

What the film crew or the Apple staff thought of Yoko's role in the band was immaterial. All of The Beatles were fully aware, however, of the damage that could be caused to their reputations. If a respected musician such as Billy Preston were to reveal the poor state of John's physical and mental state and Yoko's degree of involvement in the band, it would stick. John, though, was not in the least bit stupid when it came to matters pertaining to The Beatles. For all his drug-induced partial stupor, he was well aware of the ridicule they would suffer if Yoko was seen as the 'fifth

Beatle'. It would be seen as a mere extension of his own and Yoko's ego, so like it or not, he had to toe the line – the break-up of The Beatles could wait a bit longer.

The question that comes to mind is, during the *White Album* The Beatles couldn't be made to be or play together in the same room even using a chair and a whip, so why had they committed themselves to being together in one room at Twickenham sound stage with no escape? Under those conditions, they lasted a week in each other's company. Maybe the simple answer is that they couldn't think of anything better to do. As much as John and George complained about going to Twickenham, they were grown men and nobody twisted their arm. In the case of John, part of his reason may have been that his muse was running dry in a big way. If discontent can be the spur for creativity, which was certainly the case for John with his time on the *White Album*, now John's discontent had, with the 'help' of heroin, developed into a full-blown animosity to The Beatles. These factors were to put a cap on his songwriting ability.

From the beginning of the *Let it Be* album until the break-up of The Beatles, John completed six new songs. His songs that were later used by The Beatles but written before *Let it Be* were: 'Polythene Pam', 'Mean Mr Mustard', and 'Across the Universe'. John also wrote 'I Want You (She's So Heavy)', the heart-aching 'Don't Let Me Down', 'Because', 'Sun King' and 'I Dig a Pony'. Alongside these was 'Come Together', title courtesy of Timothy Leary, music courtesy of Chuck Berry; the extremely poor 'Dig It', a full band composition, and 'One After 909', which had been written some ten years previously with Paul, 'I've Got a Feeling', a welded-together effort of a song of Paul's refrain from John. There was also John's first single since 'All You Need is Love', 'The Ballad of John and Yoko'. The music and chord sequence came from Paul's 'Paperback Writer'.

For someone with the musical gifts of John, that only six songs were produced during the period from his return from Rishikesh in April 1968 to September 1969 and the demise of The Beatles was a poor haul, even given that his 'Child of India' would be rewritten and reappear later as 'Jealous Guy'. Maybe this judgement is unfair, in that it is not comparing like with like; but just over three years previously, John had almost single-handedly completed the *Help!* album. The reasons for John's lack of input into The Beatles' music catalogue in 1969 are manifold. The most obvious one was the complications of him being a high profile, avant-garde artist and peace campaigner. He'd put himself in the public eye as never before. John's view that being a celebrity with a cause was easier than being creative was true. Shifting gear back into writing music would bring its own problems. Storr's insight into the creative block that John was going through suggests that:

> A work may be over 'determined': that is it may become so much a matter of life and death to the creator that he dare not complete it.

The issue for John was that procrastination took on epic proportions. Song-writing ceased to become songwriting as he once knew it, and became instead a constant battle for self-validation. Fear of failure becomes tortuous, as Storr continues:

> If the whole of one's self-esteem comes to be bound up in the production of a particular work, it is too dangerous to risk its exposure, and it may therefore be put off and put off by means of one excuse after another. More commonly it becomes impossible to proceed at all, although the reason for the block is generally unconscious. The torments which people suffer, and the compulsive way in which they force themselves to engage in a task which brings no pleasure, but only pain, is often highly distressing.[9]

John was in a dilemma. His music had helped him cope with his poor mental health, but since the touring stopped, a series of personal and musical crises evolved. These were his crumbling marriage, his excessive use and dependency on drugs, Paul's musical ascendancy and last but not least, the complex relationship with Yoko. All of these, not surprisingly, had profound repercussions on his friendship and working relationship with the rest of the band. All these issues turned the notion of writing songs to combat the regular waves of hopelessness he felt on its head. Now the fear of tackling songwriting brought on only further despond-ency and melancholia. The only way out was to write without fear of rejection. This is where the Plastic Ono Band served its purpose. The Plastic Ono Band, together with John and Yoko's involvement in rock-chic politics, would be the main elements which would provide John a bolt-hole from The Beatles.

The Beatles' musical differences and animosities at this time seemed to move seamlessly from the recording studio to the boardroom with bankers, financers and accountants. The financial complications of that year saw not only a split between The Beatles concerning who managed their finances, but also who was to control the rights to John and Paul's songs.

When John and Paul's recording career began, Brian had arranged for Ardmore & Beechwood to handle their royalties, but was dissatisfied by their lack of promotion of their first single 'Love Me Do'. Brian approached George Martin for the names of an alternative publishing company. He was supplied with a number of recommendations, one of which was a newly formed company owned by ex-band singer Dick James and his financial backer and silent partner, Charles Silver. After meeting Dick James, Brian signed up John and Paul to a contract of a new-ly-formed company to look specifically after their songwriting. The company was given the name Northern Songs. The basis of this company contract was 50 per cent to go to Dick James, 20 per cent to John and Paul and ten per cent to Brian. For his 50 per cent, Dick James was responsible for promoting John and Paul's music and handling the collection of the songs royalties and any requests for cover versions.

Later on, in an attempt to pay less tax and to generate income for the shareholders of Northern Songs, the company went public. The result was several hundred thousand pounds in the coffers of Northern Songs. The division of ownership now changed to (approximately) Dick James (and Silver) 37.5 per cent, John and Paul 15 per cent each, Brian seven and a half per cent with George and Ringo 0.8 per cent. This meant John and Paul had gone along with the offer of selling 25 per cent to outside 'partners' in London's financial sector. This arrangement lasted until not long after The Beatles finished recording the *Let it Be* album.

A request by Allen Klein for a meeting with John was accepted, and arranged through Derek Taylor. At the meeting, John was impressed with Klein's street savvy track record of artist representation and blue collar background. Klein had done his homework and stroked John's ego by demonstrating his familiarity with all of his work. He also flattered Yoko when he showed an interest in her work and offered to promote her exhibitions. John wanted to sign with Klein as his business representative and informed the other Beatles. Another meeting was arranged, and while George and Ringo agreed, Paul disagreed with having Klein represent them and contacted Linda's father for legal advice. Klein co-managed The Rolling Stones, so Paul also contacted Mick Jagger to seek his opinion of him. Sandwiched between these meetings, The Beatles were to make their last public appearance together, filmed by Michael Lindsey-Hogg as part of the *Let it Be* project. They made their last public appearance in an unannounced 40-minute set on top of Apple's Savile Row office on 30 January 1969.

The advice from Mick Jagger to Paul's enquiry about Klein was to steer clear. But when Jagger was called to a meeting of The Beatles at the Apple boardroom he folded under the pressure of John's enthusiasm for Klein and told The Beatles, 'he's alright, if you like that kind of thing'.[10] Paul may have understood that his own behaviour in taking over the studio during the past couple of years was selfish and tried to rectify it by accommodating John's and, indirectly, Yoko's, needs. But he wasn't prepared to extend this appeasement to John's wishes to have Klein as The Beatles' new manager. This consequently brought Paul's future brother- and father-in-law into the mix.

The power struggle for control of The Beatles was in some ways akin to two bald men fighting over a comb. All four members wouldn't have bet that the band would be in existence beyond the year's end. It could have easily ended on half a dozen occasions in the previous month. So why argue over what already seemed to be a *fait accompli*? Essentially, the feud within The Beatles just moved location from the studio to the boardroom. John understood just how much The Beatles meant to Paul. Klein gave John an opportunity to challenge Paul and to take control of something that John decided long ago he didn't want – The Beatles. This in turn would make good for all the perceived injustices that Paul had visited on him.

A month later, Klein began to represent the three other Beatles. Paul took on representation from the Eastman's law firm. Klein's brief was to look into increasing The Beatles' finances by renegotiating royalty payments while the Eastman law firm was to investigate the legal side of the The Beatles and Apple. At this time Clive Epstein, Brian's brother, approached The Beatles with an offer to sell the NEMS management contract (owned by Brian's mother, Queenie) that Brian had signed with The Beatles. The asking price was £1 million. The contract that Clive Epstein was offering guaranteed NEMS 25 per cent of The Beatles' income until 1973. This also included Brian's share of Northern Songs. Klein recommended that The Beatles should consider raising the money, some £2 million, needed to buy up the floating 14 per cent of shares on London's stock market.

John Eastman Senior erred towards caution and said that a letter should be sent to Clive Epstein seeking to find out the financial position of NEMS before any purchase. Unfortunately for John and Paul, the letter from Eastman was drafted in a heavy-handed way which implied a lack of integrity in NEMS' handling of The Beatles. Distraught by the implication that his dead brother was a crook, and before The Beatles could raise the necessary capital, Clive Epstein sold his mother's 70 per cent share in NEMS to the merchant bank Triumph Investment Trust.

Events were to get more complicated due to the relationship with 'Uncle' Dick James. After the death of Brian and the launch of Apple, John and Paul began to view their share of Northern Songs as disproportionately small. Discontent set in in their relationship with James and when John began a very public and controversial artistic and personal relationship with Yoko, James began to have grave concerns as to the value of his shares. While newly-married Paul and Linda were on their honeymoon, and coincidently at the same time as John and Yoko were on theirs, 'Uncle' Dick James and his partner sold their Northern Songs shares to Associated Television (ATV)'s Lew Grade in a deal worth £3 million made up of ATV shares and cash. Predictably, both John and Paul reacted furiously. They would have fully expected Dick James to have given them first option to buy *their* songs.

Dick James assured John and Paul that it was in their interest for him to sell to Lew Grade by 'broadening the shares base'. The reality of the situation was that if James had offered John and Paul the opportunity to buy the shares, the concern in the city over why James would want to sell would in all likelihood have pushed down their price. There was no guarantee that John or Paul could raise the capital or even want to buy the shares. There was also the issue of Allen Klein. Dick James would no doubt be concerned over a maverick like Klein, with his 'kick over the table' style of management. Klein would want to go through the Northern Songs agreement that John and Paul had signed with a fine tooth comb, so Dick James jumped ship.

Relationships between John and Paul during the fight for Northern Songs reached a new low. At one point during a business meeting, they very nearly came to blows. Klein was prepared to pay up $750,000 of his own MGM film stock in an attempt by buy back the shares of Triumph Investment Trust, thus giving John and Paul controlling interest. Paul, unlike John, would not put in his shares as collateral. To make matters worse, Paul had been buying Northern Songs shares without John's knowledge. John in turn didn't help matters when he was widely reported as saying, 'I'm not going to be fucked around by men in suits sitting on their fat arses in the city'. He followed this incendiary comment by telling the *Daily Express*, 'I am back to work, recording with The Beatles. I need the money... Right now, in cash, I have about £50,000'.[11]

Considering The Beatles were in a life-or-death situation regarding their multi-million pound bids, a revelation like this may not be the best piece of gossip for a national daily. Eventually, despite all the efforts to bring control of Northern Songs under the umbrella partnership of John and Paul, it was Lew Grade's ATV who gained the ruling 51 per cent plus. The Northern Song episode only added to John's already fraught relationship with the rest of the band and all but broke his financial and legal connections with Paul. The Forthlin Road 'eyeball to eyeball' songwriting partnership of John and Paul, begun over a decade earlier, was coming to a sad, destructive and ignominious end.

Amidst this financial wrangling, John still found time to continue his newly-found campaign for peace. He spent a week in bed at the Amsterdam Hilton giving interviews to journalists. John's efforts for world peace seemed to be genuine enough, but due to his lifestyle of having his every whim satisfied, the practical nature of some of his peace efforts failed to materialise and fell into farce, a prime example being when he and Yoko sent all the world leaders an acorn to grow for peace. The task was turned over to the personnel at the Apple offices. Unfortunately it was out of season for acorns, and the staffers were reduced to putting advertisements in the newspapers offering a pound an acorn. When this didn't produce the expected results, they went to the parks of London to dig holes in an attempt to find where the squirrels had buried their acorn stash.

Despite the poor relationship between John and Paul, it was amazing and a credit to them that they could still write songs together. As a follow-up to The Beatles' last single 'Get Back/Don't Let Me Down', they met at Paul's Cavendish Avenue home and while Ringo was filming and George was abroad, John and Paul made between them the last collaborative single. This partnership was made possible by John's seemingly exceptional ability to compartmentalise his emotions, which were to switch from rage to smiles within a heartbeat. This, together with Paul's willingness to accommodate John at almost all costs, encouraged the process. Whether Paul was disposed to support John with 'The Ballad of John and Yoko' due to feelings of guilt is uncertain. Although Paul was not brought up Catholic, his mother was and his extended family on his mother's side were and this could easily have distilled a Catholic guilt complex. When the break-up was at its worst and it looked like Paul was against the world, he revealed to Miles:

> I remember thinking, in many ways, I wish I was a lorry driver, a Catholic lorry driver, very, very simple life, a firm faith and a place to go in my lorry, in my nice lorry.[11]

To all intents and purposes, this could well have been the last time that John and Paul would record together, but what helped them drive them apart in the shape of financial issues would be the same issues that would force them back into the studio for one last time.

CHAPTER NINETEEN

1969
Tittenhurst

AS THE RECORDING sessions for *Let it Be* at Savile Row finished, an unspoken agreement was made to leave the completing the production of the album until one of The Beatles could muster enough courage to go back to the desperately needed, but painful, job of improving the quality of the tapes. After the break-up, John's own view of the quality of the album was simple: 'I thought it would be good to go out'. Here John is speaking of the rough version, 'the shitty version because it would break The Beatles. It would break the myth'.[1] John's agenda was simple, to build his own new career on the back of The Beatles' managed decline, accumulating publicity and musical clout for himself and Yoko, while meeting the needs of the growing market of the increasingly sophisticated, politicised generation of listeners.

John's time away from the band was split between his own work and his peace campaigning which put him firmly in the public eye. A month after the *Let it Be* recording sessions were complete, John and Yoko gave their first live musical performance together at a concert in Cambridge University. Here John performed with electric guitar feedback accompanying Yoko's vocals. The performance was recorded and later used as part of the album *Life with the Lions*. The second side of the album was made at Queen Charlotte's Hospital, where Yoko had miscarried. This side consisted of them recording themselves on a portable cassette recorder, chanting out press cuttings about themselves. Additional material consisted of the recording of the baby's heartbeat, followed by two minutes of silence.

The problem with avant-garde, by the sheer nature of it aims, is that it's not usually marketable, at least not in the lifetime of the artist. The Beatles' financial wrangling over management was going to drag on into the immediate future. So, finance for John was unpredictable. Peace campaigning wasn't going to pay for the newly acquired Grade Two listed Tittenhurst stately home, kitted out with tennis courts and 72 acres of gardens (and, later, a recording studio), which they had bought for

£145,000. John had become a revolutionary with a mortgage. Financially, he had to seriously consider a return to being a successful rock star, and this is where the Plastic Ono Band would come in. But before that there was the matter of the demise of The Beatles.

Like John's, Paul's life in the previous 12 months had been turned upside down. Unlike Paul, John had the best part of a year to prepare himself to leave The Beatles. It's fair to say that due to his faith in The Beatles, Paul was the last to understand the imminent break-up of the band and as events unfolded, he was left totally flummoxed.

Not long after Paul and Linda married, John and Yoko were seeking to 'get hitched' too, but this was not without its difficulties. 'The Ballad of John and Yoko' gave a lyrical itinerary to John's problems of getting married and a protest against their public ridicule. It was written by himself with the help of Paul. The song provided John with a platform for righteous indignation. It was a rant about what he perceived as the persecution that he and Yoko had been subject to. The persecuted Christ-like John comparison was obvious. John's time as a Beatle had been based on the avoidance of suffering, not the acceptance of it. The years that John's unchallenged demands had been provided for would not be changed in an instant. He would not be the first creative talent to have perceptions of a tortured soul amplified into canonisation. It would have taken more than the few months to become Saint John of Tittenhurst.

'The Ballad of John and Yoko' was conceived and recorded in a matter of days. The use of the chord sequence to Paul's 'Paperback Writer' gave 'The Ballad' its structure. George was out of the country and Ringo was unavailable, filming, which just left John and Paul to finish recording the single. Both George and Ringo didn't seem to mind being overlooked. Typically droll, George explained, 'I don't mind not being on the record because it was none of my business. If it had been "The Ballad of John, George and Yoko" then I would have been on it'.[2] In America, the single was released with a cover that showed John, Paul, George, Ringo and Yoko.

Those in the studio also recall John and Paul now totally at one, best friends, as it were, laughing and joking. Just four days later in the Apple boardroom John was being restrained from trying to beat Paul up. This was due to the discovery of Paul buying shares of Northern Songs without John's knowledge.

Further trouble was to follow. On the same day as John and Yoko's *Life with the Lions* was released, an ill-tempered meeting took place at the Apple boardroom between The Beatles, Yoko, Klein and Lee Eastman. The conflict surrounded the representation of The Beatles. All but Paul had signed a contract to be represented by Klein. After the meeting, a night session in Olympic recording studios had been booked. Paul arrived first and waited. Then the other Beatles arrived and continued to confront Paul. He should sign the contract and have Klein as his representative – Paul refused. Klein, who was about to board a New York bound plane, was contacted by pager – John was on the phone. The message from him was simple: 'Paul's making trouble. You have to come back to Olympic'.[3] Even after Klein's return, Paul still refused to be managed by him until he had had time to consult his lawyer. John, George and Ringo stormed out of the studio in disgust. The situation was moving towards The Beatles only coming together as a group at business meetings or at 'work' in the studio.

John and Yoko were left with more time to pursue their peace campaign. The main front for their 'assault' was America. With John's drugs conviction, entry to the country proved difficult. They needed to be as near as they could to the country to make it easy to attract the American press. With this in mind, their first port of call was the Bahamas. Unfortunately the oppressive heat made this a short-lived venue. The next option was Canada, and so John and Yoko flew to Montreal and booked into the Queen Elizabeth Hotel, where they would have a 'Bed-In'. The event would see wall-to-wall journalists and news teams camped outside. At times the couple would be facing 150 journalists a day. In the USA alone, 350 radio stations were recording the events as they happened.

John's Bed-In at the Queen Elizabeth Hotel was by far and away the most famous of all his peace protests. This came about due to the recording of the anthem 'Give Peace a Chance' in the bedroom. Joining in the ad hoc recording with John and Yoko were a host of their guests, including amongst others, Timothy Leary, the Smothers Brothers and Allen Ginsberg. The spontaneity and fervour of the song immediately captivated the listener. 'Give Peace a Chance' was without a doubt the highlight of John's solo performance as a Beatle and, arguably, as a non-Beatle.

'Give Peace a Chance' was singularly the coolest, hippest protest song ever. Its delivery didn't even initially sound like a protest song, more like something that would be getting played on one of Paul's childhood mystery tour charabancs with an old-time, singalong, raucous chorus, which sounded like something to do with giving The Beatles' first drummer another go. Never mind your Barry McGuire, Joan Baez or Peter, Paul and thingy, 'Give Peace a Chance' was the real McCoy. The track was a young Bob Dylan stuck in a lift with Lonnie Donegan. That day in the Queen Elizabeth bedroom was to be John's very own personal Shea Stadium.

After John's tour of (peace) duty, there was the little matter of getting back to work and earning some money with The Beatles. Before John returned to Abbey Road studios for the band's final album, he decided to take Yoko, her daughter Kyoko and his son Julian to visit his family. He set out to visit Aunts Anne and Harriet on Merseyside and then move on to his cousin Stanley and Aunt Mater in the Scottish Highlands. Before this trip, John had already introduced Yoko to Mimi at Mimi's home in Poole. This visit by John and Yoko was filled with disapproving comments. On their arrival at Mimi's house, when Yoko was introduced as John's new wife, Mimi recalls:

> I took one look [at her] and thought, 'My God what is that?' Well I didn't like the look of her right from the start. She had long black hair, all over the place, and she was small. She looked just like a dwarf to me. I told John what I felt: while she was looking across the bay I said to him, 'Who's the poison dwarf John?' The best John could do in protest was to give an uncomfortable laugh.

Following this, Mimi then proceeded to make a comparison with the Duke of Windsor and Mrs Simpson. The Duke of Windsor lost popularity with his subjects due to his intention to marry Simpson, a twice-divorced American. 'He thought that he could get away with it,' Mimi said, 'because he was so popular. But he lost his popularity and John, you'd better know that'.[4]

The comparison wasn't lost on Yoko, nor was it meant to be: 'I'm the Mrs Simpson,' she exclaimed.[5] What Mimi left out of her spiteful comparison was that, not long after losing the popularity of the British people, the Duke of Windsor abdicated and he and his bride Mrs Simpson found favour in Hitler's Fascist Germany. Publicly celebrated by top-ranking Nazis, they were both ostracised by the British royal family. They never set foot in Britain again.

During the same visit to Poole, Mimi also declared:

I didn't like [Yoko] and he knew. I was a good judge of character. I couldn't see what he saw in her and I thought it was wrong and nothing good would come of it.[6]

Mimi's comments, made long after John had been murdered, showed neither understanding nor compassion towards Yoko. Mimi was perhaps showing off for the journalist – playing to the balcony, mistaking ignorance and prejudice for wit and forthright speech. John's accommodation of her wishes in his childhood never really left him, to the point of having Yoko insulted by her eliciting only an awkward laugh and a clearing of the throat.

Mimi's criticisms came against a backdrop of John and Yoko being publicly vilified. From all corners of the media and general public, no 'joke' insult or abuse was left unused against them. John's benign response to Mimi's nastiness during their first visit to Torquay was in stark contrast to any slights perceived or otherwise towards Yoko in Abbey Road or the Apple office.

As John and Yoko continued on their journey to the Scottish Highlands to his Auntie Mater and Uncle Bert's home, the party needed a change of car. The small Austin Mini that John was driving was swapped for a larger Austin Maxi. This was provided courtesy of chauffer Les Anthony driving up from London for the exchange of cars. The stay at his aunt's was to be a short one of just a few days. The reason for this was a disagreement between John and Auntie Mater over John's intentions to sue Cynthia for the custody of Julian; his aunt believed this to be a bad idea and words were exchanged. Whether due to John's poor driving skills or still being upset over the argument with his aunt, John drove the car off the road while trying to negotiate a bend.

The result of this accident was 17 stitches to John's face, a damaged back for Yoko and 14 stitches to her head. Kyoko needed four stitches and Julian escaped with minor injuries and shock. John was in hospital for five days. When Cynthia arrived at the hospital to find out what had happened, John refused to see her. During his stay in Scotland, John's 'big brother' Stanley was quick to notice the change in him since they last met. The first thing Stanley picked up on was John's glue-like attachment to Yoko and Yoko's total unwillingness to engage in conversation with any members of the family. There was also a reluctance by either John or Yoko to step in against the constant bullying of Julian by Kyoko. It was left to Stanley's mother to intervene. The reluctance of Yoko to talk to anyone beyond John could have been a sense of solidarity, only wanting to be with John. It could also have been the development of a 'bunker mentality' in which the couple's union was strengthened by their own isolation. It seemed that in the exclusive 'John and Yoko Club' there was a limited membership of two. Cousin Stanley wasn't impressed and later made a visit to John's new home:

> I went to visit them at a huge mansion in Ascot that John bought. He took me outside and we mucked around on this vehicle he had bought that could drive through lakes and over rough terrain. It was like we were boys again. As soon as we got back to the house, and her, John just clammed up and withdrew again. It was heart-breaking.[7]

It's likely that John's 'bunker mentality' found its root in Mimi's Mendips of black-and-white thinking and judgemental attitude towards others. John believed others judged him in a negative way. He developed the misplaced strategy of judging others in a similar way, a cruel form of defensive elitism which was meant to increase his own self-esteem. It did, but it was always short-lived. The bouts of guilt, self-loathing, chronic self-criticism and depression that followed resulted in a series of critical thought patterns embedded so deep, that even when John was in a healthy frame of mind, the tendency to exhibit offensive language and behaviour was always ready to surface.

Examples of John's prejudices, learnt during his childhood, were revealed in his collection of jokes, verse and cartoons that he circulated at Quarry Bank in the shape of the *Daily Howl*. John came out with: 'Some Scotchmen [sic] live in caves and are still cannonballs [sic] (wot eat men). They walk on their hands to save their shoes (not that their [sic] mean). They eat porrage [sic], and something food also, to, as well. Some Scotchmen have tarton [sic] hair instead of a kilt, silly niggers'.[8]

It could be argued that John was a product of his times. Britain of the 1950s still believed in the right to rule an Empire populated by non-whites and therefore 'naturally' inferior. Prejudice in the country was rife but for a 16-year-old schoolboy to put the 'n****r' word on paper and freely circulate it with moral impunity gives rise to the charge of 'I blame the parents', or in this case Mimi. John's indifference as to what did or didn't constitute as unacceptable returned five years later in a letter to Stu while he was in Hamburg with this nonsense, racist verse. 'Uncle Norman has just driven up on his moustache,' and 'PS Mary Queen of Scots was a Nigger'.[9] This is not to make the case that John was a racist; he wasn't, but he was ignorant of other people's feelings.

The major problem in understanding John's complicated outlook and actions centres around the manner in which he seamlessly separated one set of values from another without seeing any obvious contradictions. An example of this can be found in the negotiations with Lee Eastman over the management of Apple. Prior to the meeting taking place, John had discovered that Eastman's name was previously Epstein. Throughout the meeting and in the presence of the other Beatles, Yoko and Klein, John proceeded to address Eastman as Epstein. John found this term of address highly amusing and chuckled at every mention. The root or subtext of John's humour came because Eastman was a *Jew, like Brian.* John didn't make the connection between his own abuses to that which Yoko had been constantly bombarded. The abuse that came along with her name – *Oh no, that one, Oko Nono!* – had seemingly no connection in his mind between that of his own 'joke' towards a Jewish name.

As John carried on with his works with the Plastic Ono Band and his peace campaign, the battle for the rights over Northern Songs continued. Gaining control over the rights to Lennon and McCartney songs meant the need for cash, and EMI still presented the best way of obtaining enough of it to buy the remaining floating shares to secure ultimate control of the company. The problem for John was that this meant a return to the studio with the other Beatles, something he hoped he could avoid. Klein and The Beatles were fully aware that the director of EMI, Joseph Lockwood, would never commit to an improved recording contract if The Beatles weren't a 'fully operational unit'. So to prove their intention, they had to resume business as usual. So on 2 July 1969, The Beatles decided to return to Abbey Road Studios, to what they all felt was likely to be their last recording session as a band.

What John had done over 12 months before leaving The Beatles, particularly the release of his controversial nude cover of himself and Yoko on the *Two Virgins* album, set off a chain of events which tied him to The Beatles longer than he wanted. The cover scared Dick James into believing that such controversial projects and the possibility of more, together with John's drugs bust and rumours of bad blood between John and Paul, would send the price of his Northern Songs shares crashing. From a business point of view, it wouldn't make sense to offer the shares to John and Paul, for two reasons. James knew as well as anyone the state of John and Paul's finances – they would not be in a position to buy the shares. They would have had to try to raise the necessary funds. Any attempt to sell James' shares to John and Paul would surely get out. James selling off what were once seen as gilt-edged shares, in turn, would send a message to the financial dealers, and the consequence would be a fall in Northern Songs' shares. James would also have to consider that John and Paul would not wish to purchase his shares. This would have again alerted the City and resulted in a fall in price. Although it seems improbable that John and Paul would not like to own a bigger percentage of their songs, to James it didn't seem that long ago when he first met John and Paul that they both believed you couldn't own songs, that they could be used by anyone free of charge. Also there was an outside chance that their attachment to their songs may not have been strong enough to go into debt to the tune of millions of pounds. The end result was to be a convoluted financial battle that continued up to and after The Beatles completed the final album.

As The Beatles entered Abbey Road for their month-long session, progressive rock and heavy metal groups such as Pink Floyd and Led Zeppelin were gearing up to take over the mantle of stadium rock stars – a mantle that The Beatles first held five years earlier. The Stones, whom John would have loved to have fronted, caught the zeitgeist of the late 1960s just as The Beatles had done at the beginning of the decade. As The Beatles began to record their last album and Mick Jagger was pleading to be given shelter with one more jolt of heroin, Mal Evans was endlessly banging away on an anvil in Studio Two in imitation of 'Maxwell's Silver Hammer'. Paul was delighted with his use of the word 'pathaphysical' (to complement the song's lyric of 'Joan was quizzical studied...'. John needed to move on.

Meanwhile, Yoko was still suffering from the results of the car accident and needed bed rest. She found this rest in the confines of a Harrods bedstead newly delivered to Abbey Road's Studio Two. Yoko tucked herself away, pulled up her duvet and then arranged for a microphone to hang over her bed in order to accommodate any requests for food and drink, or to give any necessary observations as to The Beatles' progress and improvement of the recording of the present album track. It was the turn of Paul, George and Ringo to start looking for the door signed 'Exit'.

The iconic album cover of *Abbey Road*, conceived by Paul, was given just a ten-minute time span to shoot by local police, who arranged to hold up the traffic. Photographer Ian MacMillan perched on top of a step ladder. John, resplendent in his Christ-like white suit (a purposeful replication of flowing robes) and flowing beard, strides with hands dug deep into pockets, eager and earnest to get on with the shoot. He would then get back to more important matters, like saving the world from military destruction. *Abbey Road* turned out to be one of the most successful of all The Beatles' albums, spending 11 weeks at the number one spot in the UK charts. Also it became the bestselling album of 1969. The response in America was just as good. By the time The Beatles had disbanded, the album had sold over seven million copies.

After the completion of *Abbey Road,* John was invited to play at the Toronto Rock 'n' Roll Revival festival. Included on the bill were John's old heroes in the shape of Little Richard, Gene Vincent and Chuck Berry. Acting 'in the moment', John hastily arranged a band to accompany him as the Plastic Ono Band to Canada, which included Eric Clapton, old Hamburg pal Klaus Voorman on bass and session drummer and soon-to-be member of Yes, Alan White. Also travelling were Mal Evans and Anthony Fawcett, Yoko's personal assistant.

His use of heroin and cocaine and the lack of it on the ten-hour flight made for a strung-out version of John on his arrival at Toronto airport. The egos of John and Yoko meant that even the likes of Eric Clapton, whose legend of 'Clapton is God' was painted on the walls of London, was treated just like any other 'flunky'. 'It was raining, and we were standing around waiting for the luggage,' Clapton recalls, 'when a huge limo rolled up and John and Yoko jumped into it and drove away, leaving the rest of us standing in the rain without a clue as to what to do next. Well, that's nice, I thought'.[10]

What we see with the dismissive treatment of Eric Clapton and the rest of the group is John's ability to socially and emotionally exclude people when it suited him. John had spent most of the transatlantic flight chatting and rehearsing with the band and yet saw nothing wrong with leaving them on the runway in the pouring rain; then he seamlessly picked up where he left off with the band on-stage at the night of the concert. John seemed capable of wounding and joking almost in the same breath. With his combination for peace campaigning and his history of belligerence, it seems John's love was for causes, not for his fellow man.

The mixture of nerves at performing in front of a crowd of 20,000 and his rock 'n' roll heroes standing in the wings saw John go into meltdown. Not being able to risk bringing any drugs into the country, matters weren't helped by a misunderstanding on arrival at the concert venue. When greeted by the young promoter, who asked John and his entourage did they need anything?, John's reply was a whispered, 'Any coke?' The response to the request was a half turn and the shout of, 'Hey Jerry, six Cokes over here!'.[11]

Eventually John got through his first night nerves and withdrawal symptoms to put on a set which included 'Blue Suede Shoes', 'Money', 'Dizzy Miss Lizzy', 'Yer Blues' and a version of 'Cold Turkey'. This was John's confessional nightmare about the horrors of heroin addiction. Yoko assisted John by holding up a sheet of paper for him with the song lyrics pencilled on. This was his first public appearance in front of a large audience since Candlestick Park. Ronnie Hawkins recalls:

> The unrehearsed performance of 'Cold Turkey' and a number of oldies like 'Blue Suede Shoes' was not a great blast of the Beatles magic which everyone was waiting for .[12]

Even so, the concert gave John cause for satisfaction: 'I can't remember when I had such a good time,' he said. 'It was fantastic'.[13]

On the downside was the performance by Yoko, who gave a set accompanied by John's howl of distorted fuzz box guitar. This was the introduction of a set which combined rock music and avant-garde performance art, with a series of Yoko's guttural shrieks interspersed by John's guitar feedback accompaniment. 'People were surprised when I suddenly used to start screaming during our concerts,' Yoko recalled, 'but they didn't realise I had vocal training'.[14] The audience wasn't impressed. Press articles of her performance report howls of derision from the audience following her act. Larry LeBlanc, a Canadian reporter at the show, remembers:

People were polite. They were bewildered but everybody knew she was an artist she'd taken photographs of bums and things like that. We figured whatever she was doing it would eventually end. But it fuckin' didn't end.[15]

Yoko's wailing clocked in at 17 minutes 22 seconds.

When John and Yoko had last played together at Cambridge University (with a not too dissimilar performance to Montreal from Yoko) it was half-expected that their set would not be 'straightforward', so the content of their performance could have been expected to be controversial. But the second-half performance by Yoko at the Toronto concert was about as welcome as King Herod in Mothercare. 'I remember the show, people were throwing bottles at Yoko Ono,' recalls Little Richard. 'They were throwing everything at her. Finally she had to run off the stage. Oh, boy, it was very bad'.[16] It's hard to rationalise what was going through John's mind at Toronto.

The clue to the audience's expectations was in the title – Toronto Rock 'n' Roll Revival. It could have been blind ignorance that *he*, John Lennon of Beatles fame, should command those in the audience to appreciate the talents of his wife. Or it could have been that John's mind had become so addled at this time by his drug use that he really wasn't 'on his game'. It could also have been that he was so terrified of returning to the stage he got carried along by what Yoko had suggested. Even in the days of Beatlemania, John never displayed such a high degree of self-importance and lack of self-perception.

A few months before the Toronto Rock 'n' Roll Revival, John was interviewed by David Wigg for BBC Radio. The amenable interviewer asked John about his peace campaign and its effects, to which John replied: 'Me and Yoko are like the wind, you don't see us but when we pass you know we've been there'.[17] Even accounting for Woodstock and the Age of Aquarius, it could be argued, his comment does come across as a just a tad pretentious. But John believed that what he said was not only true, but profoundly so. The simple reason for his conviction was that there was no one willing to tell him otherwise. At this time in his life, no one thought more of John than John.

On his trip to Canada, John had announced to Eric Clapton and Klaus Voorman that he was about to quit The Beatles and start a new band.

Were they interested in joining? John asked them to keep his decision a secret until he had informed the rest of The Beatles. True to his word, at a meeting with the rest of The Beatles and Klein, John announced his decision to leave the band. After the initial shock and attempts to have him change his mind, Allen Klein pointed out the financial implications of leaving at this particular time, with negotiations for a lucrative deal with Capitol Records underway. Not lost on them was that the USA provided The Beatles with 75 per cent of their royalties. John took on board Klein's advice and postponed the announcement of his departure until a more financially appropriate time. Hammering a further nail into The Beatles' coffin, five days later ATV gained a majority share of Northern Songs. Klein's advice to John and Paul to this change in circumstance was to sell their own shares, which they eventually did for £3.5 million, in the form of ATV shares.

On the last day of October 1969, the tracks 'Something' and 'Come Together' were released. For all the internal difficulties – personal, musical and financial – the success of *Abbey Road* and The Beatles' latest single suggested to the general public that it was business as usual for the band. What wasn't usual was the week after 'Something' and 'Come Together' hit the charts, John and Yoko's third album, the *Wedding Album*, was released.

The remarkable feature of this period was the exposed situation John put himself in. When going through the dozens of interviews for his peace campaign, he stretched himself too far and he left himself open to ridicule. This was the case when he and Yoko were giving interviews from inside a bag, in Vienna's Hotel Sacher.

QUESTION: How long is your hair?

JOHN: You'll have to guess. It's not important – it's only what I say we're here for.

QUESTION: But you're not really saying much, are you?

JOHN: Well if the questions are banal you're going to get banal answers.

QUESTION: Are you in that bag to hide your pimples?

JOHN: I don't have any, actually.

QUESTION: Can you prove that to me, please?

JOHN: Take my word for it.

QUESTION: Can you give me a recipe against pimples?[18]

As the novelty of the peace campaign began to wear off, John became an easy target for cruel questions and comments by journalists. In all likelihood, he would have expected some ridicule and maybe sometimes welcomed it as a public exposé, given his 'persecution complex'. Nevertheless it was pressure, and it was the first time John had been under this intense media scrutiny since the uproar of his 'more popular than Jesus' comments. At that particular time, John had the other Beatles and Brian to share his load. Now he was not just defending himself, he was also defending Yoko. At another Bagism, in which the couple gave interviews from inside a canvas bag, a reporter from the *London Evening Standard* asked John the cheap and unfunny question, was there another bag in there with him?

In the case of John returning his MBE, he left himself open to being seen as not only naïve but at the same time self-serving. His now-famous letter to Prime Minister Harold Wilson smacks of indifference and tastelessness:

> I am returning my MBE in protest against Britain's involvement in the Nigeria-Biafra thing, against our support of America in Vietnam and against 'Cold Turkey' slipping down the charts. With love, John Lennon.[19]

The phrase '"Cold Turkey" slipping down the charts' seems to be what many people recall about John's letter, but over one million civilians died in the war in Biafra. For John to be so insensitive as to label it 'the Nigeria-Biafra thing' was ignorant beyond belief. John's previous experience with The Beatles was of dealing with a press conference made up of usually friendly journalists wanting an upbeat, human-interest type story. When John opened up to journalists for support in his peace campaign, the previously friendly ones were no longer that friendly; the questions put to John, for example, included asking why he had bothered sending his MBE back:

> QUESTION: It just struck me that it diminishes you, sending back something that was worthless, calling an award so grotesque and horrible.
>
> JOHN: Okay, it's worthless.
>
> QUESTION: It won't work.
>
> YOKO: But people are getting killed every minute.

QUESTION: What I am saying is you are no better for what you did, so why did you diminish yourself? People thought you did it as a gag.

JOHN: But people also thought we did the bag event for a gag, but we changed their minds.

QUESTION: Did you! Did you!

A few minutes later John tries to explain, in a slightly confused way, that he uses publicity for peace:

JOHN: If it gets on the front page of the paper that I don't like apple pie for peace.

QUESTION: Is that all you care about!

JOHN: Listen! Listen! Listen! If I'm going to get myself on the front page I might as well get there with the words 'peace'...

QUESTION: You're a fake.

JOHN: Okay that's your opinion...

QUESTION: There are people who know that a protest movement doesn't involve chauffeured cars sending back medals you despised in the first place.

YOKO: You're embarrassing him.[20]

The question about the chauffeured car hit the mark. Yoko's retort of 'You're embarrassing him' could be countered with the question 'How am I embarrassing him?' The simple answer is, John's luxury lifestyle.

John had stated that he didn't mind 'playing the fool' if it achieved his efforts towards world peace. Being attacked by journalists who were out for cheap laughs and cheap copy was one thing, but when John came up against genuine and probing questions about his intentions, there were times that he floundered. Six months later, in an interview with the French journal *L'Express*, he revealed that he only accepted the MBE because 'our manager wanted it', and 'for the others'. John's blind spot was assuming that whatever his views were, they were not up to being *questioned*. John took the MBE and never thought too much about it until he engaged on his peace campaign. If he had looked into returning it, he would have found that he couldn't – once accepted, the title has to be kept for life.

John did put himself under pressure. He did suffer from his peace activities, but most of it wasn't intentional. Being ferried in a chauffeur-driven Rolls Royce to peace campaigns, his luxurious estate of Tittenhurst and the whole package of luxury rock star lifestyle was brought under the microscope by the media alongside John's time spent and commitment to his causes of those worse off than others. His peace campaign and the time that this entailed were fine, as long as it didn't cause him any inconvenience.

The 'open season' by the media on John and Yoko and the pressure that came with their cause, resulted in the view by the couple themselves as being 'under siege'. If this 'siege' was self-imposed, it was in many ways courageous and praiseworthy, but the constant pressure and intrusion was increasing emotional pressure and physical strain. One way of 'coping' was drugs. After the motor accident in Scotland, both Yoko and John were using heroin. It was while in hospital at this time that Yoko claimed to come off heroin. Yoko said:

> We wouldn't kick in a hospital because we wouldn't let anybody know [...] We just went straight cold turkey. The thing is, because we never injected, I don't think we were sort of – well, we were hooked, but I don't think it was a great amount. Still, it was hard. Cold turkey is always hard.[21]

It could be argued that being an addict or 'hooked' is not one of degrees, you can't be a 'bit hooked'. Whichever way Yoko wants to dress it up, she and John at this time were junkies.

Close friends of John and Yoko, Neil Aspinall and Ray Connolly, recall Yoko's version of 'getting clean' differently. They recollect being visitors to John and Yoko at a private London clinic, where both were receiving treatment for heroin addiction. The problems that the couple had with heroin would not be contained with this course of treatment. It would reappear for many years to come. John was later to reveal:

> It's a very difficult situation, drugs... The worst drugs are as bad as anybody's told you. It's just a dumb trip, which I can't condemn people if they get into it, because one gets into it for one's personal, social, emotional reasons. It's something to be avoided if one can help it.[22]

As *Abbey Road* dominated the album charts and 'Something' and 'Come Together' became constant plays on the jukeboxes of pubs and clubs in the run-up to Christmas, John and Yoko released their third album. This followed on from their *Life with the Lions*; their next effort was another unconventional offering; the *Wedding Album*. The contents revealed them to be calling out each other's names for over 20 minutes, improvised songs and audio sequences of press interviews along with room service phone recordings. The album was presented in a box containing a copy of the couple's marriage certificate, press cuttings and a cardboard wedding cake. It failed miserably, selling very few copies. The *Wedding Album* was seen as an extreme example of artistic values wrapped up in full blown ego-centricity – the Emperor's New Clothes in neon light. Even though some people found John's efforts in his venture into avant-garde laudable, many more questioned its seriousness or value, and others found it laughable.

When 1969 tumbled into 1970, another piece of The Beatles' tradition and 'culture' was to end. Since 1963, the monthly issue *The Beatles Book* kept tens of thousands of fans up to date with the comings and goings of their favourite Beatle – the band's music, their tour dates and their personal lives, their wives, their children. Now this monthly dose of Beatle gossip had come to an end, John, Paul, George and Ringo couldn't maintain the pretence of The Beatles family any longer. So, as the decade ended, so did another connection that linked The Beatles with their fans and their past.

CHAPTER TWENTY

1970–71
Dakota Building

THE NEW YEAR would begin where the last year ended, with John getting up in the morning, going to his bedroom window and scanning the horizon for 'enemies'. In the short space of 12 months, The Beatles were to be a thing of the past. Despite the pronouncements of John that he had outgrown The Beatles, for the past 13 years Paul, George and later Ringo had been an integral part of his life. The byzantine business dealings that accompanied The Beatles' demise only served to accentuate the hurtful way in which the break-up was conducted. It left a residue of bitterness that spread well into the 1970s.

With a change of band from The Beatles to the Lennon/Ono Band, John also went for an alteration of image. At this point, there was a proliferation of Blues Rock Bands, mostly made up of well-educated Home Counties and London based blues and jazz aficionados with names like Spooky Tooth, King Crimson and Jethro Tull (named after the man who invented the seed drill in 17th-century England). These names seemed designed to separate the university-educated aficionados of 'prog rock' from the 9–5 factory and office worker oiks. Those previously sporting broad-belted hipsters, casually carrying albums of Marvin Gaye and The Small Faces, would be replaced by those wearing army surplus overcoats, religiously clutching copies of albums like *Ten Years After* and *Ginger Baker's Air Force*. John wasn't going to be taken in with some glass plate or red brick university band playing their 15-minute guitar solos – John was making his way to the barber who had 'done' his hair on the set of *How I Won the War*.

John started his musical career as a watered-down version of a working-class Teddy Boy, changing into an art school hard case, then moving to the denim-clad rough neck look. This was followed by John's Hamburg leather-clad Wildman, which transmuted itself into a Pierre Cardin Beatle suited scream machine, until eventually, emerging as a braid coated Lonely Heart moving noisily on to his Stations of the Cross mode. Now it was back to the future, with hair shorn, bib and braces, roll-your-own ciggies welded between the fingers of a fist, big boots, spit on the floor, *Friggin-workingclassmate!* Just when the university-educated liberals – with their Marcusian *One-Dimensional Man* notions and equality-for-all bollocks all tied up with the patronising of the masses – thought it was safe to come out and play, 'Jack' Lennon was coming down the cobblestoned streets: John Lennon, 'Working Class Hero', was on the move.

Oddly enough, John's metamorphosis into one of Orwell's 'proles' began with an attempt to eliminate one of his 'working-class vices' – smoking. John travelled to Holland to visit Yoko's ex-husband Tony Cox and their daughter Kyoko. While there, he sought help to end his heavy addiction to nicotine. While attempting to kick his at times 60-a-day habit, the nonconformist in John decided long hair was now passé. When bank clerks began to compete in hair length, it was time to bail out, and so he had his shorn. Along with this almost down-to-the-wood haircut came a taste for denim – denim jeans, denim shirt and denim jacket.

John's public first venture of 1970 came with the Plastic Ono Band on an edition the BBC's *Tops of the Pops*, promoting their latest single 'Instant Karma'. As John bashed out chords on the piano, singing about being knocked off your feet by your own deeds coming back to visit you, Yoko sat patiently on a stool to the side of the stage, knitting away while blindfolded. Whether this was meant to be a symbolic protest against the socially-conditioned, sightless submission of the domesticated female or just Yoko knitting is hard to say.

The shearings from John's head while in Holland were collected and bagged. John had a home for the hair, back in Britain, in the shape of Michael X, whose real name was Michael de Freitas. Born in Trinidad and Tobago, he was a self-appointed London community leader, and a victim of prejudiced white society. In reality, he was a shyster wrapping himself in the flag of black power and racism victim who a few years later would be executed in Port of Spain for the murder of a British tourist. John found himself involved with Michael X when he marched into The Beatles' Apple offices demanding money from John for the pain *his people* had suffered at the hands of white people, and The Beatles in particular – 'for ripping off the music of the black man'. John duly handed over £5,000 in cash to pay for the publication of Michael X's memoirs on his life in racist Britain. No receipts were handed over. No drafts were handed over and no memoirs were produced – identifying with oppression is one thing, paying for the 'right' to be associated with it is another.

Apple Press officer Derek Taylor recalled John's involvement with Michael X, which in his view resulted in John been seen as 'such a pathetic and silly figure, he destroyed his last shred of credibility with the press'.[1] The low point of John's love affair with the press came at the black cultural centre, the Black House, that Michael X ran in Camden Town. The press, badgered along by Derek Taylor, assembled for the handover of John's hair which was to be auctioned off. In turn John was presented with a gift by Michael X – allegedly a pair of Muhammad Ali's blood-stained boxing trunks. 'The next morning,' Peter Brown recalls, 'for the first time in Beatles history, not one photograph of the event appeared in any of the London papers'.[2]

At this time, Yoko found herself pregnant (but again was to miscarry); John had her booked into a private London hospital. John and Yoko insisted that the confinement to hospital was entirely related to her pregnancy, but close confidant Magic Alex recalls staff administering the heroin substitute, methadone, to her while one visitor friend and journalist Ray Connolly remembers John shouting at one of the medical staff, 'Don't give her that – she's a junkie'. John and Yoko continued to struggle with heroin addiction. Commenting on him and Yoko at this time, John admitted, 'When we're not working, we get pretty depressed'.[3]

Time and again, John referred to his poor mental health without being prompted. He referred to being suicidal, which could be perceived as 'just John's personality' and dismissed. But John's personality involved many lengthy periods of being in a deep state of depression. Others, except for Cynthia and Yoko, couldn't pick up on it. John's perceived position as 'Leader of The Beatles' paradoxically left him vulnerable and reluctant to confide in others of his depressive state, meaning that he could be aggressive, resentful and belligerent when coming out of it. It's no coincidence that when John knew the game was up with The Beatles, he began seeking professional psychiatric advice. But perversely, this advice would result in increasing amounts of hurtfulness to those around him and distancing himself further from any elements of compassion or support.

As The Beatles wound down, John could have very easily made a quiet life for himself. Instead he chose a high profile career as peace campaigner and controversial anti-establishment artist. It could have been the relative

fallowness of his creativity after *Sergeant Pepper* which gave the 'opportunity' for his depression to return. The response was to substitute the
need for the maintenance of *self* by using music to using celebrity. The
only salvation from the terrors of depression had seemed to be his music
and drugs, moving from pot to acid. These drugs were now insufficient to
deal with his mental anguish, and so John moved on to being a steady user
of heroin. He was to declare of heroin: 'It was not much fun. I never
injected it or anything. We sniffed a little when we were in real pain'.[4] The
complacency in which John tries to hide the importance of his reliance on
the drug in many ways was an effort to hide his shame and vulnerability
from being an addict.

An obstacle in dealing with John's pain was his reluctance to engage
with any psychiatric support, at least until the introduction of Dr Janov.
John's persona would not allow him to be seen 'bleeding in public', so any
intervention had to be kept away not only from journalists but from
friends and colleagues. A book that arrived by post at Tittenhurst gave
John cause for hope. This was Janov's *The Primal Scream*, which set out
a new way forward in dealing with neurosis. The basic concept of primal
therapy is that neurosis has its roots in the suppressed pain brought about
by childhood trauma. Janov focused on the origins of mental health issues
found in a person's childhood. Due to traumatic events, these grow and
present themselves in adulthood as full-blown neuroses. This in itself was
not original. What was original was the treatment he proposed for dealing
with this mental distress. According to Janov, re-experiencing this pain
was the only possible way to nullify the suffering brought on by the
childhood trauma. Relief was to be delivered by reliving the actual events
so that Janov's scream therapy could begin its healing process.

John devoured Janov's work in a day; he found the contents fascinat-
ing. Almost immediately, he made contact with the psychiatrist. He at last
considered that his mental health problems lay in his childhood. 'Not to
take one's own suffering seriously, to make light of it or even to laugh at
it, is considered good manners in our culture,' explains Alice Miller. She
continues:

> This attitude is even called a virtue, and many people are proud of
> their lack of sensitivity toward their own fate and above all toward
> their own childhood. I have tried to show in my books why the fatal

belief that such an attitude is desirable can so stubbornly persist, as well as the tragic conditions it helps to conceal.[5]

John asked Janov to come to England to carry out the therapy. Janov, though, was unwilling to fly to London due to commitments with other patients. Eventually, and reluctantly, Janov and his wife made the trip from their clinic in Los Angeles. After initial talks and treatment it was agreed that John and Yoko would follow this up with further sessions back in Janov's clinic.

In Los Angeles, John was encouraged to curl up into a ball and scream as he delved back into his childhood in an attempt to relive the pain and suffering – in the hope of purging his deep-seated negative emotions. During these sessions, John encouraged Yoko to join him in the therapy, but she declined. She viewed Janov as too dominant in his dealings with her husband. The makeup of John's neurosis was complex. As a young child he had been made to choose between Freddie and Julia as to whom he wanted to live with. His sense of rejection when handed to Mimi by his mother was followed by a low sense of worth. While living at Mendips he became eager to please, eager to seek validation, desperate not to disappoint and constantly reminded that his parents had given him up. All this left an emotional hole that John felt his music could fill. But the need to increase his self-image and reduce self-criticism was firmly rooted in the insecurity of his childhood and a desperate need to accommodate the wishes of his aunt:

> If a man habitually says 'Yes' in order to please others, he is in danger of disappearing as a separate entity. The maintenance of individuality requires at least a minimum of self-assertion. But the practice of an art gives a man an opportunity to express himself without any immediate need to fit in with the opinions of others.[6]

The phenomenal success of The Beatles kept his depressive and neurotic condition at bay. That is, until such time as a correlation began to appear with John's self-doubts as a creative artist. This was being matched by Paul's polar opposite confidence as songwriter and highly proficient studio musician. This last factor was essentially the main reason for The Beatles' demise.

John was to accuse George Martin and Paul of butchering his work in the studio. If John believed this was the case, then the question is, why did he allow it? The answer may be to do with John's own perceptions of himself and an effort to distance himself from what he saw as the competition of recording. When asked a question, post-Beatles, about recording studio techniques, John answered, 'I like singles and not LPs. I like the idea of saying everything in three minutes'.[7] John's comment suggests that, in the main, his art depended on working in the moment – getting in, getting out. This was unlike the methodical nature that Paul could apply to recording.

As The Beatles ceased to be a functioning band, following on from his marathon 'peace happenings', John undertook a number of brutally honest and controversial interviews. There was now a major difference concerning John's previous comments about 'Jews', 'spastics' and 'queers' up to 1967. Up until that earlier period John was in many ways indiscriminate, in that he had no goal other than to give vent to his built-up frustrations and bitterness. Post 1967, he developed a sharpening focus which then became a blueprint for a searing, almost never-ending series of accusations, insults and destructive comments. John had a 'shopping list' of disappointments – Brian had let him down. Paul had let him down. George had let him down. George Martin had let him down. Julia and Freddie had let him down. The public hated him. Businessmen ripped him off. Everyone hated Yoko, and nobody appreciated his art and music.

John's interviews at this period show a total disregard for how he will be perceived by readers. John tells the journalist what he wants and more. The person putting the questions asks him what the time is and John tells him how to make a watch. Due at times to John's lack of confidence, he needed people to take an interest in him and one of the ways he did this in interviews was by being sensational. John compensated for his insecurities by his aggression, but in a way this aggression in the interviews was in fact passivity. John was subconsciously pleading to be liked by accommodating the interviewer with good copy. John's analogy of himself as a 'performing flea' even applied to interviews.

Looking at the interviews which John gave post-1968, large tracts are public confessions, in which he defies the person who is asking the questions to disbelieve his pained response. John repeatedly states that he is a 'genius', he's 'suffered' and he's 'working-class'. John's suffering, political affiliations and his genius seem to be the three most common topics. The honesty and naivety in John's interview answers is amazing. In some interviews, he compares himself with tortured artists such as Van

Gogh and Oscar Wilde. In others, he compares himself to the 19th-century Dorset workers exiled to Australia for their membership of a trade union, the Tolpuddle Martyrs. These comparisons lost some of their potency when some years later John revealed, 'I used to do embroidery. My auntie told me how to do little flowers like that'.[8]

There are the usual contradictions in some of John's interview comments but some bordered on the ludicrous and worrying; when asked for his views on Fascism: 'I don't know much about Fascism except the result, so I can't really comment.' John was clearly not a believer in the view 'when in a hole, stop digging' – he ploughs on:

> I'm not saying there should be sadism in the streets, unless everybody said, 'Okay, let's have sadism in the streets.' I think it should be a community allowance. People should be allowed to do whatever they like.[9]

John is clearly out of his depth here, but rather that flag up his ignorance, he takes a stab at a political belief which has resulted in the death of millions and ends up confusing it with sexual deviancy.

John wanted to be accepted by the counter-culture community of New York, just like he did with the young rock 'n' roll, working-class community of Liverpool 15 years before. Just like then he had to adopt a radical change of persona. His comments like 'I mean it's just a basic working-class thing' to 'hate and fear the police as a natural enemy' seem strange.[10] Just as John had to be over the top with his Teddy Boy image in art school so he went over the top in portraying himself as the idealised working-class warrior.

After he left The Beatles, John declared himself a genius. In the case of Jann Wenner's *Rolling Stone* interview of 1970, John refers to himself as a genius not once but seven times in the space of a few minutes. John's belief in his own brilliance was unshakable, but his conviction left him with many blind spots which manifested themselves in some of his most abysmal behaviour and comments.

Social research studies have revealed that the students taking academic tests respond in unusual ways when taking their tests. In his book *The Age of Absurdity*, Michael Foley offers an example that is particularly relevant to John's perception of himself. One group of students was informed by the researchers that they achieved their good results due to being 'naturally clever'. A second group of students who also achieved good results were informed that their efforts were due to 'hard work'. Following this, a second set of tests was arranged. This time the 'naturally clever' group fell behind their previous results while those who were told they worked hard saw their marks increase. The 'moral' of this example of research could be applied to John. It would suggest that he didn't have to try to be a genius by the sheer fact that being a genius was natural. On the other hand, John felt, at times, that he just had to sit around and wait for his muse to drop in. Paul, on the other hand, would chase his muse. This is not to say Paul's creative work was better than John's, more that it's better to try to be creative than wait to be creative. John clearly subscribed to the view that creativity was natural and spontaneous, rather than something that requires hard work, a view that is evident in his comment about Paul: 'Paul has a special gift for making up tunes'.[11] Paul certainly did have 'a special gift' but he also had a great deal of discipline and commitment to his tunes. The result of John's wait for his muse left too much time on his hands and this time turned to a negative self-reflection.

John spent four months with Janov in Los Angeles. The psychotherapy gave him hope, but it was not as successful as he thought. One of the reasons for this was his inability to see beyond his parents as the source of his trauma, while to all intents and purposes the *real parent* was Mimi. All John's efforts towards primal scream therapy were misplaced. 'In the case of "normal" persons, it is to be assumed that they receive enough supplies of love from those who care for them for self-esteem to become built-in,' Alice Miller argues. 'Alternatively, one could say that normal people become conditioned by receiving enough love as small children to expect that others will give them approval and thus proceed through life with confidence.' Miller concludes:

> People who remain in the depressive position have no such built-in confidence. They remain as vulnerable to outside opinion as a baby is vulnerable to the withdrawal of the breast. Indeed, for such people, the good opinion of others is as vital to their well-being as milk is to the infant rejection and disapproval are a matter of life and death; for unless supplies of approval are forthcoming from outside, they relapse into a state of depression in which self-esteem sinks so low, and rage becomes uncontrollable, that suicide is a real possibility.[12]

A patently clear sign of primal scream therapy's failings came on John's 30th birthday. Janov recommended to his patients that if possible they should talk with their parents and discuss the outcome of their therapy. John would be no different. A couple of weeks before his birthday, John contacted Freddie to invite him, his wife Pauline and their young son David to Tittenhurst. Freddie accepted and on 9 October they made their way to John's home. The welcome they received was a lot less than what they expected. After making them wait, John appeared and proceeded to rant and rave at Freddie, continuing until Freddie and his family left the house. Firstly, John announced that he was cutting off Freddie's small allowance. This was followed by 'a torrent of abuse'. Freddie was accused of deserting John while Julia was continually referred to as 'a whore', then it was back to Freddie: 'You've treated me like shit, just like all the others. You've all ripped me off, the whole fucking lot of you'.[13]

During this tirade, Yoko stood alongside John, silent other than to support John on the importance of parental responsibility, which she felt Freddie had renounced. The family reunion concluded with a furious John pointing to his two-year-old half-brother as a comparison to himself, suggesting that if Freddie were to 'Lock him away from his parents and ordinary beings and see how he'll end up – he'll end up a raving lunatic just like me'.[14] The sad aspect about this fall-out was that even in a brave attempt by John to use primal scream therapy to heal himself, the chasm of pain he experienced was too wide to bridge. The therapy, far from starting a healing process, became a new way to tap into John's reservoir of bitterness and perceived betrayal.

One effect of the lack of success of the Janov sessions resulted in an inflation of his view of himself as one of life's unfortunate victims. The painful recollections that arose in the therapy sessions focused on Julia and Freddie, but they should have been focusing on Mimi. John became acutely aware of his childhood pain while at the same time leaving Mimi out the equation of responsibility. This in turn re-energised John's view of the world through Mimi's eyes.

An example of this 'world according to Mimi', came in an interview in which Mimi explains her views on Freddie, via a conversation she allegedly had with John:

JOHN: Oh Mimi, how could my mother marry a man like that? Why didn't you tell me what kind of father I had?

MIMI: Dear Boy, how would I know what kind of father you had? I didn't know him well myself. Did you want me to bring you up telling you he was a bad man who left you? Would that have made you any happier? You've been happy haven't you?

JOHN: Yes I'm the happiest person in the whole family.[15]

The supposed exchange between Mimi and John would be funny if it wasn't for the fact of the untold emotional damage caused to John by his time at Mendips.

The reason for this lost opportunity is found in John's constant ignoring of the emotional damage done to him at Mendips. In the 1970 *Rolling Stone* interview, he talked about his argument with Paul over Paul's dad wanting him to find a job after leaving school, which would interfere with Paul's commitment to playing rock 'n' roll. John confronted Paul with a choice – the band or Paul's dad. Six months later in a second interview with the magazine, this topic came up again. This time John revealed an input from Mimi: 'So I said to him [Paul], my Aunt Mimi reminded me of this the other night; she rang up and said he'd got this job and couldn't come to the group'.[16] This seems a strange comment to mention in the telephone conversation, Mimi bringing up a criticism of Paul about something that happened 12 years ago when John was at art college and Paul had just left school. One wonders how many of these telephone conversations took place revolving around the corrosive element of Mimi's 'lower types' and the grief that these 'types' were bringing to her nephew.

What did come out of Janov's month-long sessions was a return of John's muse. What poured out of his therapy was John's last solo recording while still a member of The Beatles, *John Lennon/Plastic Ono Band*. The album cover depicts John and Yoko lying in each other's arms against the backdrop of a large oak tree. The picture of such tranquillity and love is revealed on the album but the tracks of endearing self-expression are coupled with tracks which reveal a tangled-up delivery of unsuppressed rage.

The album touches on love, disillusionment, anger and trepidation, which ties in not just with John's own psyche but with the fading glow of 1960s hippy Camelot. The key track on the album is of course 'Working Class Hero', a fusion of John's protest-pained and anger theme going back to 'Help!', 'Yer Blues' and beyond. As usual, the song has John at its centre. The curious aspect of 'Working Class Hero' is that it's not a protest song like Dylan's 'Oxford Town' or Gil Scott-Heron's 'Whitey on the Moon' or even Jarvis Cocker's 'Common People', and that's because it wasn't a protest song at all. 'Working Class Hero', surprisingly, has nothing to do with identifying with or supporting the working class.

The lyrics to the song are split in two and show the complex and contradictory nature of perceptions of class and the working class. The first three verses are about John; all one has to do is replace the second-person narrative with the first-person, and John is arguably singing about himself, the reflecting perception of himself revealed in interviews given over the previous three to four years: as soon as I was born I was made to feel small. John then throws in the notion of him being a working-class hero in the shape of the refrain. The 'golden age' of being working-class, with its rock 'n' roll, Teddy Boys, influences in cinema, art, photography, comedy and music (such as The Beatles), was now entering a stage of self-autonomy, with trade unionists flexing their industrial muscle.

Being a blue collar worker was not now about being hard-done-by but fighting back. The first three verses of 'Working Class Hero' show the heroic victim (John), deserving of a large amount of sympathy, then comes a volte-face. In the next two verses, it's grammatically difficult to simply replace a third-person narrative with a first person, nor do they elicit any of the sympathy from the listener that the first three do. John would never address himself, however veiled, as a 'peasant'. In this fourth verse, who are the peasants looking for room at the top – maybe Paul and George? John's feud with Paul at this time is well documented. Not so well documented is the fact that in the ten years until John's death, George and he never spoke: 'You can't tell George anything,' commented John bitterly.[16] When asked about George's court case concerning the use of The Chiffons' 'He's So Fine' to the tune of 'My Sweet Lord', John responded with, 'Well, he walked right into it. He knew what he was doing'. When questioned further, his droll comment was that, 'maybe he thought God would just sort of let him off'.[17] Yet these comments were made after John himself had been successfully sued for using Chuck Berry's 'You Can't Catch Me' for the tune of 'Come Together' and after he (legitimately, although not going public) used the chord progression and melody of the folk ballad 'Stewball' as the basis for 'Happy Xmas (War is Over)'.

'Working Class Hero' has largely been seen as a tirade against the caustic effects of a hegemonic consumer capitalist system. Played dirge-like on guitar – along the lines of Dylan's 'Masters of War' – it was a bald statement of fact about the impending class war, with John taking the role of an Uncle Sam type recruiting officer for the coming revolution. The development of 'Working Class Hero' could have been John slipping into lyrics which unconsciously deliver a complex mix of a plea for help, a contempt for and a seemingly contradictory empathy for the working class. Commenting on 'Working Class Hero' a few months after its release, John explained, without any irony whatsoever, and with a dexterity of abusive language that manages to be both homophobic and sexist in one sentence, 'I just think its concept is revolutionary, and I hope it's for workers and not for tarts and fags'.[18]

His working class awareness stemmed, not surprisingly, from his years at art college and his time hanging around the cafés of Liverpool and playing local clubs, most notably The Cavern. His fascination with Liverpool, the hardship the city had endured, its sense of otherness with its back to the mainland and facing the sea – 'A city born between slavery and famine'[19] – and all the different influences the port brought, John could associate with the emotional hardships he had endured and his own sense of isolation and being an outsider.

After the touring ended, John had more time on his hands than was healthy. It was then that his deep-rooted depressive nature would really kick in and search for all the familiar aspects of his life which had let him down. The main one he found was himself. He berated himself for being something he wasn't. Why did he pretend to be something he wasn't in the shape of a working-class Teddy Boy or a working-class rock 'n' roller on the streets of Liverpool? He resented himself for being scared of real working-class rock 'n' rollers such as drummer Johnny Hutchinson. He resented *those* people for 'forcing' him *to talk, act and speak like them.* 'One has to completely humiliate oneself to be what the Beatles were, and that's what I resent'.[20] What John resented was the contradictory impasse he found himself in. In all his efforts to find his Self, he sold himself out as in the adage of the writer, 'Better to write for yourself and have no public than write for the public and have no self.' John's take on it was 'I mean I did it, I didn't know, I didn't foresee; it just happened bit by bit, gradually, until this complete craziness is surrounding you and you're doing exactly what you don't want to do with people you can't stand, the people you hated when you were ten'.[21]

The question is, what had these people done to him when he was ten years old? The people that John couldn't stand, who he hated, he hadn't met when he was ten. All he knew about them was what Mimi had told him. What she had told him as a child was 'he should avoid people like that'.[22] Those people were 'Liverpudlians' – working-class people. John relates an incident as a lustful teenager with his having the 'hots, as they say, for a rather lower-class female on the other side of the road'. Sounding like a cad seducing a chamber maid in a Barbara Cartland novel he follows this up with: 'I always think I should have done it. Presumably she would have allowed it'.[23] It would be excusable if these offensive remarks were isolated, but they're not. John makes a great show of flaunting his offensive terminology as he did as a teenager in Liverpool.

John's love-hate relationship with 'lower types' is at times contradictory beyond belief. While living in New York not long after recording 'Working Class Hero', John undertook a series of interviews with Peter McCabe and Robert Schonfeld, two of the small handful of journalists who weren't overawed by John's status. McCabe's observations were that John viewed the world as black-and-white. People were either the salt of the earth or the devil's spawn. Conversations about equality for women, poverty and left-wing politics could be easily accompanied by illogicality as McCabe and Schonfeld reveal. In an incident at the Saint Regus Hotel restaurant, McCabe says, 'Once when we were having dinner, he got so caught up in his (John) monologue, talking full steam, that he thought nothing of asking the waiter to cut up his steak into bite size pieces'.[24] Again we see John being a master of total self-absorption.

During his early years as a teenager he found a desperate need to be involved with the cut and thrust of inner-city life within a working-class city. The excitement that lay there was at odds with the pretentiousness of what was going on inside Mendips. The emotional confusion this caused intensified the internal and external conflict he was experiencing because of Mimi. When his 'fall from grace' came in the shape of Paul taking over de facto leadership during *Sergeant Pepper,* John found himself moving from 'I'm from Liverpool and proud of it' to internally criticising himself for seemingly letting himself 'be conned' into riding on the back of the image of a 'sexy working-class council house kid made good'. John resented the notion of lowering himself in this guise of sheep in wolves clothing. Yoko, at this stage, together with her affluent background, supported John's move away from his Liverpool roots and into the largely middle-class arena of counter-culture art.

John became interested in the fashionable working class: Michael Caine, David Bailey, Albert Finney types, not like Mimi's perception of the 'ordinary working-class types' choking up betting shops with cigarette smoke, laying tarmac roads or up before the magistrate. When major working-class movements such as trade unions, which began to organise high-profile strikes, and working-class political activism took shape and blue-collar workers began to look sexy, John jumped ship, denigrating the middle class.

Commenting on American rock groups in the early '70s, John denounced them: 'they're all middle-class and bourgeois and they don't want to show it. They're scared of the workers',[25] once again identifying himself with the working class. John seems to have no problem at all in holding two sets of conflicting ideas and switching and substituting these ideas at will. This is revealed in the large amount of emotional energies and in the verbal gymnastics John used in declaring with righteous indignation of his points of view. The convoluted mix of values and emotions meant that John couldn't out-run his appetite for his own self-destruction.

It seems that most of John's life was driven by a frantic attempt to escape from longing and sadness. Although at times he claims his upbringing was a happy one – 'My childhood wasn't all suffering'[26] – his occasional claims to an idyllic upbringing were way off the mark. Even John's comment above could lead one to interpret this remark as meaning *only parts of my childhood were without suffering*. For most of his life, he endured memories that felt painful. The sense of rejection never left him and consequently promoted his dire need to be wanted.

Considering all that John had endured as a child, his generosity of spirit was more than evident for much of his life, as was his humour and his passion for life and fun. Examples of this generous nature included taking Paul on an all-expenses-paid trip to Paris on his 21st birthday, or answering the door at Kenwood to an unsolicited request for funding from students and immediately scouring the house for all the money there was. Pete Shotton recalls, 'When John had a dozen sweets in a bag and there were three of us around him, he'd share them all out equally'.[27]

John's love for life was found in the establishment in his leadership of The Beatles. Close confidant and friend from the early days, Neil Aspinall, remembers with feeling:

My happiest memories of being with the band were some of the laughs that we had backstage and in the dressing room, when nobody else was around and we were swapping jokes together. No big deal really. It was those little personal things that are my favourite moment and still are today. We did all enjoy one another's company and we had a laugh. That was one of the big things right the way through everything, even today – we enjoy a laugh.[28]

It was this sense of having a laugh and camaraderie that John found in The Beatles which gave him ballast towards the whirlpool of emotions that dogged his whole life. The tragedy for John was that he had spent his life creating music as a bulwark against his melancholy and never severed this dependency which became an umbilical cord between his art and his mental wellbeing. The question that ran through his life, like a monkey on his back, was – if the creative process validates the artist and endows contentment and happiness, what happens when their creative process can't be found? As The Beatles broke up, John transferred the vehicle for his emotional rescue from Paul, George and Ringo to Yoko. With Yoko, he tried to apply his creativity during the *White Album* in typical John fashion, jumping head-first into his own version of 'challenging art' and radical politics – but novelty and controversy tied up with a rock 'n' roll lifestyle where never going to equate to revolution.

'Rebellion against the past, and therefore against parents and all they have stood for,' remarked Anthony Storr, 'is another way in which creativity can sub-serve the expression of aggressive impulses'. Storr continues:

Revolutionary genius is not the only form of genius; but it is certainly a very important one. Bernard Berenson once defined genius as 'the capacity for productive reaction against one's training'.[29]

Storr's notion of rebellion against the past to service the needs certainly applies to John with the break-up of The Beatles. In a *Playboy Magazine* interview with John and Yoko, published after his death in 1981, John corrects the interviewer when he puts forward the view that when John met Yoko: 'that's when you knew you were starting to drift from The Beatles.' John replies: 'No what I did... in my own cowardly way was to *use* [John's emphasis] Yoko... it was like now I have the strength to leave...'.[30] Nearly ten years after the break-up John admitted that he used Yoko to achieve this. John could have easily answered 'yes I was drifting apart and I wanted a future, artistically with Yoko and without The Beatles.' But in true John fashion he shoots from the hip, he goes and informs the interviewer far more than the question asked. It almost seems that he's taking satisfaction in revealing that he started the band and he ended it, and that he roped in his wife to achieve this.

Maybe at the time of the interview John felt an unconscious urge to declare and re-establish his control and sense of purpose within The Beatles' history. The elephant in the room, though, is the question of how? How in actual fact did he use Yoko to break up The Beatles? The interviewer doesn't ask, either because John's forceful disposition prevented such a 'personal' question or because the interviewer felt people already knew the answer, they didn't need to be told by John. Yoko never had the influence but John did and, by involving her in almost every aspect of The Beatles' studio work, he created animosity within The Beatles to such an extent that the other three felt the continuation of the band wasn't worth the effort. After the break-up of the band John would claim it was because Paul, George and Ringo wouldn't accept Yoko as an equal in terms of her position as an artist – and there was continued animosity shown to her – but in reality the last thing John wanted was acceptance of Yoko within The Beatles, it was the non-acceptance he wanted and the turmoil this non-acceptance would cause. Interestingly, considering that she takes pains to present herself as an independent artist and feminist, Yoko makes no comment as to being used in this way.

The disaster of John's genius was that it all but destroyed him as a person of contentment, in touch with his feelings. Being damaged by insecurity and pessimism, John was left with an over-reliance on his art to deflect and forestall the terrifying arrival of the never-ending well of deep despair and the disposition toward suicide. When Paul's own natural leadership ability together with his growing strength in the studio and his writing skills led to him inadvertently becoming the pivotal point of The Beatles, he took away John's last real lifeline to a healthy state of mind. The Beatles were, without a shadow of doubt, John's band, and its demise sent him into decline, artistically and mentally.

The 'defence mechanism' that no one could suffer like him was not only untrue, but detrimental to John's own wellbeing. An example of his inability to empathise and see outside his own pain was when he witnessed Judy Garland performing her signature tune, 'Over the Rainbow', and it sent him into a spate of loud insults, despite the fact that it was widely reported she had had a 'nervous breakdown' and showed signs of cuts to her wrist.

Although John's different personal outlook made him original in his music, it was also this sense difference that made him so unhappy. In *A Trip to Echo Spring* (*Why Writers Drink*), Olivia Laing cites the instance of John Berryman, in hospital due to his alcoholism. At rehabilitation group therapy sessions, another group member noted:

> When he tried to relate to other people he did make friends but he couldn't ever be wholehearted about belonging with the rest of us; he was constantly retreating into his uniqueness, but really though it was all he had that made him worth anything. So he stayed shut out he couldn't make it alone.[31]

Towards the end of The Beatles and in subsequent interviews, we find John throwing leading statements about his mental health around like confetti. When he flags up his cry for help, the response is either ignored by the interviewer or ignored due to the fear of where subsequent questions may lead. Further reason for a lack of pursuit in this area could well have been the awareness of John's mood-swings and temper, or even the perceived lack of interest from the readers of the interview.

All too often his painful declarations of pain went unheard or unheeded:

> It's like black space out there... Being an artist is torture. If I had the capabilities of being something other than I am I would. If I could be a fuckin' fisherman, I would.[32]

But even when The Beatles achieved everything and more that John wanted, it still wasn't the lifebelt he needed – it still wasn't enough to give him peace of mind.

There are numerous examples like this with John reaching out for sympathy and understanding. But, even though invited to comment on his mental health 'confessions', John's fearful personality and temper meant matters pertaining to his personal disposition were largely left unquestioned and therefore no help followed. John had slowly built an emotional wall of toughness and masculinity around himself, and this eventually transformed itself into a prison.

Irish writer Edna O'Brian, commenting on 'those at the bottom' and her reasons for leaving Ireland, believed her personality and that of many others was formed by:

> a fear of church, fear of gombeenism, fear of phantoms, fear of ridicule, fear of hunger, fear of annihilation, and fear of their own deeply ingrained aggression that can only strike a blow at each other, not having the innate authority to strike at those who are higher.

John's leaving of Mendips is at one with Edna O'Brien's own leaving her tainted childhood, but the damage was done, as 'leaving is only conditional. The person you are is anathema to the person you would like to be'.[33]

Temporary salvation came for John with art college and immersion into Liverpool culture. The impact of Liverpool on John with its self-mocking wit provide an antidote to the sombre mood of Mendips, but his 'going native' as a Scouser eventually resulted in a complex aversion to what he had changed into. Hamburg had been about tearing out the foundations of his life up to then – six years later this demolition of himself as a Beatle would be repeated as he saw Paul becoming the yardstick by which he would become measured.

And yet for all his deeply held resentment against Paul towards the end, it was Paul who rescued him in a, at times, not too subtle way, corralling his talents towards stardom for them both. John could be brutally honest when it came to his opinions, especially when it came to his opinions of himself and his feelings. Interviewed shortly before he was gunned down and asked the perennial and mundane question on the process of songwriting with Paul, John gives a lengthy response which finishes with:

> It's like a love affair... But after 15 or 20 years, a different kind of sexual *and* intellectual relationship develops, right? It's still love but it's different. So there's difference in creativity too. As in a love affair, two creative people can destroy themselves trying to recapture that youthful spirit, at 21 or 24, of creating without even being aware of how it's happening. One takes to drugs, to drink, to knock oneself out.[34]

Without any prompt, succinctly, eloquently, and after barbed comments about Paul, John lays bare the true essence of their failed friendship.

On reflection, it's surprising when looking at John's life to see the wheel turn full circle, trying so hard as he did to escape the substitute mother figure of the dominant Mimi, with her class-dominated ideology, to the safe haven of Yoko as 'mother'. John had battled against in the shape of Mimi's traditional deference toward her betters. He now found himself seeking security in Yoko's privileged background. The reason for this seems obvious – John's mental health and his fear of disintegration of his own personality through his loss of creativity, a creativity that flourished with the blistering competition of Paul's music – this, at one time much-needed, competition became a poisoned chalice. John's command of his craft, his genius born from the solitude of his childhood writing and his worldwide success should have offered a way out, but sadly they didn't. Commenting on fiction, Edmund Wilson pointed out that the:

> Perhaps most novels are an adjudication between the rival claims of daydreaming and memory of wish-fulfilment and the repetition compulsion, Freud's term for the seemingly inexplicable re-enactment of real-life experiences (he argued that we repeat them in order to gain mastery over them). And as with music, the more ingenious, the more familiar the melody, the more elegant and palatably ingenious can be the variations.[35]

Maybe with John's 'In My Life', 'Strawberry Fields' and 'Julia' he was looking for just this – a repetition and attempt at the 'mastery' of his childhood played out to music in order to make sense of why.

Epilogue

JOHN WAS KILLED on 8 December 1980 outside his home in New York, across the Atlantic from his old home in Liverpool – both cities whose development was heavily influenced by the slave trade and the Irish famine, with cultures energised by their roles as major gateways for immigrants. In Liverpool it was this legacy which struck a powerful chord with John, shaping his understanding of himself as an outsider within a city of outsiders. Throughout his career, the contradictions of his upbringing can be seen in his identification with the underdog, the ways he went against the grain, ready and proud to be a member of the awkward squad. The resonances between New York and Liverpool provided an easy recall to the history of his hometown and the influences of his youth.

It seems a perverse twist of fate that John should have begun his life and then have it ended in a port city: Liverpool and New York, sailor towns indifferent to norms, celebrators of change, conduits of the radical. The complexities of John's life were dictated by his attempts to find strength as an outsider while at the same time harbouring a desperate need to be wanted and loved, although his attitude to others could be inconsiderate in the extreme. His childhood dealt him a 'bum hand' but how he survived and coped with the emotional fallout is what gave us The Beatles and John Lennon's musical brilliance.

The last ten years of John's life without The Beatles began with hopes of a renaissance in his songwriting. His first album as an 'official' ex-Beatle was the critically acclaimed and financially successful *Imagine*, released in September 1971. However, *Imagine* was followed in 1972 by the politically radical but poorly received double album *Some Time in New York City*. The next few years were something of a mixed period for John – difficulties in his relationship with Yoko, the alcohol-fuelled 'lost weekend' of the mid-1970s, guest appearances with David Bowie and Elton John, sporadic hits with 'Mind Games', 'Whatever Gets You Through the Night' and 'Number 9 Dream', and the birth of his and Yoko's son, Sean, in 1975. Some argue that, during this period, John's creative well seemed to be running dry. But it has to be remembered the tenacity with which Pablo Picasso's maxim that 'every act of creation is first an act of destruction' is borne out in John's creative life.

As The Beatles broke up and John settled in New York City, with a new wife and eventually a new son, he stated that he wished he'd been born in the City. His life in the vibrant seaport of New York could have been used in much the same way as he used as his maritime home town of Liverpool as a crucible towards the forging of what became his mantle as the one of world's greatest songwriters. After a mixed decade, musically, in the 1970s John looked forward to the new decade of the '80s with optimism. But the night of December 8 was to dictate a different course of events, one which saw John leaving the Record Plant Studio, where he and Yoko had worked on Yoko's 'Walking on Thin Ice'. The journey back to their home at the Dakota building would prove to end in a nightmare for millions of Beatles fans around the globe.

A decade earlier, John's Plastic Ono Band album (which also contained 'Mother') included the track 'God'. The raw and emotional content of the album, released only three weeks before Paul's application for a High Court dissolution of the group, saw the song 'God' as a lament to the end of The Beatles, the lyrics interwoven with (a coda of) sensitivity and perception towards John's life outside the band he formed back in Liverpool all those years ago. The second half of the song, given in a mournful delivery, declares that, the dream is now over – a dream that no doubt, for John, included Julia, Stuart, Brian, Beatlemania, and Love and Peace. Later John sings/confesses to being (just) 'John', addressing the listeners as dear friends with a request that they'll just have to carry on; this is followed by, and echoes, John's first line regarding the dream being over. This is all heartachingly sad and poignant when moving forward through the years to the backdrop of a dark, New York, December's night in 1980 when the tragedy which was John's life would eventually be cut short below the carved stone entrance of the Dakota building. In a few moments of sudden violence a life was snuffed out – that of one of history's greatest and most persistently misunderstood poets, musicians and rebels: John Lennon, rock 'n' roll genius.

Endnotes

Preface Quotations

1 Quarry Bank High School Report in Evans, (2009) p. 21.

Introduction

1 J. Lennon in *Anthology* (2000) p. 13.
2 P. Sutcliffe in *The Real John Lennon* (2000 TV)
3. P. Morley, The North (*and Almost Everything in It*) (2013) p. 393–94.
4. J. Lennon in Du Noyer (2007) p. 26.

Chapter One

1 J. Lennon in Wenner (1972) p. 182.
2 R. Crane in *City of Radicals* (2011) p. 89.
3 Lane (1979) p. 15.
4 H. Melville in Lane (1979) p. 62.
5 T. Eagleton, *City of Radicals* (2011) p. 45.
6 J. Lennon in Evans (2009) p. 279.
7 F. Lennon in Davies (1992) p. 74.
8 O'Neill, *The Iceman Cometh* (1993) p. 5.
9 J. Lennon in Wenner (1972) p. 180.
10 Medical Officer of Health in Lane (1979) p. 66.
11 Crouch, *History of Jazz*, PBS (2001 TV)

Chapter Two

1 W. Churchill in *Merseyside in Crisis* (1979) p. 47.
2 C. Black in Coleman (1990) p. 370.
3 P. McCartney in Du Noyer (1997) p. 7.
4 F. Lennon in P. Lennon (1990) p. 17.
5 Headmaster in P. Lennon (1990) p. 18.
6 Reporter in Lane (1997) p. 2.
7 M. Smith in Spitz (2006) p. 21.

Chapter Three

1 G. Smith in Goldman (1988) p. 36.
2 J. Baird, *Imagine This* (2007) p. 22.
3 M. Smith in Spitz (2006) p. 24.

4 Relative in Spitz (2006) p. 24.
5 Bedford (2011) p. 52.
6 Davies (1992) p. 66.
7 J. Baird in Bedford (2011) p. 50.
8 M. Smith in Norman (2009) p. 29.
9 J. Baird in Bedford (2011) p. 54.
10 J. Baird in Bedford (2011) p. 54.

Chapter Four

1 Tory Supporter in Marwick (1980) p. 73.
2 *Liverpool Echo*, 29 November 1950.
3 J.B. Mays in Mays (1955) p. 44.
4 J. Lennon in Miles (1980) p. 9.
5 P. McCartney in Miles (1997) p. 44.
6 P. McCartney in Miles (1997) p. 121.
7 Gallup Poll in Sandbrook (2005) p. 87.
8 L. Harvey in Goldman (1988) p. 34
9 J. Baird in Bedford (2009) p. 54.
10 P. Lennon (1990) p. 83.
11 M. Smith in Norman (2009) p. 9.
12 M. Smith in Spitz (2006) p. 32.
13 Spitz (2006) p. 32
14 L. Harvey in Spitz (2006) p. 32.
15 M. Smith in Norman (2009) p. 138.
16 R. McKibbin in Hennessey (2007) p. 87.
17 Cynthia Lennon (2005) p. 143.
18 M. Smith in Norman (2009) p. 31.

Chapter Five

1 P. Norman (2009) p. 49.
2 D. Sandbrook (2005) p. 410.
3 J. Lennon, *Anthology* (2000) p. 8.
4 J. Lennon in Braun (1964) p. 37.
5 C. Lennon (2005) p. 37.
6 J. Lennon in Shelf (1981) p. 134.
7 J. Lennon in *Anthology* (2000) p. 10.
8 W. Fienburgh in Kynaston (2010) p. 114.
9 S. Parkes, <www.triumphpc.com/mersey-beat/beatles/johnlennon-men loveavenue4.shtml>

10 M. Smith Pritchard and Lysaght (1998) p. 3.
11 S. Parkes, <www.triumphpc.com/mersey-beat/beatles/johnlennon-men loveavenue4.shtml>
12 L. Garry in Riley (2011) p. 27.
13 J. Lennon in *Anthology* (2000) p. 283.
14 Miller (1990) p. 162.
15 <www.liverpoolecho.co.uk/whats-on/music/there-are-places-we-remember- 35532>
16 J. Lennon in Sheff (1981) p. 131.
17 S. Parkes, <www.triumphpc.com/mersey-beat/beatles/johnlennon-men loveavenue4.shtml>
18 *Liverpool Post and Mercury*, 12 November 1930.
19 S. Parkes, <www.triumphpc.com/mersey-beat/beatles/johnlennon-men loveavenue4.shtml>
20 J. Lennon in *Anthology* (2000) p. 231.
21 J. Lennon in *Anthology* (2000) p. 7.
22 J. Lennon in *Anthology* (2000) p. 8.
23 J. Lennon in Evans (2009) p. 282.
24 J. Lennon in Evans (2009) p. 280.
25 C. Lennon (2005) p. 81.
26 H. Davis in (1992) p. 60.
27 J. Lennon in Wenner (1972) p. 163.
28 P. Shotton (1984) p. 27.
29 J. Baird in Bedford (2009) p. 52.
30 J. Lennon in Davies (1992) p. 84.
31 J. Lennon in Wenner (1972) p. 27.

Chapter Six
1 J. Lennon in H. Davies (1992) p. 82.
2 P. Shotton (1984) p. 29.
3 P. Shotton (1984) p. 29.
4 P. Shotton in Giuliano (1998) p. 195.
5 J. Lennon in Davies (1992) p. 82
6 S. Parkes, <www.triumphpc.com/mersey-beat/beatles/johnlennon-men loveavenue5.shtml>
7 J. Lennon in *Anthology* (2000) p. 9.
8 M. Smith in Norman (2009) p. 27.
9 Lynne Varcoe, <www.britishbeatlesfanclub.co.uk/2011/09/interview-with-lynn-varcoe.html>

10 M. Smith in Goldman (1988) p. 36.
11 J. Baird in Bedford (2009) p. 54.
12 J. Lennon, *Anthology* (2000) p. 12.
13 J. Lennon in Pritchard and Lysaght (1998) p. 8.
14 J. Lennon in *Anthology* (2000) p. 9.
15 W. Pobjoy in Pritchard and Lysagth (1998) p. 9.
16 J. Lennon in Davies (1992) p. 82.
17 J. Lennon in Norman (2009) p. 33.
18 J. Lennon, *Anthology* (2000) p. 99.
19 J.B. Mays in Mays Page (1955) p. 41.
20 J. Baird in Pritchard and Lysaght (1998) p. 15.
21 J. Lennon in Wenner (1972) p. 156.
22 P. Shotton in Spitz (2006) p. 98.
23 C. Hanton in Norman (2009) p. 33.
24 M. Smith in Davies (1992) p. 22.
25 M. Smith in Norman (2003) p. 36.
26 M. Fishwick in Norman (2009) p. 150.

Chapter Seven

1   J. Lennon in Davies (1992) p. 117.
2   A. Ballard in Clayson and Sutcliffe (1994) p. 48.
3   A Ballard in Clayson and Sutcliffe (1994) p. 48.
4   P. Hartas in Norman (2009) p. 127.
5   R. Murray in Clayson and Sutcliffe (1994) p. 48.
6   A. Mason in Spitz (2006) p. 104.
7   J. Lennon in Davies (1992) p. 120.
8   J. Lennon in Peebles (1981) p. 56.
9   J. Lennon in Peebles (1981) p. 56.
10 H. Anderson in Spitz (2006) p. 53.
11 A. Ballard in Clayson (2003a) p. 48
12 P. Sutcliffe in *The Real John Lennon* (2000 TV)
13 L. Garry in Pritchard and Lysaght (1998) p. 25.
14 P. McKenzie in *The Real John Lennon* (2000 TV)
15 G. Harrison in Norman (2009) p. 171.
16 A. Williams in *The Real John Lennon* (2000 TV)
17. A. Clayson (2003a) p. 52.

Chapter Eight

1   J. Lennon in Davies (1992) p. 79.
2   J Hutchenson in Norman (2009) p. 173.
3   A. Williams, *The Real John Lennon* (2000 TV)
4   D. Wilkie in Norman (2009) p. 74.
5   C. Lennon (2005) p. 81.
6   G. Harrison in Miles (2002) p. 25.
7   P. McCartney in Miles (2002) p. 25.
8   W. Burroughs in Campbell (1999) p. 199.
9   C. Lennon (2005) p. 73.
10 J. Lennon in Shevey (1990) p. 165.

Chapter Nine

1   M. Smith in Davies (1992) p. 169.
2   P. McCartney Snr in Davies (1992) p. 170.
3   J. Lennon Anthology (2000) p. 14.
4   S. Parkes, <www.triumphpc.com/mersey-beat/beatles/johnlennon-men loveavenue5.shtml>
5   R. Galvin in Leigh (1998) p. 63.
6   P. Delaney in Leigh (1998) p. 64.
7   G. Harrison in Miles (2003) p. 39.
8   B. Epstein in Coleman (1990) p. 381
9   B. Epstein in Coleman (1990) p. 381.
10 K. Redfield Jamison in Duke and Hochman (1992) p. 182.

Chapter Ten

1   EMI in Spitz (2006) p. 312
2   G. Martin, *The Real John Lennon* (2000 TV)
3   Wooler in Leigh (1998) p. 49.
4   P. Best, *The Real John Lennon* (2000 TV)
5   B. Wooler in Wooler Leigh (1998) p. 48.
6   J. Lennon, *Anthology* (2000) p. 72.
7   B. Harry in Leigh (1998) p. 49.
8   J. Lennon in Davies (1985) p. 211.
9   B. Harry in Leigh (1998) p. 49.
10 B Wooler in Spitz (1998) p. 302.
11 J. Lennon in Wenner (1972) p. 90.
12 M. Lister, <www.beatlesinterviews.org/db1968.0606.beatles.html>

13 R. Starr in Clayson (2003) p. 97.

14 R. Starr in Spitz (2006) p. 501.

15 R. Starr in J. Baird (2007) p. 190.

16 C. Lennon (2005) p. 43.

17 C. Lennon (2005) p. 98.

18 J. Lennon in C. Lennon (2005) p. 152.

19 J. Lennon in *Anthology* (2000) p. 98.

20 P. McCartney in Norman (2004) p. 307.

21 P. McCartney in Doggett (1997) p. 595.

22 A. Durband in Pritchard and Lysaght (1998) p. 25.

23 L. Grant, *The Guardian*, 10 July 1999.

24 B. Harry in Leigh (2002) p. 185.

25 J. Lennon in Badman (2000) p. 60.

26 Miller (1991) p. 69.

Chapter Eleven

1 Taylor (2001) p. 97.

2 J. Lennon in Spitz (2005) p. 302.

3 J. Lennon in Coleman (1990) p. 324.

4 M. Smith in Coleman (2000) p. 132.

5 J. Lennon in Coleman (2000) p. 132.

6 Du Noyer (2007) p. 25.

7 Chris Hutchins, *Mr Confidential* (2005) p. 56.

8 G. Harrison in Badman (2000) p. 17.

9 J. Lennon in *Anthology* (2000) p. 105.

10 M. Cleave in Braun (1964) p. 65.

11 *London Evening Standard* in Braun (1964) p. 64.

12 G. Harrison in Pritchard and Lysaght (1998) p. 145.

13 G. Harrison in Braun (1964) p. 86.

14 P. McCartney in Miles (2007) p. 26.

15 Willets-Pitts in Du Noyer (2007) p. 25.

16 Reporter in J. Baird (2007) p. 190.

17 E. Sullivan in Shevey (1990) p. 34.

18 S. Bernstein in Braun (1964) p. 89.

19 B. Epstein in Coleman (1990) p. 17.

20 T. Strongin, *The New York Times*, in Braun (1964) p. 110.

21 Reporter in Braun (1964) p. 102.

22 S. Graham in Braun (1964) p. 110.

Chapter Twelve

1   J. Lennon in Skinner Sawyers (2006) p. 91.
2   P. McCartney in Braun (1964) p. 45.
3   Dr R. Short in Braun (1964) p. 137.
4   J. Lennon in Clayson (200) p. 134.
5   J. Lennon in Norman (2009) p. 354.
6   R. Starr in Clayson (2003) p. 88.
7   C. Gillett in Evans (2009) p. 66.
8   V. Montgomery in Braun (1964) p. 69.
9   W. Shenson in Norman (2003) p. 239.
10 D. Jacobs in Norman (2009) p. 239.
11 J. Mulhearn in Kenny (2006) p. 149.
12 P. Sutcliffe in *The Real John Lennon* (2000 TV)
13 M. Smith in Norman (2009) p. 31.
14 G. Orwell (2001) p. 88.

Chapter Thirteen

1   J. Lennon in Norman (2009) p. 395.
2   S. Bernstein in Pritchard and Lysaght (1990) p. 197.
3   R. Starr, *Anthology* (2000 TV)
4   Presley in Miles (2002) p. 170.
5   <www.quotesworthrepeating.com/quote-by/j/john-lennon/superb-words-of-john-lennon>
6   G. Harrison, *Anthology* (2000) 181.
7   C. Lennon (2005) p. 81.
8   J. Lennon in Wenner (1972) p. 84.
9   Forward and Buck (2002) p. 21.
10 J. Lennon in Miles (1997) p. 56.
11 Styron (2001) p. 80.
12 J. Lennon Evans (2009) p. 282.
13 J. Lennon in Miles (1980) p. 56.
14 B. Dylan in Evans (2009) p. 184.

Chapter Fourteen

1   J. Lennon in Evans (2009) p. 223.
2   N. Smith in G. Giuliano (1999) p. 67.
3   N. Smith in Pritchard and Lysaght (1998) p. 202.
4   M. Cleave in Norman (2009) p. 638.
5   J. Lennon in Coleman (1990) p. 357.

6   J. Lennon in Coleman (1990) p. 358.
7   N. Weiss in Coleman (1990) p. 358.
8   M. Cleaves in Skinner Sawyers (2006) p. 90.
9   J. Lennon in Cleave (2006) p. 88.
10 *The Times Literary Supplement* in Sauceda (1983) p. 3.
11 J. Lennon, *Anthology* (2000) p. 176.
12 J. Lennon in Sauceda (1985) p. 157.
13 J. Lennon in Shotton (1984) p. 47.
14 Jamison (1991) p.145
15 J. Lennon in Giuliano (1999) p. 66.
16 J. Lennon in G. Giuliano (1999) p. 66.
17 P. McCartney in Miles (2002) p. 93.
18 Badman (2000) p. 238.
19 G. Harrison in Badman (2000) p. 219.
20 J. Lennon in Wenner (1972) p. 20.
21 G. Harrison in Clayson (2003) p.178.
22 G. Harrison in Sandbrook (2006) p. 435.

Chapter Fifteen

1   A. Marwick in Sandbrook (2009) p. 340.
2   P. McCartney in Sandbrook (2006) p. 435.
3   J. Lennon in Badman (2000) p. 250.
4   J. Lennon in Badman (2000) p. 254.
5   J. Lennon in Miles (2002) p. 224.
6   J. Lennon in Miles (2003) p. 174.
7   B. Miles in Heylin (2007) p.132.
8   A. Storr (1993) p. 109.
9   P. McCartney in Miles (1997) p. 40.
10 Dr M. Sorenson in Storr (1993) p. 109.
11 J. Lennon in Sheff (1982) p. 166.
12 J. Lennon in Heylin (2007) p.132.
13 G. Martin in Giuliano (1999) p. 33.
14 J. Lennon in Wenner (1972) p.52.
15 C. Lennon (2005) p. 147.
16 J. Lennon in Evans (2009) p. 221.
17 Storr (1993) p. 109.
18 J. Lennon in Wenner (1972) p. 52.
19 J. Gustafson in Coleman (1990) p. 386.

Chapter Sixteen

1   J. Lennon in Wenner (1972) p. 54.
2   J. Lennon in Miles (1997) p. 170.
3   P. McCartney in Miles (1997) p. 171.
4   A. Storr (1993) p. 109.
5   F. Lennon in Davies (1992) p. 187.
6   C. Lennon in P. Lennon (1990) p. 133.
7   J. Lennon in P. Lennon (1990) p. 135.
8   J. Lennon in C. Lennon (2005) p. 256.
9   C. Lennon (2005) p. 260.
10 J. Lennon, http://www.johnlennon.it/john-lennon-quotes-it.htm
11 A. Storr (1993) p. 112
12 A. Koestler in Heylin (2007) p. 179.
13 A. Miller (1997) p. 163.
14 Julian Lennon in *The Daily Telegraph*, 23 May 1998.
15 J. Lennon in Badman (2000) p. 324.
16 J. Lennon in Norman (2003) p. 341.
17 P. Shotton in Norman (2003) p.540.
18 J. Lennon in Wenner (1972) p. 174.
19 C. Lennon (2005) p. 284.

Chapter Seventeen

1   J. Lennon in Wenner (1972) p. 51.
2   K. Redfield Jamison (1996) p. 241.
3   Y. Ono in Johnstone (2005) p. 15.
4   J. Lennon in Norman (2009) p. 624.
5   A. Storr (1993) p. 109
6   A. Storr (1993) p. 109.
7   J. Lennon in <www.beatlesinterviews.org/db1968.05ts.beatles.html>
8   G. Harrison in Doggett (2009) p. 37.
9   J. Lennon in <en.wikipedia.org/wiki/Unfinished_Music_No._1:_ Two_Virgins>
10 J. Lennon in Miles (1997) p. 337.
11 J. Birch Society magazine in Skinner Sawyers (2006) p. 141.
12 J. Lennon in Emerick and Massey (2006) p. 243.
13 J. Asher in Evans (2009) p. 200.
14 A. Taylor in Taylor (2001) p.217.
15 G. Emerick in Emerick and Massey (2006) p. 258.

16 R. Starr in Giuliano (1999) p. 128.

17 J. Lennon in Norman (2009) p. 534.

18 W. Styron (2001) p. 46.

19 J. Lennon in Badman (2000) p.368.

20 http://en.wikipedia.org/wiki/Transference

21 Shotton Doggett (2009) p. 45.

22 J. Lennon in G. and B. Giuliano (1998) p. 118.

23 K. Kesey (1986) p. 309.

24 K. Kesey (1986) p. 309.

Chapter Eighteen

1 J. Lennon in *Anthology* (2000) p. 317.

2 J. Lennon in Sheff (1981) p. 162.

3 J. Lennon in Sheff (1982) p. 162.

4 J. Lennon in Badman (2000) p. 405.

5 D. Taylor in Brown and Gaines (1983) p. 313.

6 P. McCartney in Doggett (2009) p. 59.

7 R. Starr in Clayson (2003d) p.134.

8 J. Lennon in Doggett (2009) p. 63.

9 Storr (1993) p. 111.

10 M. Jagger in Miles (2002) p. 228.

11 J. Lennon in Miles (2002) p. 292.

12 P. McCartney in Du Noyer (2007) p. 31.

Chapter Nineteen

1 J. Lennon in *Anthology* (2000) p. 322.

2 G. Harrison in Doggett (2009) p. 77.

3 J. Lennon in Doggett (2009) p. 85.

4 M. Smith in Norman (2009) p. 558.

5 Y. Ono in Norman (2009) p. 559.

6 M. Smith in Norman (2009) p. 558.

7 S. Parkes, *The Real John Lennon* (2000) TV

8 J. Lennon in Doggett (2009) p. 9.

9 J. Lennon in Norman (2009) p. 177.

10 E. Clapton (2008) p. 125.

11 J. Lennon in Shelvey (1990) p. 156.

12 R. Hawkins, <beatles.ncf.ca/live_peace_in_toronto>

13 J. Lennon in <beatles.ncf.ca/live_peace_in_toronto_p1.html>

14 Y. Ono in Doggett (2009) p. 100.

15 L. LeBlanc, <beatles.ncf.ca/live_peace_in_toronto_p1.html>
16 Little Richard, <beatles.ncf.ca/live_peace_in_toronto_p1.html>
17 J. Lennon in D. Wigg, BBC radio interview, 8 May 1969.
18 Reporter in G. and V. Giuliano (2001) p. 122.
19 J. Lennon in G. and V. Giuliano (2001) p. 54.
20 Reporter in G. and V. Giuliano (2001) p. 109.
21 Y. Ono in Brown and Gaines (1983) p. 319.
22 J. Lennon, <http://www.johnlennon.it/john-lennon-quotes-it.htm>

Chapter Twenty

1   D. Taylor in Brown and Gaines (1983) p. 235.
2   P. Brown in Brown and Gaines (1983) p. 326.
3   J. Lennon in Brown and Gaines (1983) p. 326.
4   J. Lennon in Doggett (2009) p. 110.
5   Miller (1991) p. 5.
6   Storr (1993) p. 109.
7   G. and B. Giuliano (1998) p. 137.
8   J. Lennon in Peebles (1981) p. 39.
9   J. Lennon in G. and B. Giuliano (1998) p. 54.
10 J. Lennon in G. and V. Giuliano (2001) p. 137.
11 J. Lennon in Giuliano (1999) p.66.
12 Miller (1993) p. 105.
13 J. Lennon in P. Lennon (1990) p. 179.
14 Lennon in Coleman (2000) p. 4.
15 M. Smith in Wenner (1972) p. 163.
16 J. Lennon in G. and V. Giuliano (2001) p. 29.
17 J. Lennon in Sheff (1982) p. 127.
18 J. Lennon in Wenner (1972) p. 110.
19 *Merseyside in Crisis* (1979) p21.
20 J. Lennon in Skinner (2006) p. 233.
21 J. Lennon in Wenner (1972) 20.
22 M. Smith in Norman (2009) p. 31.
23 J. Lennon in Norman (2009) p. 74.
24 P. McCabe in McCabe and Schonfeld (1984) p. 14.
25 J. Lennon in Evans (2009) p. 279.
26 J. Lennon in *Anthology* (2000) p. 7.
27 P. Shotton in Davies (1992) p. 375.
28 N. Aspinall in Thompson in Gutman (1987) p. 166.
29 Storr (1993) p. 111.

30 Sheff (1981) p. 130.
31 B. Peddie in Laing (2013) p. 259.
32 J. Lennon in Giuliano (1999) p. 69.
33 O'Brien, *Mother Ireland* (1976) p. 146.
34 J. Lennon in Sheff (1982) p. 120.
35 E. Wilson in Laing (2013) p. 171.

Bibliography

Badman, Keith. *The Beatles: Off the Record*, Omnibus Press, 2000.

Baird, Julia. *Imagine This: Growing Up with My Brother John Lennon*, Hodder & Stoughton, 2007.

Bedford, David. *Liddypool: Birthplace of The Beatles*, Dalton Watson Fine Books, 2011.

Belchem, John and Biggs, Bryan (eds), *Liverpool: City of Radicals*, Liverpool University Press, 2011.

Braun, Michael. *Love Me Do: The Beatles' Progress*, Penguin, 1964.

Brown, Peter and Gaines, Steven. *The Love You Make: An Insider's Story of The Beatles*, Macmillan, 1983.

Campbell, James. *This is the Beat Generation*, Martin Secker & Warburg Ltd, 1999.

Clapton, Eric. *Eric Clapton: The Autobiography*, Arrow, 2008.

Clayson, Alan and Sutcliffe, Pauline. *Backbeat: Stuart Sutcliffe – The Lost Beatle*, Pan, 1994.

Clayson Alan. *John Lennon*, Sanctuary, 2003.

Clayson, Alan. *Ringo Starr: Straight Man or Joker?*, Sanctuary, 2003.

Clayson, Alan. *George Harrison*, Sanctuary, 2003.

Clayson, Alan. *Paul McCartney*, Sanctuary, 2003.

Cohen-Portheim, Paul. *England, the Unknown Isle*, Duckworth, 1930.

Coleman, Ray. *Brian Epstein: The Man Who Made The Beatles*, London, Penguin, 1990.

Coleman, Ray. *Lennon: The Definitive Biography*, Pan Books, 2000.

Davies, Hunter. *The Beatles: The Authorised Biography*, Arrow Books, 1992.

De Botton, Alain. *The Consolations of Philosophy*, Penguin Group, 2001.

Doggett, Peter. *The Art & Music of John Lennon*, Omnibus Press, 2005.

Doggett, Peter. *There's a Riot Going On: Revolutionaries, Rock Stars and the Rise and Fall of '60s Counter-Culture*, Canongate, 2007.

Doggett, Peter. *You Never Give Me Your Money: The Battle for the Soul of The Beatles*, The Bodley Head, 2009.

Du Noyer, Paul. *Liverpool – Wondrous Place: From the Cavern to the Capital of Culture*, Virgin, 2007.

Duke, Patty and Hochman, Gloria. *A Brilliant Madness: Living with Manic Depressive Illness*, Bantam, 1992.

Emerick, Geoff and Massey, Howard. *Here, There and Everywhere: My Life Recording the Music of The Beatles*, Penguin Books, 2006.

Evans, Mike (ed). *The Beatles: Paperback Writer: 40 Years of Classic Writing*, Plexus, 2009.

Fawcett, Anthony. *John Lennon: One Day at a Time*, New English Library, 1977.

Fitzgerald, Michael. *The Genesis of Artistic Creativity: Asperger's Syndrome and the Arts,* 2005.

Finucane, Michael. *The Liverpool Irish*, Zingaro Press, 2002.

Foley, Michael, *The Age Of Absurdity: Why Modern Life Makes It Hard To Be Happy*, Simon & Schuster, 2010.

Forward, Susan and Buck, Craig. *Toxic Parents: Overcoming their Hurtful Legacy and Reclaiming Your Life*, Bantam, 2002.

Giuliano, Geoffrey and Giuliano, Brenda (eds). *The Lost Lennon Interviews*, Omnibus Press, 1998.

Giuliano, Geoffrey and Giuliano, Vrnda (eds). *Things We Said Today: Conversations with The Beatles*, Adams Media Corporation, 2001.

Giuliano, Geoffrey. *Two of Us: John Lennon and Paul McCartney – Behind the Myth*, Penguin Studio, 1999.

Goldman, Albert. *The Lives of John Lennon*, Great Britain, Bantam Press, 1988.

Gould, Jonathan. *Can't Buy Me Love: The Beatles, Britain and America*, Piatkus, 2008.

Griffiths, Robert. *The History of the Royal and Ancient Park of Toxteth,* The City of Liverpool, 2002.

Harry, Bill. *The Book of Lennon*, Aurum Press, 1984.

Harry, Bill. *Bigger Than the Beatles*, Trinity Mirror, 2009.

Harry, Bill. *The John Lennon Encyclopaedia*, Virgin, 2000.

Hennessy, Peter. *Having It So Good: Britain in the Fifties*, Penguin, 2007.

Heylin, Clinton. *The Act You've Known For All These Years: A Year in the Life of Sgt. Pepper and Friends*, Canongate, 2007.

Higginson, Steve and Wailey, Tony. *Edgy Cities*, Northern Lights, 2006.

Hoggart, Richard. *The Uses of Literacy: Aspects of Working-Class Life*, Penguin Books, 1957.

Hutchins, Chris. *Mr Confidential,* Blake Publishing, 2005.

Jamison, Kay Redfield, *Touched with Fire: Manic-Depressive Illness and the Artistic Temperament*, Free Press Paperback, 1994.

Johnston, Nick. Yoko Ono Talking, Omnibus, 2006.

Kelly, Michael, *Liverpool's Irish Connection*, Formby, 2006.

Kesey, Ken. *Demon Box*, Viking, 1986.

Kurlansky, Mark. *1968: The Year That Rocked the World,* Vintage, 2005.

Kynaston, David. *Family Britain, 1951–57*, Bloomsbury, 2010.

Laing, Olivia. *The Trip to Echo Spring: Why Writers Drink*, Canongate Books, 2013.

Laing, R.D. *The Divided Self: An Existential Study in Sanity and Madness*, Penguin Books, 1957.

Lane, Tony et al. *Liverpool: Gateway of Empire*, Lawrence & Wishart, 1987.

Lane, Tony *et al. Merseyside in Crisis*, Manchester, Manchester Free Press, 1979.

Leigh, Spencer. *Drummed Out! The Sacking of Pete Best*, Northdown, 1998.

Leigh, Spencer. *The Best of Fellas: The Story of Bob Wooler*, Drivegreen Publications, 2002.

Lennon, Cynthia. *John*, Hodder & Stoughton, 2005.

Lennon, Pauline. *Daddy Come Home: The True Story of John Lennon and His Father*, Angus & Robertson, 1990.

MacDonald, Ian. *Revolution in the Head: The Beatles' Records and the Sixties*, Vintage Books, 2008.

Marsden, Gerry. *I'll Never Walk Alone: An Autobiography*, Bloomsbury Publishing, 1993.

Marwick, Arthur. *Class: Image and Reality in Britain, France and the USA since 1930*, Collins, 1980.

McCabe, Peter and Schonfeld, Robert D, *John Lennon: For the Record*, Bantam Books, 1984.

Melly, George. *Revolt into Style: The Pop Arts In Britain*, The Penguin Press, 1970.

Miles, Barry. *The Beatles: A Diary*, Omnibus Press, 2002.

Miles, Barry. *Paul McCartney: Many Years from Now*, Martin Secker & Warburg Ltd, 1997.

Miles, Barry (ed). *John Lennon: In His Own Words*, Omnibus Press, 1980.

Miller, Alice. *Banished Knowledge: Facing Childhood Injuries*, Virago Press, 1991.

Miller, Alice. *For Your Own Good: Hidden Cruelty in Child-Rearing and the Roots of Violence*, Virago Press, 1987.

Miller, Alice. *The Untouched Key: Tracing Childhood Trauma in Creativity and Destructiveness*, Virago Press, 1990.

Morley, Paul. *The North (and Almost Everything in it)*, Bloomsbury, 2013.

Murphy, Michael and Rees Jones, Deryn (eds). *Writing Liverpool: Essays and Interviews*, Liverpool University Press, 2007.

Neises, Charles P. *The Beatles Reader*, The Pierian Press, 1984.

Norman, Philip. *John Lennon: The Life*, Harper Collins, 2009.

Norman, Philip. *Shout! The Beatles in their Generation*, Pan, 2004.

O'Brien, Edna. *Mother Ireland*, Harcourt, 1976.

O'Neill, Eugene. *The Ice Man Cometh*, Nick Hern Books, 1994.

Peebles, Andy. *The Lennon Tapes: John Lennon and Yoko Ono in Conversation with Andy Peebles*, BBC Books, 1981.

Pritchard, David and Lysaght, Alan. *The Beatles: An Oral History*, Hyperion, 1998.

Riley, Tim. *Lennon: The Definitive Life*, Virgin Books, 2010.

Roylance, Brian (ed). *The Beatles Anthology*, Cassell & Co, 2000.

Sandbrook, Dominic. *White Heat: A History of Britain in the Swinging Sixties*, Abacus, 2006.

Sandbrook, Dominic. *Never had It So Good: A History of Britain from Suez to The Beatles*, Abacus, 2005.

Sauceda, James. *The Literary Lennon: A Comedy of Letters – The First Study of All the Major and Minor Writings of John Lennon*, Pierian Press, 1983.

Sawyers, June Skinner. *Read The Beatles: Classic and New Writings on The Beatles, their Legacy, and Why They Still Matter*, Penguin, 2006.

Sheff, David. *The Playboy Interviews with John Lennon & Yoko Ono*, New English Library, 1982.

Shevey, Sandra. *The Other Side of John Lennon*, Sidgwick & Jackson, 1990.

Shotton, Pete. *John Lennon: In My Life*, Coronet Books, 1984.

Southall, Brian and Perry, Rupert. *Northern Songs: The True Story of the Beatles Song Publishing Empire*, Omnibus Press, 2006.

Spitz, Bob. *The Beatles: The Biography*, Aurum Press, 2006.

Storr, Anthony. *The Dynamics* of Creation, Ballantine Books, 1993.

Sounes, Howard. *Fab: An Intimate Life of Paul McCartney*, HarperCollins, 2010.

Sulpy, Doug and Schweighardt, Ray. *Get Back: The Beatles' 'Let it Be' Disaster*, Helter Skelter Publishing, 2003.

Taylor, Alistair. *A Secret History*, John Blake, 2001.

Taylor, Derek. *It Was Twenty Years Ago Today*, FireSide Book, 1987.

Thomson, Elizabeth and Gutman, David (eds). *The Lennon Companion*, Macmillan Press, 1987.

Trynka, Paul. *The Beatles: 10 Years that Shook The World*, Mojo, 2004.

Wenner, Jann S. *Lennon Remembers: The Rolling Stones Interviews with John Lennon and Yoko Ono*, Franklyn, 1972.

Womack Kenneth. *Long and Winding Roads: The Evolving Artistry of The Beatles*, Continuum, 2007.

Womack Kenneth (ed). *Cambridge Companion to The Beatles*, 2009.

Picture Acknowledgements

Luath Press would like to thank Roger Hull of Liverpool Record Office, Liverpool Libraries for his extremely diligent work in locating the atmospheric period photographs used in this book's picture section. Our thanks go to him and The Liverpool Record Office for these photographs and the permission to reproduce them.

We would also like to thank John Darch, Lipinski and Repon1x for making their photographs of Mendips, 20 Forthlin Road and The John Lennon Art and Design Building available for us to use on Wikimedia Commons.

Luath Press Limited

committed to publishing well written books worth reading

LUATH PRESS takes its name from Robert Burns, whose little collie Luath (*Gael.*, swift or nimble) tripped up Jean Armour at a wedding and gave him the chance to speak to the woman who was to be his wife and the abiding love of his life. Burns called one of 'The Twa Dogs' Luath after Cuchullin's hunting dog in Ossian's *Fingal*. Luath Press was established in 1981 in the heart of Burns country, and now resides a few steps up the road from Burns' first lodgings on Edinburgh's Royal Mile. Luath offers you distinctive writing with a hint of unexpected pleasures.

Most bookshops in the UK, the US, Canada, Australia, New Zealand and parts of Europe either carry our books in stock or can order them for you. To order direct from us, please send a £sterling cheque, postal order, international money order or your credit card details (number, address of cardholder and expiry date) to us at the address below. Please add post and packing as follows: UK – £1.00 per delivery address; overseas surface mail – £2.50 per delivery address; overseas airmail – £3.50 for the first book to each delivery address, plus £1.00 for each additional book by airmail to the same address. If your order is a gift, we will happily enclose your card or message at no extra charge.

ILLUSTRATION: IAN KELLAS

Luath Press Limited
543/2 Castlehill
The Royal Mile
Edinburgh EH1 2ND
Scotland
Telephone: 0131 225 4326 (24 hours)
email: sales@luath.co.uk
Website: www.luath.co.uk